BREAKTHROUGH STRATEGIES FOR GROWTH

Tony Grundy

FT
PITMAN
PUBLISHING

PITMAN PUBLISHING
128 Long Acre, London WC2E 9AN

A Division of Pearson Professional Limited

First published in Great Britain 1995

© Pearson Professional Limited 1995

British Library Cataloguing in Publication Data
A CIP catalogue record for this book can be obtained
from the British Library.

ISBN 0 273 62046 0

1 3 5 7 9 10 8 6 4 2

Typeset by Pantek Arts, Maidstone, Kent.
Printed and bound in Great Britain by
Biddles Ltd, Guildford and King's Lynn

*The Publishers' policy is to use paper manufactured
from sustainable forests.*

CONTENTS

'Tony Grundy has linked the techniques and elements of the strategy process and shown how they impact on today's imperative of creating shareholder value. This obviously isn't just another book on strategy theory. It is a very practical and reflective guide on how to do it.'

Simon Hart, Head of Strategic Planning, Rolls-Royce plc

'A must for any manager or student of business strategy seeking to use the processes and tools, rather than seat of the pants thinking, to derive winning solutions and avoid potential oblivion.'

Mike Jackson, Chief Executive, Birmingham Midshires Building Society

PREFACE

This book addresses a very important management issue.

There is often a bewildering choice of ways of growing your business. Each of these is likely to have quite varying degrees of likely success and risk. Managers often have to make these choices with limited data and in tough time constraints. But they certainly do not want to get these critical decisions wrong – either at the decision stage or during implementation.

Breakthrough Strategies for Growth takes you step-by-step through the competitive and financial issues which need to be addressed in growing your business – and to help you reach for sustainable value.

There is a multitude of books dealing with strategic management and key management disciplines, including marketing, organization and finance. However, it is not possible to find a single book which provides an overview of all the key disciplines, and how they all fit together and make this work in a practical context.

The key strategic management books purport to achieve the goal of integrating perspectives. However they are typically not sufficiently linked to one or more of the other key management disciplines. They either have a marketing or organizational or (more rarely) financial emphasis but never all three.

Nor are they perhaps sufficiently well linked to management practice to help overcome the problem of transforming learning from a theoretical to a real setting. Although all the best books do have case studies even here there is very little (if any) live demonstration of how to use tools and frameworks in practice. Not only is this book replete with illustrations but each chapter also concludes with summary checklists.

This book addresses this major gap by providing an overall framework for managing the whole of strategic development. It is also very much concerned with corporate dynamics rather than with relatively *static* analysis. The case studies and exercises all focus on achieving breakthrough strategies for growth.

Who should read this book?

The book is primarily targeted at these people.

- The general manager who faces specific and difficult choices in achieving tough strategic and financial goals.
- The mid-career functional manager who wishes to broaden their understanding of how business growth can be managed cross-functionally.
- Heads of business, market or product development.
- Managers who face implementation barriers and are seeking routes forward which will offer genuine breakthrough.
- Non-financial managers who would like to gain a better understanding of how finance can and should shape strategy – without undermining competitive advantage through tactical or purely numbers-based thinking.
- Financial managers and analysts who are seeking a strategy driven view of business opportunities (rather than purely by financial analysis).
- The younger, high potential manager who wants to stretch their understanding of strategy, finance and implementation (as if he or she in the CEO's shoes – to feel what this is really like).

It will also be of interest to students of management.

For MBA (and undergraduate) courses it is of particular value in:

- supporting core texts (such as '*Exploring Corporate Strategy*', Johnson and Scholes, 1989), particularly in showing how to use the book.
- providing stimulus to thinking for students on their course work across corporate strategy, marketing and financial analysis and international management.
- supplying examples which can be used as essential pre-examination revision.
- helping students make the link to their own businesses through worked examples of real cases.

Finally, I would like to acknowledge the help of both Professor David Asch, Dean of the Open Business School, and of Professor Robin Wensley of Warwick Business School in their invaluable comments on the early chapters of the book. I would also like to thank the innumerable managers I have worked with who have contributed to this thinking, to Pat Edwards for her assistance on this and other books, and to my family for their amazing tolerance of a strategy-holic.

Part I

INTRODUCTION

*'Senior managers ... are now
suddenly expected to exhibit
'holistic vision' in tackling
strategic and related issues
and decisions.'*

1

STRATEGIES FOR GROWTH – A PROCESS WASTELAND?

Key concepts covered in this introductory chapter include:

- Managing *both* competitive and financial advantage.
- Developing (organizational) capability.
- What is 'strategy'?
- Strategic options.
- Deliberate, emergent and unrealized strategies.

Even in the mid 1990s many middle managers believe that evolving strategies for growth is the primary, if not exclusive, concern of the chief executive and the top team. But as we near the year 2000 it is evident that primarily top-down strategy no longer fits with our flattening organizations, more fluid cultures and faster competitive change.

When faced with the competitive challenges into the late 1990s and beyond, even some very senior managers find themselves ill equipped to manage sustainable growth strategies more effectively. They are frequently confused by business schools, management books and gurus, and by wave after wave of 'born again' management consultants.

These senior managers have frequently come up a functional ladder – from marketing, finance, IT (information technology) etc – but are now suddenly expected to exhibit 'holistic vision' in tackling strategic and related issues and decisions. (Holistic vision is really quite simple – it is the ability to look at a business problem or opportunity from many different angles simultaneously, and over different time scales.) Some managers exercise holistic vision naturally – but they are few. Many struggle to achieve and sustain it. Others are even past saving. This guide is probably not for them.

To shift the mindset of future top managers we need to provide more structured and practical education for those who have ambitions to lead businesses or business functions, and to achieve growth which actually realizes value.

These managers are sometimes students of management. We need to sensitize them at an early stage in their career to holistic vision before it is too late. But in order to raise this group's awareness of strategic development issues, we need to put them, as it were, in the corporate driving seat, and this cannot be done just by abstract learning or concepts. It needs to be made concrete. For instance, what would you do if you were the chief executive of Apple, BMW, IBM, Rover, Tesco or Marks & Spencer? There are no definitive answers but you may well be able to explore the differences faced in strategic development by asking just these kinds of questions.

But more frequently there are managers in senior positions who are not fully comfortable with some of the big and strategic choices which they face. For instance, how do they reconcile the strategic with the financial priorities? And how, then, do they evolve effective implementation plans? This book is for them, too.

So, this book is about achieving breakthrough strategies for growth. It is about reaching for value, because growth in itself may dilute economic value. It is about *breakthroughs* because it seeks new ways of thinking about your business, or sets of businesses. It is also geared to implementation – to making things happen. You will find rich case material from Marks & Spencer, Tesco, Hanson, ICI, Sketchley, BMW and Rover, and Cellnet to practise on.

The book contains a wealth of tools which are carefully explained. Some are found in other books and several are actually new. But the really important thing is that they can be used at a variety of levels. First, they can be used formally as part of the core management process. Second, they can be used (again formally) in workshops – whether these are set up principally as business-driven or learning events (or as both). Third, they can be used by individuals – again formally, to analyse key issues. Fourth, they can be used *informally* and intuitively by managers – either singly or in groups.

The fourth use – internally and intuitively – is perhaps likely to be most frequent. However, there will be times when the going gets tough or your intuition gets foggy when you need to apply them formally, either individually or in groups.

In this initial chapter we now explore the rationale for having a process for managing strategies for growth. This is then related to the key management disciplines and also to the relevance to students of management. This is illustrated through a short case study of London International Group. We then examine how strategies for growth can be managed through the five forms of strategy which link to Mintzberg's original strategy types.

DO WE NEED A PROCESS?

Modern management techniques have become an industry in their own right over the last 30 or more years. Yet much of what is preached either degenerates into near-empty rituals and fashions, or is applied in a very patchy manner. But most managers face even more bewildering choices (and frequently constraints) than ever before, especially in the sphere of strategies for growth.

The first port of call for the student of strategies for growth is perhaps strategic management. In the classic strategic management books (for instance, Johnson and Scholes, 1989), we were taught to perform strategic analysis, choice and implementation. But this systematic view of the strategic process appears to be frequently in a separate world to that inhabited by real, practising managers. Indeed, the real organization world often seems to bear more resemblance to chaos than it does to the ordered world of the 'design school' strategic management theorists, who preach the virtues of rational analysis.

Organizations internally can become increasingly chaotic, uncertain and ambiguous, whatever happens to their environments. However, there is *more* value in having a set of tools for managing strategies for growth, and not less. When there are more and more choices, and quality of information deteriorates, you need to spend *more time* understanding what is going on, and what you can do to shape it.

This does not imply doubling the size of the strategic planning department (or, for that matter, doing an upgrade on the chief executive's brain). It implies developing a flexible process for managing strategies for growth which taps into the network of minds in the organization. To achieve this network demands sharing of assumptions which, in turn, requires a common language and a workable toolkit.

Although analysis and implementation tools exist for managing growth strategies, they are often found scattered around in different pieces of advice. This book addresses that problem by bringing the key perspectives together. But besides frameworks, there appear to be further hurdles to be addressed. Although these tools have been around for quite some time, they appear to be hardly ever used formally, and only occasionally informally. Why is this?

First, managers often seem uncomfortable about using any formal tools or process. Are they afraid of looking silly in front of their colleagues? Or is it because they want to use the tools absolutely right first time, thus inhibiting experimentation? It is probably a mixture of these two causes.

There is a third reason why strategies for growth are often managed through gut feel and with little formal design – managers fear that 'process' implies tight control. Also they may fear that control means possibly tight control of a financial nature. Financial control might be good or bad, depending upon how it is applied. It might be good because it provides a disciplined check on pet strategic projects. Equally, it may be poor because it assumes that financial reductionism is feasible, that 'everything can be reduced to financial measures, *and* this can be achieved with precision'.

Finally, there are internal, political reasons why analysis and implementation tools are hardly ever used. These tools provide much greater transparency than may have previously existed. This visibility is often threatening to players, especially where they perceive they may well 'lose out' as a result of their business area being assigned a 'harvest strategy' (one which seeks maximum short and medium term cash flow, and least investment).

The issue of managing the politics cannot be dissolved merely through a strategic toolkit (or even process). But the effects can be greatly reduced by more open and astute management. (Chapter 5 deals with these issues directly.)

GROWTH BREAKTHROUGH OR BREAKDOWN?

Companies that do not address growth opportunities in a strategic way pay dearly for their inability. From the many corporate failures during the late 1980s and early 1990s we know that untested and unchallenged judgement – which constitutes corporate acts of faith – frequently leads to corporate breakdown. In the UK for instance, we witnessed spectacular corporate collapses, such as Maxwell Corporation and Polly Peck, all due in part to a single strong entrepreneur with an overriding but unchecked strategic vision. (In the US, whole industries – like airlines – have been in crisis.)

But even more cautious companies may become the victims of a shared, but myopic, mindset or 'groupthink', particularly in unwise diversification (for instance, Boots's foray into out-of-town do-it-yourself retail). Yet even after these disasters (whether well or poorly publicized) there remains to emerge a clamour for a more effective process for managing growth strategy.

This process wasteland seems very odd when contrasted with the superstructure of modern management fashions. Initiatives like Total Quality Management (TQM – vintage 1980s) and Business Process Reengineering (BPR – vintage early 1990s) have spread through corporations with an impressive speed. (Perhaps these approaches could be called 'Tidal Wave Management' – because they come in waves and these waves sweep through quickly, sometimes leading to benefits but very frequently resulting in waste and confusion.) Yet it is very rare to find themes like 'quality', 'simplification' and 'process management' percolating through to the process of managing strategies for growth. As one general manager of a telecommunications company put it:

> *'It does irritate me. We have all these initiatives like TQM ... we end up worrying about the quality of the paperclips, and such like. What I would really like to see is us applying process-type principles to big decisions such as which major business development opportunities should we go for, on what criteria, and how we prioritize these.'*

Working in this spirit, this guide gives strategies for growth a workable process without giving it a top-heavy superstructure of unnecessary theory.

WHAT ARE THE OBJECTIVES OF GROWTH?

To begin our journey, we first need to define what we mean by 'strategies for growth'. Strategies for growth involve 'exploiting business opportunities for both financial and competitive advantage, and to develop capability'.

Strategies for growth aim to achieve three objectives simultaneously. They seek financial advantage (as this provides the incentive to invest money and effort in often uncertain opportunities). They also involve building a longer term competitive advantage externally. Finally, they entail developing a well-chosen set of underlying capabilities which will support existing and future competitive advantage.

Strategies for growth can take many forms in reality. For instance, there are the bigger moves, such as major acquisition, strategic alliances and product/market diversification. Or there are more incremental strategies for development which extend existing product/market penetration or development of existing capabilities.

So, breakthrough strategies for growth therefore embrace a number of key management disciplines, shown in Figure 1.1. First, corporate strategy offers us tools for developing a strategic vision and supporting business strategies (Chapters 2 and 3). Then, financial strategy (Chapter 4) helps us analyse the potential economic value of different business strategies, options and projects. Implementation analysis highlights the likely difficulties of "making it happen". This in turn is supported by internal development (which we call 'Organizational Strategy') in Chapter 5.

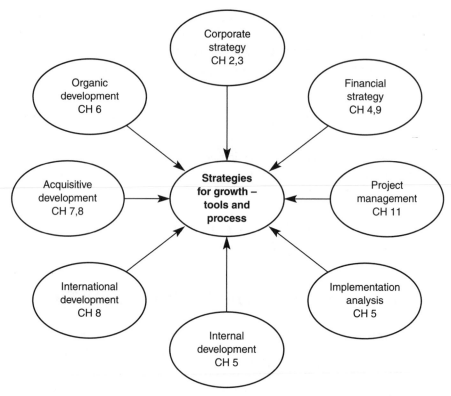

Fig. 1.1 Strategies for growth – the key management disciplines

Applications of our process include:

- organic development (Chapter 6 – with Tesco);
- acquisitive development (Chapter 7);
- international development (Chapter 8 – with BMW and Rover).

On many MBA programmes, corporate strategy itself is seen as *the inte-grating discipline*. Figure 1.1 suggests that while corporate strategy is indeed a crucial discipline, to make better sense of the whole it may be more fruitful to look at the wider ingredients of strategies for growth (as implied by Figure 1.1).

STRATEGIES FOR GROWTH AT
LONDON INTERNATIONAL

Here is an actual case example of growth strategies that offers many lessons. Although this case examines a group which very nearly failed, it needs to be set in the context of the business climate of the heady 1980s, a time that many other companies fell into similar traps. It does not imply that management was inept. If you believe that the following strategic events cannot happen to you, then they probably will.

In the mid to late 1980s, the London International Group ('LIG') was an apparently successful group which had reasonably healthy financial results. It also had an enlightened attitude to innovation and staff development, and a number of very well known, branded products. Best known for its contraceptives, particularly Durex, the group had exploited its core competence in rubber technology by growth in the fields of surgical gloves and other products.

But several clouds had begun to appear in the corporate sky. First, the UK regulatory body, the Monopolies and Mergers Commission (MMC) placed significant constraints on LIG's access to and share of the UK market. Previously LIG had a virtual monopoly of this market, thus generating a very healthy stream of profits and cash flow.

Understandably, LIG management began to look further afield – both outside their core markets and ultimately outside their existing core competencies to target new areas of development.

They decided to focus on the photoprocessing market, presumably because it was relatively fast growing in the mid and then later 1980s. Also, as a not so enormous group (its total turnover by 1988 was £302m) it would have been more difficult to enter a much bigger market. So, LIG elected to grow via niche development.

As the existing photoprocessing market was fragmented, LIG acquired a number of companies with different geographic markets and sometimes differing customer groups.

It appeared that these acquired businesses possessed no particular advantage over their competitors. Nor was it apparent what value this corporate parent brought to these businesses – their being outside LIG's core competencies, and also their more specific and distinctive areas of competitive advantage.

So, while LIG put more and more time, effort and resource into developing photoprocessing, this diluted the attention on core businesses relative to what it might have been otherwise. This was unfortunate, as new entrants, including the entrepreneurial Virgin Group, captured significant share of the contraceptives market during a time when this was growing – due to AIDS and the associated publicity.

And unforeseen by LIG management, the photoprocessing industry was hit very hard indeed by the early 1990s recession. Purchases of processed film are very dependent upon discretionary spending on leisure and travel. So they are very likely to be the first thing to be cut when consumer income drops.

By 1992 results overall were severely affected by photoprocessing, which was evidently dragging down the financial performance of the group. Yet in the 1992 report and accounts the (then) board of directors were still – at least on the surface – confident that photoprocessing would be turned around. Indeed, even as late as these very accounts, LIG Group made an acquisition of another photoprocessing company – serving the specific needs of estate agents.

It looks, at least from the outside, as if LIG found it hard – if not impossible – to conduct an objective and realistic reappraisal of their strategies for growth. This was very unfortunate because in and around 1993 the group subsequently came very close to financial collapse.

The LIG experience clearly illustrates the problems of appraising new strategies for growth where management is inevitably learning about new markets, and developing capabilities and recipes on the go. It also flags up the changes of what might be called a 'lobster pot strategy' – where the temptation is alluring, but once in, you get deeper and deeper and find it impossible to reverse out.

This case shows that it may be a necessary but certainly not a sufficient condition of corporate success, that a group is innovative, develops its employees, or for that matter has a formal strategic planning process. It would be hard to believe that LIG was not following a strategic plan (indeed it appears that LIG had a director of planning). But it also highlights that successful strategies for growth involve linking thorough strategic analysis with a careful appreciation of the financial realities and the crucial hurdle of implementation.

It is clear from the London International case that strategies for growth are concerned with both exploiting existing business potential and also with developing new business. It is concerned with achieving both improvements in competitive advantage and at the same time with financial advantage. If managed effectively, both competitive and financial advantage are complementary. Finally, it is also about developing the organization capability to do new things, or to do existing things differently and better. This is about moving the organization from where it is now to where it wishes to be/needs to be in the future, which invites us to explore the question of 'What is strategy?'

WHAT IS STRATEGY?

Figure 1.2 aims to demystify the idea of strategy. This will help clarify both what strategy means and its implications for how to manage strategies for growth. Here are some givens to start off with.

- It is thought that you are currently at point A. (But is it worth challenging this?)
- It is also thought that point B is attractive, and you therefore want to go there. (But will this actually be worth while – will it satisfy key stakeholders?)
- The environment is ambiguous and uncertain, but you suspect that you need to negotiate a river estuary to get to B. (But again, perhaps you should consider not such obvious options like a subterranean tunnel.)

We can adopt a working definition now that:

Strategy is about getting from where you are now to a place where it is worthwhile being. Strategy is also about getting there through competitive advantage, with least difficulty and in least time.

Figure 1.2 suggests a number of specific concerns which you may need to think hard about:

- Are the two little matchstick men in the south-west friends or foes? (Competitors or strategic alliances)
- There seems to be a storm brewing in the north-east of the map which could be a major threat. (An environmental threat)
- There seems to be a dam or bridge across the river. But this might turn out to be a rope ladder that has been partly hacked away by guerillas – is this an attractive strategic route or one fraught with risk? (An environmental opportunity)

Fig. 1.2 What is strategy?

- Those strange things in the estuary seem to be windsurfers – or are they actually sharks cleverly disguised as windsurfers? (Ambiguous signals)
- Is there a major advance of enemy tanks about to occur in the south-east? If so, what would be an appropriate alternative route? (Strategic options)

The environment in Figure 1.2 is very fuzzy and requires further intelligence, questioning and conjecturing before proceeding. Developing and implementing strategies for growth are exactly like this in practice (as we saw at London International).

Besides illustrating the problems posed of analysing and interpreting the external environment, Figure 1.2 can also generate some very fruitful debates over options for strategies for growth.

Obvious options might exist, for example swimming down the estuary or an overland march. Also more innovative or technology-led options might include:

- a submarine option (to go beneath the obstacles);
- a microlight – or a very small aeroplane – (to go over them);
- a *Thunderbirds* option – perhaps using a mechanical mole (tunnelling beneath the constraints).

Each of these options would have very different degrees of difficulty, risk, speed and costs, and would thus have to be carefully appraised against existing and possible environmental conditions. This must include some appreciation of how the other players on the scene (customers, competitors, allies, suppliers, 'referees' or regulators) may behave. Also, there would not be a one right strategy, which was independent of the environment and change in that environment.

One of the key lessons from the London International case was that you need to steer your strategy as environmental change occurs. In Figure 1.2 you would be foolish to set a strategic course and stick to it even though things had changed. Also, as this change happens quickly you need to aim for the future environment, not the past. As with clay pigeon shooting, you need to aim for the clay's future position rather than where it is now.

Having explored Figure 1.2 to the full, it can now be seen how important it is to do a thorough review of the environment for any major strategic development project.

After exploring how strategies for growth are often fraught with uncertainty and ambiguity, it is useful to look at types of strategy.

WHAT TYPES OF STRATEGY EXIST?

Traditionally strategy has been characterized as being possibly of a 'deliberate' nature (the analytical, rational model) as emergent (Mintzberg) or as unrealized (Mintzberg, 1985).

Mintzberg suggests that strategy operates on a rich continuum between deliberate and emergent. Mintzberg says that strategy should move 'on two feet' – one deliberate and one emergent. He expands his analysis to cover a number of manifestations along the deliberate–emergent continuum, especially as follows.

- **'Planned' strategy**, where the route is laid out in great detail and over a lengthy period of time.
- **'Entrepreneurial' strategy**, where the strategy's main target is specified, but where the route is left very flexible and fluid, and is very responsive to new opportunities.
- **'Ideological' strategy**, which is pushed outwardly from a central and firmly held idea and set of values.
- **'Umbrella' strategy**, which sets down the parameters that guide strategic decisions and implementation.
- **'Process' strategy**, which sets down the 'rules of engagement' for evolving and implementing strategy, but does not dictate the outcomes or decisions.
- **'Unconnected' strategy**, where decisions are made and implemented in relative isolation from one another.
- **'Consensus' strategy**, which is forged gradually by building agreement, rather than by central direction.
- **'Imposed' strategy**, which is introduced from the outside and where there is little discretion over its content (the 'what') and process (the 'how').

Mintzberg's typology is useful because it highlights that planned strategies are only one variant, yet managers often equate plans (and planning) with strategies. More frequently, effective strategy takes the form of an umbrella/process strategy – especially when facing an uncertain and ambiguous environment (for instance, at Mercury Messaging, a division of Mercury Communications (Grundy, 1994a)).

But still the typologies may seem rather abstract from a practical point of view. This invites some simplification and relabelling, which is now explained.

My simplified five forms of strategy (see Figure 1.3) are: deliberate, emergent, submergent, emergency and detergent.

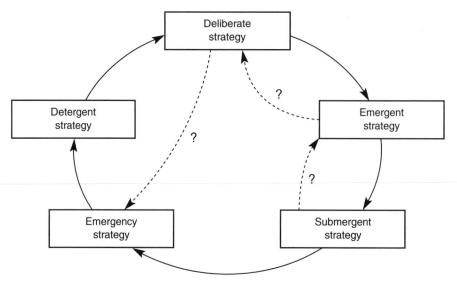

Fig. 1.3 Strategy forms – a menu

Deliberate strategy

A deliberate strategy is one which has a very clearly formulated idea of how to get from A to B. Deliberate strategies, if innovative and skilfully crafted, can offer a more direct route to breakthrough strategies for growth. The proviso here is that any deliberate strategy needs to anticipate both pending external change *and* complexities of implementation.

Deliberate strategies vary considerably, however, in the extent to which (1) A is actually where you are now, (2) whether B is worth going to, (3) whether the strategy actually exploits your competitive advantage, (4) whether the implementation issues are sufficiently thought through, (5) whether your commitment to a particular strategic route is sufficient to withstand setbacks, (6) whether the strategy has sufficient flexibility to respond to change or not. (EuroDisney is a classic case of partly thought through deliberate strategy by its parent, which did not take sufficiently into account local climate or culture.) Deliberate strategy maps closely on to the 'planned' form of strategy in Mintzberg's earlier account. But it may also take the combined form of umbrella and process forms.

Deliberate Strategy: A short story – The Lego Strategy Fails

My eight-year-old son enjoys building sophisticated Lego models or, at least, he enjoys watching me build them for him. Sometimes the Lego designs are complex and intricate. It can take a good two hours to build a space-station, or a set of pirate ships or a tropical island. Imagine my horror when, the very next day, someone has accidentally kicked to bits all the hard work. Now it is very easy to start again, repair all the hard work and then come back the next day to find another mess once again. This time the cat wanted to have a go!

What is the lesson? In a turbulent environment very intricate strategies do not last long. Avoid the Lego strategy (or move the Lego to a safer environment).

Emergent strategy

An emergent strategy is one which is hard to detect as an explicit strategy at the time. Emergent strategies are more commonly ones whose pattern can only be detected virtually after the event, once the pattern has been knitted together. Emergent strategies vary in terms of (1) how coherent this pattern is after the event, (2) whether they exploit opportunities in different strategic directions thus, in effect, partly cancelling each other out. Emergent strategies can help achieve breakthrough in strategies for growth by exposing unlikely opportunities.

Often strategies can be deliberate at one level but emergent at a lower level. London International Group's strategy was no doubt deliberate at a very macro level but was probably much more loose and fluid at the level specific product/market strategies. Or, individual activities or businesses might have quite deliberate strategies, but at a higher level strategy can be quite emergent.

Emergent strategy thus maps closely on to the entrepreneurial and the ideological, and the consensus building strategies of Mintzberg.

Submergent strategy

A submergent strategy is one which was either originally a deliberate strategy which has gone wrong or an emergent strategy which has got itself into real trouble. The submergent strategy is an unrealized strategy which has led to damaging results. In one UK company which struggled to digest the impact of change in the early 1990s, a senior line manager reflects that:

'I don't think we really monitored where we were against the plan. We discovered this too late.... It was as if we were on the Titanic, with water levels slapping on to the deck, and you suddenly realize my God, we are sinking, and to put it bluntly we need to understand that we are shipping water, and it is self-evident that we are slipping beneath the waves...'

Submergent strategies can crystallize very gradually (as at IBM) or perhaps very suddenly, depending upon the degree of turbulence in the external environment, and the extent of recognition and response lags internally. Submergent strategies typically lead to corporate breakdown, not breakthrough.

A submergent strategy might occur when an umbrella strategy proves ineffective as it is too broad, when an ideological strategy no longer fits its environment or where an entrepreneurial strategy begins to fail. The organization may then get locked into making an inappropriate strategy happen. Or it might result from consensus building, being harder and harder (and slower and slower) to achieve.

Emergency strategy

Emergency strategies are characterized by very little longer term pattern in strategies for growth, with these being mainly reactions to short-term pressures or temptations. Emergency strategies are off the highway of achieving breakthrough strategies for growth. An emergency strategy would hardly count as a strategy at all unless it was so prevalent as it is in reality.

Emergency strategies are very frequently the result of the unconnected form of approach to strategy.

Detergent strategy

A detergent strategy is often called 'refocusing' strategy. The idea of detergent strategy is perhaps more powerful as it links directly to cleaning up the mess after an emergent, submergent or emergency strategy. A detergent strategy can be found either as part of a major and dramatic turnaround, or as a more localized attempt to prepare a more solid basis for new deliberate strategies. (Marks & Spencer's North American strategy over the last five years is probably aptly characterized as a 'detergent strategy', as was the ICI/Zeneca demerger – see Chapter 7 – and the float-off of part of Hanson's US operations in 1995.) The new management team at London International Group had, by 1994, substantially refocused the group's activities and had dealt with the photoprocessing problem. Chrysler has even had several phases of 'detergent strategy'.

Particular strategic initiatives tend to move in a cycle around the five strategy forms. For example, the Prudential's major excursion into the estate agency business in the UK was a classic deliberate strategy. However, the Prudential's implementation strategy was very much emergent during the integration/post acquisition phase. During the early 1990s recession, this corporate advance became submergent and then took on the status of being an 'emergency'. Finally, the Prudential chief executive, Mick Newmarch, put in place a decisive detergent strategy by selling off the entire business. Unlike London International Group, which found it hard to extricate itself from its 'lobster pot' strategy, the Prudential was courageous in making this painful move well before several other key players as illustrated by Figure 1.3.

A detergent strategy is a combination of planned and imposed strategies.

No single form of strategy is therefore appropriate to managing strategic development in different contexts. Emergent (and even detergent) strategies need to be managed together in a deliberate, corporate juggling act (for example, as in Figure 1.4). Success is contingent upon management's ability to learn about their strategies for growth – in effect to achieve 'strategic learning' (Mintzberg, 1985; Grundy, 1994a).

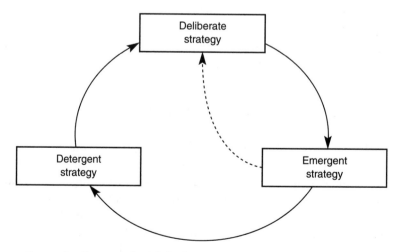

Fig. 1.4 Strategies for growth and the learning cycle

Short exercise

What kind of strategy predominates in your organization and what are its consequences (positive and negative)? Think about:

- deliberate strategy;
- emergent strategy;
- submergent strategy;
- emergency strategy;
- detergent strategy.

HOW IS THE BOOK STRUCTURED?

This management guide is split into three main parts. The first part explores in more depth what strategies for growth entail and the implications for managing them as a process. Then the relevance of strategic business and financial analysis in providing tools to analyse 'hard' content issues in strategy development (Chapters 3 and 4) is examined. This is complemented by analysing the 'softer', organizational issues (in Chapter 5).

In the second part, a number of applications are considered which go through both organic and acquisitive strategies for growth (Chapters 7 and 8) and also by integrating both in the international case study – BMW and Rover – in Chapter 9. Finally, two themes of internal change to support growth and deliver value – strategic cost management and valuing business change (Chapters 9 and 10) – are examined.

Finally, the third part concludes with a chapter which helps you to apply project management to strategies for growth. This chapter also summarizes the key themes and insights that have been explored.

CONCLUSION

Strategies for growth need to be tackled through an explicit and coherent management process – it is far too important to be left to the vagaries of day-to-day management. This process needs to weld thinking about strategic, financial and organizational issues together as a seamless whole. To achieve this, it is more relevant that strategies for growth are approached through an ongoing and critical process of self-examination. This implies moving from a 'strategic planning' mindset to one of strategic learning. To achieve this demands a complex juggling act so that different types of strategy are used in different situations. This juggling act needs to be skilfully orchestrated by top management, especially to avoid the (inappropriate) dominance of emergent (or 'emergency') strategies.

ACTION CHECKLIST

- Does the top team in your business genuinely have 'holistic' or 'helicopter' vision?

- Is it clear (and well known) what the key breakthroughs are which are being targeted (internally and externally) in your business?

- Does your management team have a common language for thinking and talking about 'strategies for growth'?

- Do they use any analysis tools – either formally or intuitively?

- Are these strategies targeted very specifically at reaching for sustainable (financial) value?

- Do you have an effective process for managing strategies for growth – from idea to decision and into implementation?

- Do you really have a clear view of 'what businesses you are in/and want to be in' and are continually revisiting this?

- Do your managers have an appropriate (or inappropriate) idea of what strategy means, and what it entails?

- Do you frequently default to emergent (or emergency) strategy?

'Managing strategies for growth for both *financial* and *competitive advantage is a difficult but necessary juggling act.'*

2

EXPLORING BREAKTHROUGH GROWTH OPPORTUNITIES

Key concepts covered in this chapter include:

- **Dimensions of growth.**
- **Financial and competitive advantage.**
- **Capability.**
- **Breakthrough.**
- **Strategic learning.**
- **Recipes for strategic development.**
- **Competing for the future.**
- **The 'onion model' of competitive advantage.**

WHAT ARE BREAKTHROUGH STRATEGIES FOR GROWTH?

The dimensions of growth

Strategies for growth which were defined in Chapter 1 involve: 'Exploiting business opportunities for both financial and competitive advantage, and to develop capability'.

Unless growth is pursued for both financial and competitive advantage, and to develop capability, what typically results is an assembly of growth tactics which will almost inevitably become an 'emergency strategy' (see Chapter 1).

This definition is best explained pictorially before we moving into more formal definition, as in Figure 2.1.

Figure 2.1 shows the inner core of each business being made up of the key business processes which both add value and drive cost. This is bounded by the three factors which should drive management – competitive

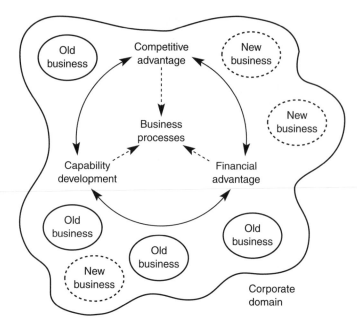

Fig. 2.1 Managing the strategic development system

advantage, financial advantage and capability development. Note that each of the three is a key part of the system – each element is closely integrated with the other two.

For instance, financial advantage is partly derived from competitive advantage. But financial advantage is a driver in its own right as it encourages the organization to compete on naturally financially attractive terrain.

Also, capability development may yield longer term financial advantage. But capability development also needs to be financially targeted: 'Which capabilities are most likely to be harvested financially in the future?' is an important question.

The two domains of new and existing business are drawn in an irregular fashion in Figure 2.1. This is deliberate. It emphasizes the uneven nature of many strategies for growth and the tendency for them to move out of any kind of 'balance' so easily.

'Business opportunities' can encompass not merely direct market interfaces, but also make improvements to activities which indirectly add value. This may include areas such as logistics, IT, finance and human resources. Individual functions need to rethink what value they add, to whom and how they achieve this. So, strategies for growth embrace not merely external development but also key areas of internal development.

Business opportunities may include both those arising out of the existing business portfolio and may involve creating new business activities. Or opportunities may arise in the form of deleting particular business areas which distract, dilute or destroy value.

This may involve repositioning existing business especially to retarget these activities to add value either in different ways, or to target different markets. Or repositioning may involve increasing business responsiveness or lowering the internal cost base. Internal areas of development are less frequently considered to be core elements of strategies for growth, even though they may play a vital, and often exciting, role.

Growth strategies delivering real value inevitably impinge on resource allocation. Resourcing involves not merely 'hard' resource (such as facilities and money), but also softer resources such as people skills, management style and also the support of key stakeholders.

What is 'financial' and 'competitive advantage'?

When dealing with resource allocation it is worth while to revisit the objective of strategies for growth, which is to exploit *both* financial *and* competitive advantage (or 'FCA') across a range of businesses. Financial advantage and competitive advantage are not opposing but are ideal complements. It is only where 'financial advantage' is pursued purely according to a short-term time perspective that tensions between financial and competitive advantage normally arise.

'Financial advantage' can now be defined as:

The art of leveraging business activities to maximize the economic value of cash flows relative to the investment in the business.

For instance, an example of financial advantage would be the ability of many financial conglomerates, like Hanson, BTR (a multinational UK conglomerate) and Tomkins, to squeeze extra financial value out of what were underperforming asset bases, cash flow streams and management.

Financial advantage is thus concerned not merely with achieving particular 'hurdle' rates of return (for instance, beating the cost of capital). It requires thinking about the range of strategies through which more financial value can be generated, or generated more quickly. This may require more rather than less investment or cost (as we will see in Chapter 9). Or it may suggest reshaping the activity or project to achieve the original strategic objectives at lower cost.

'Competitive advantage' can now be defined as:

> *Adding either more real or perceived value to target customers than your competitors or similar value with lower cost, or in a faster time.*

For instance, an example of measurable competitive advantage would be Microsoft's innovative capacity to generate products with higher value to the user than certain other competitors.

While financial advantage has a focus on more internally measurable, economic value – and the value to the business – competitive advantage considers external product/market value – how this value is added, then shared between company and customer, and how this customer value compares with competitors.

Short exercise

For *one* area of business or corporate growth over your last one to three years, ask the following questions.

- To what extent has this been a success?
- To what degree does the strategy build on both financial and competitive advantage (either via deliberate or emergent strategy)?
- How sustainable is success likely to be into the future (i.e. will the conditions for generating both financial and competitive advantage continue, why and how)?

Company capability

The final ingredient of strategies for growth is that of developing capability. This capability may be the capacity to do new things or to do existing things even better. 'Capability' is a better term than competency because 'competency' may be taken to imply some extremely specific skills. 'Capability' is perhaps a better term for capturing the most business-critical skills or capacities in a business or group.

Short exercise

For one area of business or corporate growth currently being pursued in your organization, ask the following questions.

- What key capabilities do you believe may be grown (either deliberately or in an emergent mode)?
- What is the potential value of these capabilities in terms of possible further opportunities?
- How probable is it that these opportunities will materialize and you will be able to take advantage of them?
- What will this capability cost to develop and sustain?

From corporate planning to corporate breakthrough

By defining strategies for growth in this tangible way, we avoid the artificial and frequently unhelpful trichotomy between:

- corporate strategy;
- business strategy; and
- functional strategy.

This is much more helpful because it brings managers within different strategic business units into the debate about how growth strategies are managed group-wide. Also, it helps to move us away from the more hierarchical notions of a separate level of the corporate plan. The corporate plan is often merely the aggregation of more localized business or functional plans. The corporate planner is often in a vulnerable position as they are exposed to the 'emperor's clothes' charge of 'What is in the corporate plan over and above the content of the individual business plan?'

The notion of 'breakthrough' itself now needs exploring. It is about choice and focus – choosing to focus core energies on a small number of areas of opportunity. The Japanese philosophy of breakthrough or *hoshin* (which can be thought of as being strategic common sense) distinguishes between:

- The one to three (maximum) areas which a management team can focus on in a particular time period (of say one to two years). These 'big areas' of breakthrough are ones which might achieve a very substantial contribution to corporate profit and cash flow.
- The many areas of continuous development and improvement which operational management can focus on.

This distinction greatly simplifies the process of strategic development. *hoshin* as a concept is currently applied by a number of major companies, US and European, including TI (Texas Instruments), Hewlett Packard and SmithKline Beecham.

The remainder of this chapter now illustrates strategies for growth with reference to a number of key examples and looks at how strategies for growth can be managed, beginning with issue recognition, then decision, action and interpretation of events and results. The role of past, current and future perspectives on managing and shaping strategies for growth are discussed.

The diagnostic approach to the case study on Marks & Spencer's (M&S) strategies for growth is applied and you can then think about how you would pursue M&S's strategic development.

HOW CAN GROWTH OPPORTUNITIES BE EFFECTIVELY EXPLOITED?

Beyond strategic planning to strategic learning

Achieving breakthrough strategies for growth means an important shift from traditional notions of 'strategic planning' to 'strategic positioning'. This may sound little different at first sight, but the word 'plan' contains overtones of fixity of purpose and pre-programmed response (Mintzberg, 1994), whereas 'positioning' suggests that managing growth strategies is very much an organic process rather than one which can easily and typically be intensively pre-planned.

Managing strategies for growth as an organic process does not mean abandoning the notion of deliberate strategies (which Mintzberg (1994) is fond of downgrading). These deliberate strategies typically seek to shift a business from one position to another according to some particular route. This organic process can be steered by a continual learning process (which I call 'strategic learning' (Grundy, 1994a)) to guide strategies for growth as they unfold.

Figure 2.2 now illustrates how strategies for growth can be managed as a deliberate process.

Note how both the external environment and internal environment interact in this picture. As strategic development proceeds there is ongoing collection of soft and hard data – whether formally or informally. In midflight there may be crossroads which managers pause at, regroup their thinking (reflecting on options), before deciding which strategic track to steer down.

An effective organic process of managing growth strategies is thus like the concept of the cruise missile. Cruise missile technology involves sophisticated guidance systems which enable each missile to make quick mid-course corrections based on signals from the environment. The cruise missile is

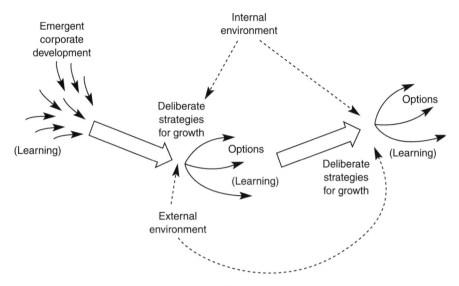

Fig. 2.2 Learning and emergent and deliberate strategies for growth

unlike its inferior counterpart the scud (which may pack a powerful bang but has fixed and less sensitive guidance systems – and is thus inaccurate).

Traditional strategic planning is very similar to the scud in that invariably it misses its target. But that doesn't mean that strategic planning is useless – indeed it contains some very potent tools. Countering Mintzberg's arguments against strategic planning, it is the way that strategic planning has been abused which undermines its value, not its potential.

Applying the cruise missile analogy to strategic development, attempts at deliberate strategies for growth can be seen (from Figure 2.2) going through a number of iterative phases. These phases are in effect cycles of corporate learning as it goes through different phases of analysis, decision, control and learning. There may be considerable feedback lags: time delays may occur between the efforts of decisions on performance; between results crystallizing; and recognition and interpretation of results; and subsequent corrective action. This cycle is depicted in Figure 2.3 (and is similar in some ways to Mintzberg and Westley's similar pictures on strategic change, 1992).

Obviously, the smooth series of cycles in Figure 2.3 can be disrupted at any point, for instance by:

- Issue recognition: by distraction.
- Decision: by simply putting off the decision.
- Action: by inaction.
- Interpretation: by misinterpretation.

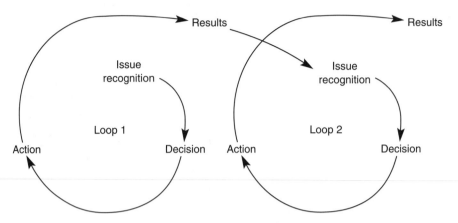

Fig. 2.3 Moving on – through learning loops

For example, in the UK, the Burton Fashion Group went through a series of phases in its strategies for growth over the last 20 years:

- as a manufacturer (and retailer) of tailored menswear (1960s and 1970s);
- as a multiple men's (and women's) retailer (early 1980s);
- as a multiple retailer (men's, women's, sportswear) and as a departmental store (with the acquisition of Debenhams) (mid 1980s);
- as a multiple departmental store and property developer – and as a trader especially prone to discounting its prices (late 1980s/very early 1990s);
- as a slimmed down multiple along with Debenhams – repositioned in the market and more reluctant to discount (mid 1990s).

These phases were championed by a number of different (and at times colourful) individuals, who brought their own personal recipes for strategic development into play. As the trading and economic environment changed, recipes which appeared to be working became recognized as inappropriate and, after time lags, the group has taken a different steer.

Turning back to Figure 2.3, in practice the reality is even messier as one learning loop may spawn several further ones. For example, as in the Marks & Spencer case described later, M&S's own credit card spawned a series of growth loops into unit trusts, personal loans, and (pending) the life and pensions business.

The frailty of corporate learning cycles accounts for the many examples of companies drifting in and out of major strategic development initiatives. Commitment to a particular direction builds faster than the corporation learns (or as Ghemawat (1991) says, 'commitment burns up faster than learning – the "burn to learn" ratio').

Surfacing recipes for strategies for growth

Another way of analysing strategies for growth is to develop a better understanding of the evolution of the company through time relative to the industry context. In more conventional strategy books, the main focus is on understanding the present and unfolding future. This focus treats the past as a given, and as something less valuable to analyse.

However, there are a small number of exceptions in the literature (Spender, 1980; Johnson, 1989), which highlight the need to uncover the drivers of past performance. Spender calls these 'strategic recipes' – being the strategic rules-of-thumb which have guided key growth strategies. Unless these recipes are uncovered then it is unlikely that senior management can really approach strategies for growth in a creative and novel way. Particular blocks to reflection are to be found, for instance, in:

- Decisions made in the past which are now regretted but which it is now perceived could not be avoided – in virtue of commitment and sticky investment in existing business.
- Strategic errors which the company has retreated from – for instance, product/market or acquisitive development which has failed and activities have now been sold off or closed down. In these cases it becomes hard now to reconsider similar kinds of activities, albeit tackled in new and more sensible ways.
- Individuals with very personalized strategic recipes – these may have been formed by personal experience either within the same company or within another company. Or they may reflect the individual style of the manager, for instance the archetypal 'steam roller' brought in to galvanize the company, lay down a new direction and force the development route forward.

Unless the past is re-examined (which is in managers' heads) there are likely to be some major difficulties in understanding the present, let alone the future. These recipes need to be re-examined so that we can begin to think afresh about corporate breakthrough. Past, present and future also need to be explored not merely in terms of company development and market development (see Figure 2.4), but also in terms of competitor development. Again, competitor intelligence, principally, focuses most on the present rather than either the past or the future. Yet unless we explore the past we will be unable to gain a truly rich understanding of competitors' strategic recipes.

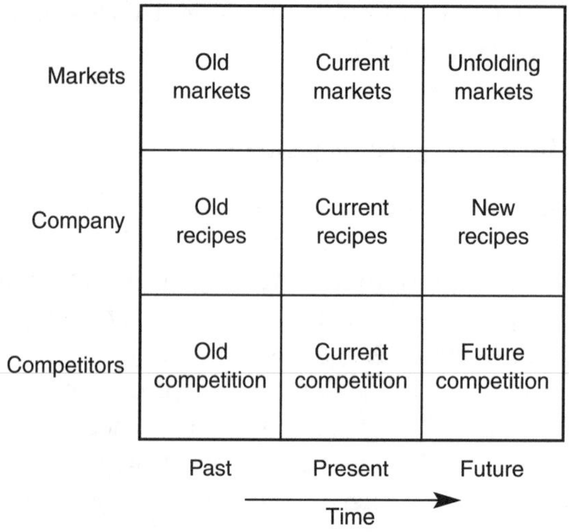

	Past	Present	Future
Markets	Old markets	Current markets	Unfolding markets
Company	Old recipes	Current recipes	New recipes
Competitors	Old competition	Current competition	Future competition

Past   Present   Future

Time →

Fig. 2.4 Managing the strategic sandwich

Looking over the horizon – competing in the future

Recent work (Hamel and Prahalad, 1994) has drawn renewed attention to the critical success factors for competing in the future. This involves understanding new markets (and emerging competitive roles), and also new competitors, and new strategies from existing competitors. Again, this counterbalances the tendency to work in a 'T–1' or 'Time-Minus-One' basis – current strategies are often dictated not by what is about to happen, nor what is happening now, but what has occurred in the past three to five years. Microsoft certainly is one which creates its own future.

Figure 2.4 is entitled 'the strategic sandwich'. The middle and vertical slices (current markets, company recipes and competition) focus on the competitive snapshot of Kenichi Ohmae (1984). The (right-hand) vertical slice (new markets – and customer needs, company recipes and competition) looks at the competitive needs of the future (Hamel and Prahalad, 1994). The past slice enables some of the key strategic assumptions about what will and will not work to be uncovered.

This analysis suggests the following process for managing strategies for growth (see Figure 2.5). First of all, the past is revisited to uncover why particular strategies for growth have been a success (or failure). This is followed by reviewing the present to understand the current position and potential for development. Then focus on rethinking the future before turning to refocusing the strategy. The final stage comprises retargeting strategic efforts.

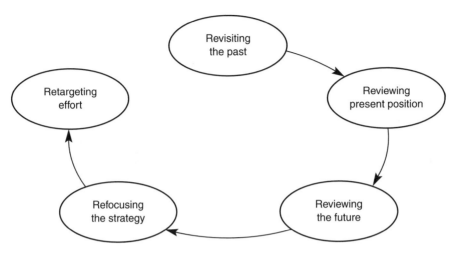

Fig. 2.5 The strategic development cycle

Before you undertake your own analysis of growth opportunities, the following example shows how the key questions can be applied.

Marks & Spencer is a good example because of its reputation as a successful company, and also because it is well known in the UK, in the US, and to many in continental Europe. It also offers major potential for strategic breakthrough, partly because of its strong (UK-based) competitive advantage and partly because of its competitive disadvantages (internationally). This case study is based extensively on publicly available data (for example, its annual reports and accounts), and a day-to-day knowledge of M&S products and services as a consumer. It has not been drafted based on any data drawn internally from M&S. The case study therefore underlines how much can be gleaned about a major company from publicly available data and an appropriately focused set of intelligent questions. (Ironically, the insights may be relatively powerful to those inside M&S, but unsurprising to ongoing M&S watchers.) The questions used to probe M&S can be used just as effectively on, for example, a customer or competitor you may know well. Afterwards we will explore M&S's *past* growth record.

MANAGING STRATEGIES AND OPTIONS FOR GROWTH AT MARKS & SPENCER

Before you start to read this case, spend a couple of minutes thinking about the following two questions.

- What do you put M&S's past success down to?
- If you were appointed to the board of M&S as director of group strategy, what ideas do you think might reinvigorate the M&S formula?

Marks & Spencer PLC is a very large, successful business with turnover of £6.5 billion and profits before tax of £851 million as at 1994. Fourteen million customers now shop at M&S each week.

Marks & Spencer is a company which has exercised strategic choice. This does not merely mean choosing to do things – this is relatively easy. (Unlike the grocery chain Sainsbury, for example, see Chapter 6, M&S has not been tempted into moves into the do-it-yourself market.)

M&S must have been exposed to many opportunities over the past 10 to 20 years which would have been strategic temptation, but has, by and large, chosen to build on its core business and capability.

Where M&S has come unstuck – in parts of its international development and in acquisition – is where it has stepped outside its (then) core capability. But these setbacks may well have prevented M&S from fully capitalizing on other avenues for strategic development, nearer to home, for example, into other service industries in the UK and elsewhere. Like BMW in the case study in Chapter 8, is Marks & Spencer now perhaps unduly attracted to the notion of becoming a 'global player'?

M&S's core business is focused on high street retailing and core products are clothing for all the family – women's, men's, children's. This 'general' business contributes nearly £3.8 billion of turnover. It has also built a very successful niche food business which now amounts to a surprising £2.6 billion of turnover (40 per cent of the group). In the 1990s M&S has successfully diversified into personal financial services (although this business is still relatively small compared with the core). Growth has been primarily of an organic nature and overseas ventures (acquisitive and organic) have met with variable success. The most successful ventures appear to have been organic and have involved partnership with local companies from whom M&S has been able to learn.

M&S's past performance

Marks & Spencer's gross profit divided by turnover (or 'gross margin') has increased from 32.8 per cent in 1990 to 35.1 per cent in 1994 – with no decreases year-on-year during the severe UK recession in the early 1990s. This is a truly impressive achievement and represents a very hard act to follow. Can M&S sustain this stretching performance into the late 1990s?

We now explore avenues for further strategies for growth which could avoid diluting M&S's financial and competitive advantage, but we need to begin by revisiting the past.

M&S's annual report and accounts do not, unfortunately, give a breakdown of operating profit by type of trading activity – indeed M&S is not (legally) obliged to. However, it is safe to conjecture that the 20 per cent of business activities (by number of activities) which have formed over 80 per cent of profit generation are (as an approximation):

- men's and women's clothing;
- the food business.

This leaves home furnishings, children's wear, men's and women's shoes, financial services and other products as generating probably around 20 per cent of profit. Also over 80 (in fact 87) per cent of activities are located in a single country – the UK. Increasingly M&S is sourcing from non-UK suppliers, having overcome its earlier hesitation.

A summary table of M&S recent results is shown in Figure 2.6. This shows a remarkable stability in the mix of corporate business over a four-year period.

Its first half interim results for the 1994 year end highlight relatively sluggish growth in food sales (at 3.9 per cent) relative to general business (posting an impressive 8.9 per cent growth). This highlights perhaps the tougher competitive constraints impacting on its UK food business. It also highlights why M&S may be tempted into a major push for growth outside the UK.

If we go back even further in time (to 1985), M&S has achieved a compound rate of growth in turnover of around 8 per cent in nominal terms over nine years. On the other hand, during much of that period we have seen fairly high annual doses of inflation, particularly in the overheated late 1980s and into the earlier part of the recession in the UK. So what is

	1994		1992		1990	
Turnover:	£m		£m		£m	
General	3786	58%	3371	58%	3221	58%
Foods	2632	40%	2358	40%	2306	41%
Financial activities	123	2%	98	2%	81	1%
	6541	100%	5827	100%	5608	100%
Operating profit	873		635		305	
Earnings per share	20.9p		13.5p		6.9p	

(Source: M&S Annual Report and Accounts, March 1994)

Figure 2.6 A brief summary of M&S recent financial performance

perhaps more impressive is M&S's stability and consistency of development rather than its percentage real growth per se.

The main driver of increased profit growth over 1985 to 1994 is the improvement in operating margin, up from 9.4 per cent of turnover to 13.0 per cent. This kind of improvement can come in a number of forms – higher prices, fewer or lower discounts, or supplier productivity improvements/M&S holding supplier prices down. It is likely that much of that improvement came through M&S exercising its very strong bargaining position *vis-à-vis* suppliers. But if that were to be the case, then has M&S still got much further scope to squeeze suppliers (or otherwise improve margins)? Does it need to seek other avenues for development to sustain its earnings growth?

M&S's current recipes for success

Marks & Spencer's success depends upon a philosophy of value for money, quality and service. It has built an extremely strong brand which has appeal to a high proportion of the 'middle market' in the UK who have high brand loyalty. (To illustrate, M&S claims to have 35 per cent of the British market for bras and knickers.) Its Marble Arch store is reputed to sell 19,000 pairs of women's knickers *per day*. Apparently one Arab customer arrived at the till with a rack of nightdresses, only to be told by the attentive M&S saleswoman 'These are all in different sizes' (he replied that so were his wives) (*The Times*, 10 December 1994.)[1]

M&S is very selective in having quality locations and relatively simple product ranges. It is also selective in the things which it does not do – for example, it has not taken other people's credit cards and avoids high fashion, etc. It is also (justifiably) famed for insisting in the absolute best from its suppliers. According to one City of London investment analyst (on Channel 4):

> *'Being a supplier to Marks & Spencer is a source of unprecedented pressure, and some might say is interference from a customer in those businesses. If you are producing products which are good enough to Marks, at a price which is acceptable to Marks, and the other conditions of being a Marks & Spencer supplier are satisfied, then being a supplier to Marks & Spencer is very, very profitable.'*[2]

In the mid 1980s M&S began to lose ground to new competitors, such as Next, which targeted M&S and offered quality clothes with just that bit more fashion. This attack was good for M&S, which as a result has since regained much of the initiative.

M&S has also had a variable track record overseas and has had a number of disappointments both in North America (for instance in Canada where M&S has traded for 22 years, according to the *Financial Times*, 1994) and in Europe. Like many companies which have developed a very strong market penetration of a single national country, M&S has found it hard to adapt its strategic and growth recipes to quite new and different business environments. For example, in Spain, it is said that while local people like M&S underwear etc., they found the original clothes offered 'ugly' (*Financial Times*, 1994). This invites the question as to whether M&S's merchandising in Spain was originally driven by a tailoring of the UK offering, rather than by working backwards from local tastes.

Indeed, in a 1994 UK Channel 4 television programme on M&S, the scenes in the Valencian store suggest that the merchandising strategy in its non-UK countries is built around the UK formula. It is as if M&S is aiming to convert non-Britons to the M&S, British formula. This is not necessarily a bad thing – chains like MacDonald's have created and imposed an international but US-based formula. But the M&S formula (especially in clothing) is likely to be heavily impacted by localized culture.

Whatever one thinks of the current international development strategy, there is no doubt that M&S is seeking to exploit these opportunities in a big, albeit cautious way.

According to an investment analyst in the City of London (Channel 4):

> *'I think a much bigger proportion of its profits will come from conti-nental Europe over the next 10, 15, 20 years. There is room for growth in France, maybe into Germany. But I also think that there are very exciting prospects in the Far East. It is already well established in Hong Kong and of course the great unknown is whether it might get into China.'*

In fact M&S intends to double its selling space in continental Europe over the next few years, with Germany and Italy (in addition to France and Spain) on the agenda. (The first German stores were announced in March 1995 – *Financial Times*, 28 March.)

According to Sir Richard Greenbury, chairman:

> *'There isn't a retailer, a big one, in the world today that can probably say that he is going to stay in his home-based economy, and just do well there. I mean all the great retailers are having to face the facts that they have yet to take their skills abroad, one way or another.'* (Channel 4)

Perhaps M&S is now much better placed to understand how to exploit its talents internationally than during its earlier experimental efforts. Maybe this could begin by recruiting more staff of other nationalities (especially in senior roles), so as to adapt the M&S philosophy to other environments. This may seem to be a minor issue at first sight but could, in the longer term, be major as it shapes the mind set of management (see Chapter 5 for more on organizational mindsets).

M&S's present platform for growth

To get a better picture of M&S's present platform for growth it is important to understand more about its underlying competitive advantage, which may be difficult.

Ohmae (1982) advocates doing a three-cornered comparison between customers, competitors and the company, to assess the following.

- How does the company add more value (perceived and/or real) to its target customers relative to its key competitors?
- Does it add value at less cost than its competitors?
- Does it add value faster or more flexibly than its key competitors?

In practice, three-cornered comparisons of customer/company/competitor can be relatively tricky. A simpler and more workable alternative is the 'onion model of competitive advantage'. which first necessitates a closer look at what is meant by 'competitive advantage'.

It is rare to find a single ingredient of distinctive competitive advantage which is responsible for a company's success. Particular sources of competitive advantage are typically easily imitated, unless of course they are:

- derived from some secret or currently patented technology;
- based on service excellence which is derived from a culture that has taken many years to build up;
- some accidental or historic advantage (in the latter case, in the early 1980s British Petroleum (BP) had two wonderful sources of competitive advantage – the huge Forties oil field in the North Sea, and also the even bigger oil fields in Alaska).

For most companies, however, competitive advantage needs to come from a number of sources and not just one. It is often because of the specific combination of specific competitive advantages that a company overall has a distinctive advantage over its competitors.

Some sources of competitive advantage are more fundamental than others – these are shown at the core of the onion. Others exist but are more easy to imitate and thus peel off. This suggests considerable similarity between the structure of competitive advantage and that of an onion – hence the onion model of competitive advantage.

Introducing the onion model of competitive advantage

In the onion model we initially brainstorm the key sources of competitive advantage. This might be done by extracting from a SWOT (strengths and weaknesses, opportunities and threats) analysis key strengths. We would then apply the Ohmae tests which help us focus whether these competitive strengths are actually based on measurably:

- superior customer value; or
- lower cost;
- greater speed, flexibility or responsiveness relative to competitors.

This can be made more concrete by defining specific criteria.

- **Value:** brand and reputation, relative market share, unique underlying skills, management skills
- **Cost:** cost base, relative market share.
- **Speed:** distribution, unique operational skills, management skills.

The danger with starting purely with a SWOT analysis is that the 'strengths' listed may not be true competitive strengths at all (unless these have been previously benchmarked). Also, the listing of SWOT items can omit key external competitive strengths relevant from a customer value perspective. Or, important issues such as the level of the cost base might be overlooked.

The rules for using the onion model of competitive advantage are as follows:

1. Only those sources of competitive advantage which are demonstrably superior to at least one other key player can be included in the onion of competitive advantage.
2. Where there is a key competitive weakness and this is demonstrably weaker than at least one other key player, then this should be counted as a source of competitive disadvantage. This will form part of the black onion of competitive disadvantage.
3. Once the demonstrably superior sources of competitive advantage have been listed, these are then prioritized in terms of the difficulty which competitors would face in imitating it. Those areas which are most difficult to imitate are positioned towards the centre of the onion, and those which are easiest to imitate at the outside.
4. Likewise, those areas of competitive disadvantage which are particularly difficult to remove are placed at the centre of the black onion.

Normally, therefore, you end up with two onions – one good onion and one black one. The size, make-up and overall visual impact of the two onions conveys very powerfully a company's underlying competitive position. A multiple layered 'good' onion of competitive advantage offers a solid platform for breakthrough strategies for growth.

The onion model also encourages a much greater challenge than that offered purely by a SWOT listing. The onion model can also highlight some fundamental problems with a company's strategic health (imagine doing one for IBM as at 1990).

So why have we chosen to focus on not merely competitive advantage (the 'good onion'), but also the black onion of competitive disadvantage? This is because frequently a company is not so successful not because it lacks distinctive and sustainable competitive advantage, but because of its *competitive disadvantage*. Sometimes I wish that Michael Porter had gone on to write his third book not on *The Competitive Advantage of Nations* but on Competitive Disadvantage – Avoiding Business Cock-Ups!

The onion model will now be illustrated by returning to the M&S case.

M&S's future platform for growth – its competitive advantage

Figures 2.7 and 2.8 draw a good and a black onion of competitive advantage and disadvantage for M&S, based once again on purely externally available data.

The centre of the onion begins with M&S brand which is extremely strong and exceedingly difficult to imitate by another company. Indeed, many companies in other service sectors aspire to have a brand like M&S.

This brand is supported by M&S's reputation for value for money and also its reputation for customer service (and its supporting culture – this is drawn for brevity as the same onion ring). Around these core advantages are clustered M&S's supplier linkages and innovation which are also core sources of competitive advantage. According to one City of London investment analyst (Channel 4):

> '*Marks has styled itself the manufacturer without factories. ... They probably do have the closest relationship with suppliers of any UK retailer.*'

Moving towards the outside of the good onion, we have included M&S systems and its high street sites. Note that we have put its prominent high street sites at the fringes, as ultimately it is possible to imitate this area of competitive advantage.

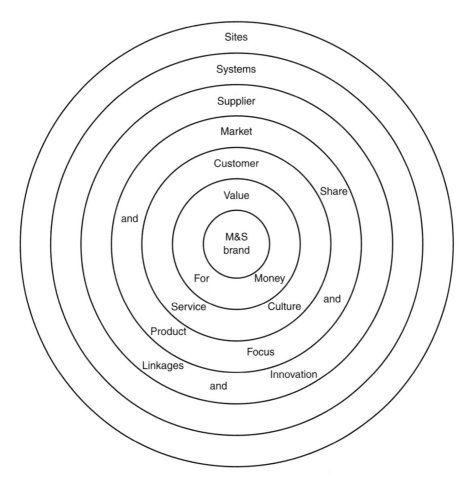

Fig. 2.7 The onion model of competitive advantage – the M&S case

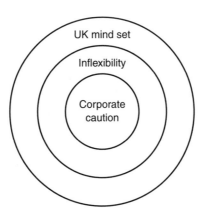

Fig. 2.8 A tentative black onion of competitive disadvantage – the M&S case

Looking at the onion picture in totality, we see that M&S currently has an impressively strong bundle of multiple and reinforcing sources of competitive advantage. The key word here is *currently*, as it is easy for a company of M&S's strength to become relaxed about its position, and unable to learn from other companies or the changing environment. One analyst reflects on this:

> *'I think they are a very self-confident company, and provided that they remain self-confident and not complacent I don't think that that's a problem. But I think that retailing is a notoriously fickle business. You have to keep on reinventing it and reinventing it year after year, season after season. You have to make sure that your clothes are fashionable, that the styles and colour are what people actually want.'* (Channel 4)

Or M&S may become too rigid as an organization. Sir Richard Greenbury, chairman, espouses the dilemmas of maintaining discipline versus encouraging individual spontaneity:

> *'You must have discipline. You can't have everybody doing their own thing. And big businesses do become bureaucratic and they do become inflexible. But the day that they become so bureaucratic and inflexible that the free thinker, the maverick, the entrepreneur, the fellow or the woman who doesn't do it the conventional way ... those people must be given an opportunity express their talents.'*

This interesting set of remarks highlights the problems of simultaneously managing two sets of opposing strategic recipes for growth. One is minded to launch a new word into the language: stratophrenia.

But does stratophrenia matter? According to one (brave) joiner from another retailer (a departmental store):

> *'People just don't say anything. No one will speak against the Chair, because they say it shouldn't be done. You can just see people's faces changing (when you say critical things). People just don't believe you, when you say something bad about Marks & Spencer, so you just don't bother.'*

Besides strategic vision and financial value, effective strategies for growth require intense entrepreneurial drive. Marks & Spencer certainly has this drive in its incremental UK-based development plans, but the key issue is can it really replicate or clone this in a tailored way internationally?

M&S's competitive disadvantages – its Achilles' heel

We now need also to address M&S's potential competitive disadvantages. These derive from:

- M&S's perhaps over-cautious approach to managing its strategic development (at least in terms of organic development in the UK – except for financial services), and its culture generally;
- its apparent lack of flexibility (for example in refusing to take non-M&S credit or debit cards (until very recently));
- its UK-centred mind-set. This does not particularly affect its UK business but may have hampered its international development, perhaps seriously.

M&S staff might well dispute this analysis (and maybe with some justification). For example, M&S's caution could perhaps now be seen as a strength in comparison with the certainly under-cautious behaviour in the late 1980s of its competitors, Next and Burtons, for instance. Note the comments of another analyst (Channel 4):

'They [M&S] will certainly tend to be dismissive of criticism from outside. When you think about it, when a company is incredibly successful and Marks & Spencer has been, and still is, then your starting base has got to be, that what anyone outside is saying is potentially wrong, and that they know the best way to do things. They have been doing it like that for 20, 30, 40, 50 years and it works for them.'

One of the most distinctive elements of this culture is the attention to microscopic detail at most senior levels. On the UK Channel 4 television programme, Sir Richard Greenbury, chairman, interjects at the start of a meeting to discuss current M&S foods to point out that:

'I had the potato and leek [soup] last night and it has got lots of cream in it and it has got no potato in it. You know, if you have potato and leek then I like it to have a sort of powerful taste *and it was, it was rich, it was too liquid it just didn't gel with me.'*

Yes, this intervention is an example of M&S's great strength ('Retail is Detail'). But how can this level of detailed intervention be possible in the future when M&S might be generating up to a quarter, a half, or even more sales outside the UK? Can M&S truly become a substantial and successful international retailer with this apparently high degree of centralized, top-down direction and control in its merchandising?

Also, the issue of M&S's refusal to take other credit or debit cards may be seen as justified in terms of the virtue of strategic choice – saying no to a costly strategy. However, the costs of excluding (or reducing) the business of many customers lacking M&S charge cards must be considerable, if unquantified. Some customers may either have found it difficult or possibly too inconvenient to acquire M&S cards (for example, tourists). It has not always been the case that on seeing a Visa, Access or American Express card M&S staff have said 'I am afraid that we can't take that particular card, but if you would like to complete an application we may be able to issue you with your M&S card in about 5–10 minutes at customer services, where we have an on-line approval system.' Since then, M&S have begun to address this issue if a frustrated customer asks the right question. Although this is now M&S's typical response, a credit card was previously seen as a threat, bordering on revulsion.

In the latter situation we might have shifted the 'say no to other companies' credit cards' from the black onion of disadvantage to the positive onion of competitive advantage.

Again, the history of M&S's attitude to non-M&S cards is symptomatic of a twin competitive strength and weakness. As one analyst (Channel 4) puts it:

> 'You are looking at a company which essentially you have to characterize as a "family dynasty", everyone is schooled in the history and in the traditions. I think the disadvantage of this kind of culture is that it can make it inward looking, it can perhaps breed a kind of arrogance. There again, if you make parallels with military power in the world, you are looking at an army of people which is incredibly disciplined, know exactly where they are going, and are a force which everyone has to reckon with.'

M&S's international position

Turning to the final issue, the UK-centred mindset, this may suggest doing the onion model of competitive advantage separately for M&S international activities. Figure 2.9 attempts to do just that, with both the positive onion and the bad onion.

Note how the pattern (within the onion model) has changed substantially. Although M&S's brand strength may still have some power, this power (as it currently stands) has shrunk greatly. Also, although M&S still has a clear market and product focus, it does not necessarily have complete fit with local cultures (or at least did not originally, as the various examples

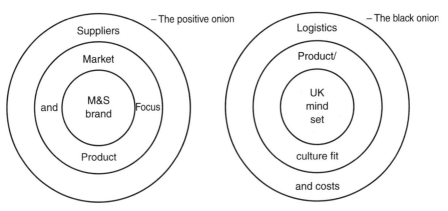

Fig. 2.9 M&S international business competitive advantage

quoted earlier illustrated). Also, although M&S still has a strong supplier base this is offset by significant difficulties of logistics and attendant higher costs internationally. It is only in the relatively recent past that M&S has been able to lift European sales. This recent success was achieved by exporting its 'outstanding value campaign' from the UK, and thus by reducing its prices and its margins significantly.

A specific competitive disadvantage in M&S international activities is the additional costs (prices are estimated as 20 per cent above the UK by the *Financial Times*) which M&S incurs because of its distance from the UK. But despite this cost disadvantage (relative to the UK) M&S still claims to be 'unbeatable value', and not just in the UK.

Harder to remove still is M&S's UK-centred culture. According to their chairman, Sir Richard Greenbury, these attitudes are changing.

> *'One of the most exciting things amongst young people joining the business today is they think internationally. They are going to have to deal with a much more competitive, much more demanding trading climate. They are going to have to deal with customers who are not short of choice, or product at any price, of any quality, anywhere in the world. The consumer today is not just king, the consumer today is dictator.'*

One detects behind Sir Richard Greenbury's statement perhaps more a vision of the future rather than a present reality. M&S still appears to take its graduate recruits from the UK rather than from the international market. And its core management echelons are staffed substantially by British managers.

Although the black onion of M&S's competitive advantage is less influential than the positive one for its international activities, this may present an over-optimistic output; the UK mindset may act as a profound disadvantage which limits M&S's international efforts.

Strategic options for growth

Overall, the M&S onion analysis suggests that M&S business portfolio is of varying competitive strength (for instance, between clothing, food, other items and financial services, UK and internationally). This calls for a review of the positioning of its businesses which is done in the next chapter to illustrate the industry attractiveness/competitive strength (or 'GE' grid). This analysis suggests that although M&S has some impressive product lines, particularly women's underwear and its niche foods business, this is offset by a number of less strategically and (probably) less financially thrilling business areas.

M&S's competitive strength in the UK gives it a platform to expand into a considerable number of potentially attractive areas in the UK. There may also be opportunities for unbundling M&S core competencies and then exploiting these selectively on an international basis. For instance M&S's very successful recipes in developing their niche food business might migrate internationally more readily than, say, its clothing. Perhaps stand-alone food stores could be pursued in selective cities? (M&S's Paris store is the second most successful after Marble Arch, with 'hordes of baguette-bred French folk cooing improbably over M&S sandwiches' (*The Times*, 10 December 1994)). Stand-alone food stores might be more rapid to develop than the general stores, which appear very slow to match to the right sites (*Financial Times*, 1994). M&S, however, is trying to expand non-food stores first, so as to provide the infrastructure for food.

Keith Oates, deputy chairman and managing director, says M&S is increasing its expansion plans outside the UK (over three years from £1 billion to £1.3 billion), perhaps at a worrying pace: 'It's hard to keep track of how much we are spending – it increases so often' (*The Sunday Times*, 4 December 1994).[3]

M&S's corporate intent is now to 'change its international image from that of a niche retailer selling a "little slice of Britain" to a high-volume, big player in Europe and East Asia' (*The Sunday Times*).

Financial services also represent a potentially attractive opportunity to M&S. When the M&S case study is run in financial services companies, most managers are very impressed by M&S's potential to make inroads into these markets. The particular strengths which M&S brings to this arena are its:

- very strong brand;
- reputation for quality (and, at the same time, value for money);
- focus on a narrower product line.

One wonders whether M&S corporate management take a similar, and even unduly measured and conservative view of their capability in financial services than their competitors do of M&S. This is an excellent example of an aspect of strategic behaviour being simultaneously *both* a strength *and* a weakness.

So, what are the key routes to exploiting these avenues to development? M&S does not seem to be in particular need to develop via acquisition, in view of its core corporate strengths and opportunities for organic development. (Rightly, M&S management stated in 1995 that there is no point in paying a lot of money for the goodwill when it is M&S's brand itself which adds the value.)

Indeed, because of M&S's very strong culture, a major acquisition may also not look like being a very sensible route, due to risks of culture clash. A way around this might be to keep any acquisition more autonomous, but of course this may inhibit value being added through integration.

An obvious course of development is to exploit M&S's existing skills in franchising. For example, in Spain M&S has teamed up with Cortefiel, an old-established business (a manufacturer–retailer) with a similar philosophy to that of M&S.

A number of areas now come to mind for Marks & Spencer to exploit, including:

- personal financial services;
- non-retail (personal) services;
- home shopping/'M&S Direct';
- stand-alone food sites (especially overseas).

Taking each main area in turn, personal financial services offers growth potential, but many areas of this market are becoming more regulated and more fiercely competitive. There might also be concerns about overstretching or putting at risk the M&S brand name. Although M&S does not operate a salesforce with highly geared commission, it might be exposed, for instance, if say its investment returns are much lower than financial services industry averages, should M&S pursue a very conservative investment policy.

Other, non-retail services might offer potential (such as up market travel), but again these need to be in areas where customers are likely to pay a premium for M&S reliability, or where high quality is rewarded by customer reluctance to shop around. One interesting and successful area of growth is Marks & Spencer's home delivery of flowers (to M&S card holders). M&S now compares with Interflora in its penetration of this UK market.

Home shopping might be an interesting avenue but may not pass the 'Is it a sufficiently big enough test?' (like home delivery of M&S wine). If we reflect on M&S's entry to financial services, this does not seem to be particularly substantial yet in relation to M&S's overall portfolio. A caveat here is the one of 'competing for the future' – maybe in ten years' time M&S could draw 20 per cent of its profits from financial services.

Turning back to home shopping this might simply cannibalize on existing M&S demand, rather than help build relative market share. Having said this, one still wonders whether M&S could not extend its market share by offering an exclusive 'M&S Direct' service to its existing cardholders, or as a catalogue. Now that M&S is relatively site-constrained, couldn't it take further market share by simply making its clothing products more accessible? Perhaps M&S is partly put off because of the corporate 'not invented here' syndrome or 'if Next do it, then we shouldn't be doing it'.

A further thought is that M&S might also find it useful to extend its existing corporate competencies in information management and logistics into the area of 'M&S Direct' – an imaginary name. One suspects that a high proportion of M&S cardholders have an IBM compatible computer which could then run a computer-based database of M&S products (maybe on CD-ROM). Perhaps this opportunity is three to five or five to ten years away, but M&S might need to begin exploring this idea now to position itself.

A bigger move into out-of-town M&S sites might be of interest, but might be poorly timed, in view of the increasing concerns about out-of-town developments. In late 1994 there was major shift in the attitude of planning authorities who are now ruling out most new applications. Maybe this might have been a fruitful opportunity once, but M&S may have missed the boat.

Stand-alone food sites might be attractive but only in very selective locations (in the UK). Overseas, however, this could offer a lot more potential, but financial viability would be contingent upon reaching critical mass. Could this concept parallel the success of the Body Shop? Would M&S be able to balance a locally tailored food offering against the need to maintain consistent product themes and core lines?

Evaluating the options

M&S might pursue several of the above options for growth, but pursuing a number of developments might run the risk of adding to M&S's business complexity. Home (or tele) shopping might provide a big contribution (with a five to ten-year horizon), but this might erode business through existing outlets.

M&S thus appears to be somewhat constrained in the medium term in the UK to modest growth. The danger is therefore of a major international push which dilutes both competitive position and value. One argument could be that M&S might be better advised to seek either UK-based opportunities parallel to its foray into financial services, rather than its very major push internationally. However, if M&S could overcome its UK control mindset and become more entrepreneurial (in its international product scope and style of operating), then perhaps international growth could genuinely add value.

In most of the larger growth opportunities M&S may contemplate, they face an increasing competitive threat. Financial services is experiencing increasing competitive rivalry generally. Home or tele shopping may also be perceived to be so attractive as to bring in new entrants, particularly from players seeking to integrate home-based information systems, telecommunications and entertainment. Finally, small niche food stores are already being experimented with by at least one other supermarket chain.

Further opportunities to refocus the business

Which other business activities naturally suggest themselves as being areas to harvest, run down or get out of?

There might be an outcry to even contemplate some major moves to move out of key activities, both from customers and within M&S. However, there might be options such as running down the range of products. Areas which might conceivably suggest themselves to be narrowed down might, for instance, be men's shoes (or conceivably women's and children's shoes).

Clearly, a number of M&S customers might conceivably decide to go elsewhere for all or part of their purchases in this event. But one would need to offset that against the other, new business activities which could be opened up. Could the lower value-added shoes be replaced by some kind of higher value personal service (maybe leisure related)? In generating radical ideas of this kind it is important to allow managers the freedom to 'think the impossible'.

Another way of looking at some of the less competitively strong areas of M&S is to see how they might be repositioned. For example, it might be possible to move men's shoes into the 'no-man's' land of shoes which lies between the commodity shoe end and the high premium priced end of the spectrum.

The strategic ideas above are largely incremental and do not involve a major rethinking of M&S's competencies. However, a substantial roll-out of an international food business would require a significant shift in skills and perhaps also in mindset. Or, if any significant acquisitions are attempted, M&S might need to buy in further skills for any international acquisitions. (M&S's track record with acquisitions is not strong – the acquisition of Brooks Brothers with 322 stores in the US has not been an unqualified success.)

Any major extension of Marks & Spencer's business scope is likely to involve significant new investment. Where this involves a business concept of a more novel nature this investment might be partly considered as an investment in corporate learning. The principal value of this investment would thus be in the learning gained in identifying what kind of future opportunities might be exploited, and how. Profits and positive cash flows would probably roll in much sooner, say, with an investment to extend M&S's niche food operation internationally relative to, say, a diversification within the services industry.

In the case of a major international expansion of food, the key risks and uncertainties would revolve around the fit of M&S's product range and presentation with local tastes. Does the existing formula (even with tailoring) actually work in a different cultural and economic environment? In the separate opportunity of (non-financial) personal services, what degree of competitive rivalry would be encountered?

The critical success factors associated with a refocused strategy for M&S (which might involve dropping certain product lines), include the need to:

- gain sufficient market penetration to become financially viable in any new products or markets;
- avoid any major operational (or regulatory) mishaps (for example, in financial services) which might detract from the M&S image of quality;
- be able to adapt M&S strategic recipes to different market and competitive conditions from those M&S is accustomed to;
- persuade senior management that the new set of strategies are financially attractive and competitively viable, and also are acceptable within the M&S culture, and politically.

An apparently simple adjustment in direction might be viewed with scepticism or cynicism within M&S as it has solidly established recipes for growth. New areas of development would need to be positioned by clear messages about their financial and competitive rationale, and timescales for development and financial returns.

The difficulty of adjusting direction could be considerable in M&S. According to one City of London investment analyst (Channel 4):

It (M&S) is a bit like a supertanker. This is a very, very big turnover company. It is the fifth largest publicly owned retail company by turnover in the world. It is very difficult to take quick decisions that will dramatically alter course. So yes, there is a bureaucracy that takes risk out of the business but perhaps also means that Marks & Spencer from time to time does miss opportunities.

Review exercise

Given your initial thoughts on what you would do if you were newly appointed as head of M&S's group strategy at the start of this case study:

- How do your own ideas for development stack up against the debated case study and analysis?
- How could your own options be further developed to make these more robust?
- What new capabilities would these ideas require that M&S develop (or require building on existing capability)?

Concluding lessons from Marks & Spencer

The M&S case represents a fascinating story of successful strategic development based on a set of relatively unchanging corporate competencies. It is probably time now for M&S to re-examine its own mindset and assumptions not only about where it can compete and grow with both financial and competitive advantage, but also how. M&S may well now need to think through what appear to be quite radical avenues for organic growth to sustain the performance improvement achieved over the past ten years. Without refreshing and novel thinking past successful recipes for strategic development may run their course and maybe even burn out. If even a traditional clearing banker like Midland in the UK was able to begin with a blank strategic page when setting up First Direct as a differentiated telephone banking service then perhaps M&S too can break the mould. Contrast M&S's conservatism with Richard Branson's exploitation of the Virgin brand, which keeps on popping up in new places – travel, Cola, and now financial services. (Maybe M&S and Virgin could co-operate? Or maybe not, given the possible culture clash.)

Testing out the strategy development process

It is now evident that a process for analysing strategic position and potential would be most helpful. The majority of other frameworks suggest that strategic analysis is primarily focused externally, i.e. outside the organization, and also on decision-making rather than on implementation. Figure 2.10, by contrast, emphasizes the equal importance of thought through design of implementation, delivery of results and also distillation of lessons. Implementation overlaps with strategic analysis and is not separate from it, hence the double-headed arrows for 'design implementation' etc. in Figure 2.10. In Chapter 5 focuses even more closely on implementation.

M&S is now used as an illustration of this process by a quick replay of its strategy for international development over the past ten years.

Diagnose situation

If we time travel backwards, in 1985 M&S was almost totally dependent on UK sales and (with the exception of its foods and possibly new ventures) nearing the peak of its high street penetration. To generate further turnover and profit growth M&S then perceived development in North America, Europe and the Far East as potentially attractive opportunities for strategic development.

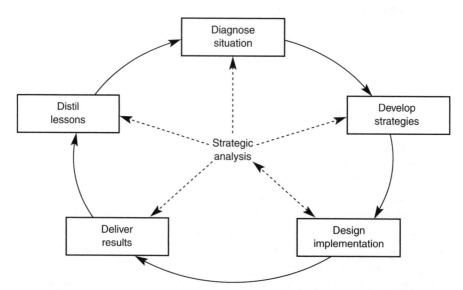

(Note: this process was developed in conjunction with Stuart Reed, formerly of Hewlett Packard UK)

Fig. 2.10 Breakthrough strategies for growth – the process

Develop strategies

As of 1985 the US market was very big but might not take so readily to the (tailored) M&S formula. Canada might be assumed to be culturally nearer to European tastes and was thus an obvious target. In Europe, France and Spain might also potentially be of interest – as evidenced by tourists from these countries visiting M&S's UK stores.

Also, there might be acquisition opportunities (such as actually crystallized in the acquisition of the Brooks Brothers chain in the US).

Franchises also offered a potential source of strategic development, provided that these did not undermine the M&S brand.

There are many lessons that M&S could have gleaned (and no doubt have, in the fullness of time) from these overseas adventures, particularly about:

- the effectiveness of its market entry strategies;
- M&S management capability (in the international sphere);
- the importance of achieving critical mass in the particular market;
- marketing infrastructure requirements (especially logistics and procurement) – not just in terms of quality of service but also its cost base;
- tailoring of merchandise – how much is typically required, and how to do it.

At all five stages in Figure 2.10 strategic analysis thus provides a potentially strong antidote to incremental thinking about strategies for growth.

The framework in Figure 2.10 emphasizes that developing strategies for growth is very much an iterative process. Most managers are inclined to resist going backwards to, for instance, revisit the situation, refine the strategies or redesign implementation. They are even less likely to perform a thorough review of causes of disappointment and past failure when delivering results and distilling lessons. Most managers' formal effort is likely to fall somewhere between 'develop strategies' and the 'design implementation' phase.

A key issue in developing strategies would clearly be implementation capability, particularly as the M&S corporate mindset (as at 1995) was bound to be very UK-centred. (Capability development appears to have not figured prominently in M&S's strategic development.)

Design implementation

Ideally, in this phase all of the implementation concerns raised in 'develop strategies' would be diagnosed in greater depth and ironed out. Given M&S's relatively slow progress to develop internationally it looks as if the implementation phase was M&S's Achilles' heel.

Deliver results

As a well-run company, M&S would no doubt have been bristling with operational and financial controls to help track results. But to what extent was progress against the international component of its strategy (including specific strategic measures, milestones and indicators of progress) monitored? In many businesses generally, 80 per cent of effort is spent on areas of controls which are only 20 per cent of the key controls needed to track the total performance of the business.

Distil lessons

It appears (from the outside) that M&S was slow to realize that its initial strategies for international development were not perhaps proving particularly effective. It is likely that M&S sought to run these ventures more efficiently ('doing things right', Drucker), rather than questioning whether they were effective (or, 'doing the right things').

CONCLUSION

Strategies for growth frequently challenge the existing allocation of resources within the organization. They are also highly dependent on the support of key stakeholders (a point which is amplified in Chapter 4).

Managing strategies for growth for *both* financial *and* competitive advantage is a difficult but necessary juggling act. The Marks & Spencer's case study highlighted the importance of gaining and sustaining competitive advantage for generating superior financial performance. This needs to be done across business units, and needs to be watched particularly carefully when undertaking rapid international expansion and business growth.

A most important issue is the extent to which capability development is explicitly targeted as one of the key outputs of strategies for growth. Arguably, this should have figured even more prominently in M&S's past efforts in international development.

ACTION CHECKLIST

- Could your planning processes be simplified by re-examining the levels of functional, business and corporate strategy, and by encouraging a more unified debate?
- What are the dominant recipes which pervade your company's thinking about what does and does not make money, and why (in both financial and strategic terms)?
- Are these recipes appropriate not only for the present but for the future?
- Has top management thought hard (and long) enough about the competitive future – what its customer's future needs will be, its future competitors, and future sources of competitive advantage?
- If you were to create your own company's onion models of competitive advantage and disadvantage, how would these compare with those of Marks & Spencer?
- What implication does this self-analysis (using the onion model) have for both existing and new strategies for growth?

[1] Published with the permission of Times Newspapers © Times Newspapers Limited 1994

[2] The world according to St Michael was produced by David Paradine Productions Limited for Channel Four Television Corporation

[3] Reprinted with the permission of Times Newspapers © Times Newspapers Limited 1994.

Part II

TARGETING STRATEGIES FOR GROWTH

The strategic analysis toolkit can help identify and evaluate opportunities both within and outside the current domain of corporate activity.

3

MASTERING THE
STRATEGIC TOOLKIT

INTRODUCTION

Strategic analysis is so frequently seen as something to be tackled in a relatively ad hoc process of meetings and discussions. Most managers feel uncomfortable using formal tools except, for instance, SWOT analysis.

Yet strategic options are now so much more complex, uncertain and demanding. Managers owe it to themselves, their staff and their shareholders to tackle strategies for growth in a professional, yet non-bureaucratic way which achieves genuine breakthrough. In this chapter we show how this is possible, giving hands-on guidance on which tools of strategic analysis to use, to test out new and existing programmes for growth.

Some (but not all) of these tools are to be found in most good books on strategic management. However, several existing concepts are taken further here. New tools and concepts are added. These tools are also explored later, particularly in Chapters 6, 7 and 8.

This chapter includes the following tools and concepts:

- gap analysis;
- SWOT analysis;
- PEST analysis;
- growth drivers (within the market);
- the five competitive forces;
- the sixth force – the industry mindset;
- the GE 'grow earnings' grid;
- profiling of competitive strength;
- differentiation, cost leadership, focus strategies;
- sustainable competitive advantage;
- STAIR analysis – simple and clear strategy, timing, advantage (internal and external), implementation (capability), resources.

This is set out as follows:

- issue analysis;
- industry analysis (with case);
- strategic positioning and development.

But first, many books exhort managers to 'think strategically' or prescribe 'strategic leadership' to helicopter out of tactical day-to-day management. But few address how to make this happen. Where strategic analysis tools are explained this is most frequently done conceptually rather than with illustrations showing how to use the tools during day-to-day management of strategies for growth.

Only a few writers on strategic management recognize the problem and reflect this in the focus of their writing. Ralph Stacey, for example (1993), suggests that at least 90 per cent of all the textbooks on strategic management are devoted to the routines of planning, rather than to the surprise and unpredictability that managers have to cope with.

This book (and this chapter in particular) is different from those criticized by Stacey. Chapters 5 to 10 all focus on implementation as well as on strategic analysis. This chapter provides a practically based overview of a complete set of strategic analysis tools.

Where appropriate, I have refined these tools (from their original sources) to make them more user-friendly and effective. An example of this is the model of key competitive forces which shapes industry structure. I introduce some new and simple models such as the onion model of competitive advantage (Chapter 2), the STAIR tool for screening a specific strategy or option, and vector analysis of growth drivers.

But, perhaps more importantly of all, you are guided in identifying in what circumstances you might use particular tools, and also how, and in targeting them directly at achieving breakthroughs. This is not however a simplistic guide which would fall into the Stacey trap of seeking to dissolve residual uncertainty and ambiguity.

Yet most of the value of strategic analysis can occur when strategies for growth programmes are re-examined and perhaps even go into reverse. By analogy, it seems that many managers would rather join a motorway queue rather than reverse up the last exit and rejoin the motorway later on. (In management terms, strategic reversing is absolutely legal – see Figure 3.1.)

Figure 3.2 highlights the need to distil lessons about how attractive strategies for growth have proven and also to revise recipes for implementation. During the diagnosis phase the results of past efforts might also need to be reinterpreted. Goals were perhaps achieved more by luck and by accidental timing rather than because the underlying strategy was robust.

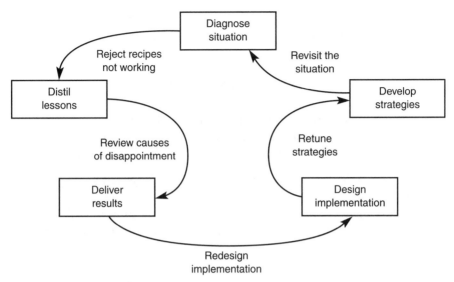

Fig. 3.1 Strategic analysis – going into reverse

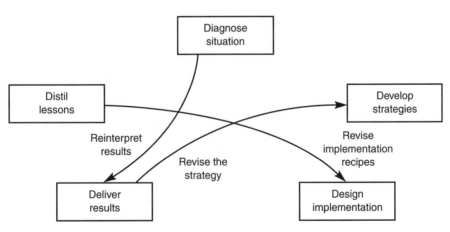

Fig. 3.2 Strategic analysis – rechecking the process

Also, monitoring results provides a continuing steer to strategy development (especially where strategy is in a partially emergent and fluid mode, as it frequently is).

The process of developing breakthrough strategies for growth thus provides a useful framework for focusing analysis effort on the right things, at the right time and in the most appropriate way. The next section looks at how strategic analysis tools can be used to drive this process.

ISSUE ANALYSIS

Figure 3.3 now displays the key tools which can be applied to the first two phases of the process. First, in diagnosing the situation there are a number of useful inputs which might provoke fresh thinking, particularly the following.

- **Gap analysis:** this assesses the gap between projected strategic development (and needs).
- **SWOT analysis:** this performs a quick snapshot of perceived strengths and weaknesses, opportunities and threats of the existing corporate and business strategies.

Gap analysis

Gap analysis is one of the least well used tools of strategic analysis. It is still quite rare to see it in formal use. Frequently corporate plans are based

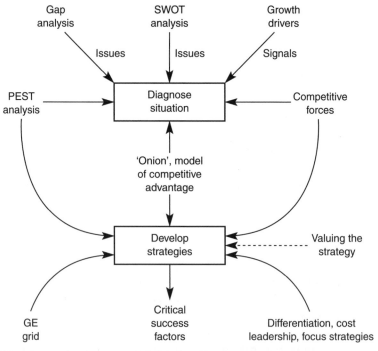

Fig. 3.3 Diagnosing the situation and developing strategies

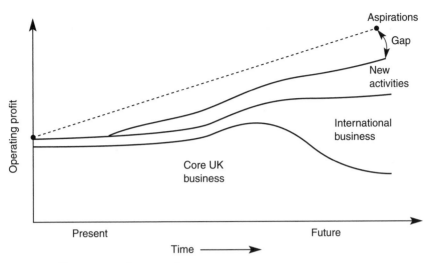

Fig. 3.4 An illustration of gap analysis

more on aggregating separate, tactical plans for achieving more profit, rather than by creating stretching, but completely viable, breakthrough strategies for growth.

An example of gap analysis for a maturing UK engineering company is illustrated in Figure 3.4. Here we see the core UK business activities facing competitive pressure and a fall in growth rate, squeezing operating profit. Although international development and new business activities may fill part of corporate aspirations, there still remains a significant gap.

Following gap analysis, a next step may be to perform a SWOT analysis. Strengths and weaknesses are more typically the internal variables of strategic position. (Opportunities and threats are more typically the external influences on a company.)

SWOT analysis

SWOT analysis is by now a frequently used and indispensable tool, providing a number of provisos for using SWOT are met. These are summarized as the following list of strategic do's and don'ts.

Strategic do's

- Make continuous and explicit comparisons with your external competitors (or internal substitutes), to reality-test your assumed strengths and weaknesses.

- Where you are unclear as to whether a particular variable is a strength or a weakness, separate these two aspects out, listing one as a strength and one as a weakness
- When dealing with product- or service-related strengths or weaknesses, make sure that you 'think customer' – assess the strength of weakness from the customer's perspective
- Rate your degree of strength and weakness on a scale (of, say, 1–5) so that you get a handle on how strong you are, or how weak
- Use this analysis to draw up a profile your overall position (see our example in Figure 3.5).

Strategic don'ts

- Do a SWOT analysis without highlighting the key areas which are most important for competing effectively.
- Be unduly self-critical of particular areas of the business when from the outside of the company you are perceived as being strong (for example, by your customers or competitors).
- Think that compiling a SWOT analysis equates with actually having a strategy.
- Assume that SWOT necessarily completes the strategic analysis (you will need to complement it with other tools, particularly those which uncover unexpected areas of opportunity or threat).

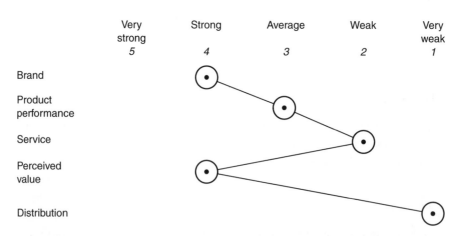

(Note: you should try to profile yourself against at least one strong or potentially strong competitor)

Fig. 3.5 Mapping competitive strengths

- Complete the SWOT analysis without standing back and saying 'What patterns have emerged about the overall business position, e.g. we are in need of turnaround, and what bigger options for strategic development does it now suggest?'

As you can see, SWOT analysis is rarely self-sufficient and needs to be utilized along with other strategy development tools. Having witnessed innumerable SWOT analyses produced without the benefit of the above 'strategic do's and don'ts', SWOT analysis reminds me of the phrase used by many estate agents to describe a property where quantity is a substitute for quality of: DECEPTIVELY SPACIOUS! So many SWOT analyses are voluminous without really distilling the really key strategic development issues and options.

INDUSTRY ANALYSIS (AND CASE)

Below are listed three complementary tools for assessing the economic attractiveness of a particular growth opportunity.

- **PEST analysis:** the key political (and regulatory), economic, social (and demographic) and technological factors shaping industry change.
- **Other non-PEST factors driving growth** inherent in the market, such as the specific drivers of customer demand.
- **Competitive forces:** the impact of entrants and substitutes, buyer (customer) and supplier power, and competitive rivalry between existing players.

PEST analysis

Taking PEST analysis first, Figure 3.6 displays the key ingredients of PEST. Note that the various PEST factors should not be analysed completely separately, but need to be looked at in terms of the pattern which emerges. For example, PEST factors might be used to predict the broad impact of recession on an industry such as retail, as follows.

- **Political factors:** following an election, interest rates go up (to choke off economic demand, which was previously overheating).
- **Economic factors:** the impact of a fall in GDP (gross domestic product) causes tax income to fall, public expenditure to rise (to fund unemployment costs) and thus income tax rates to rise. This in turn puts additional restraint on consumer demand, especially in discretionary

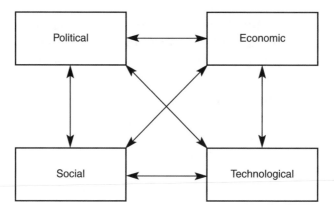

Fig. 3.6 PEST factors

retail purchases. As unemployment rises rapidly this acts as a brake on consumer spending and also shrinks those areas of the market which are highly price sensitive.

- **Social factors:** concerns about security of jobs, higher income taxes and lower real increases in pay put a squeeze on sectors like holidays and restaurants. Paradoxically this provides a boost to markets like quality ready-cooked meals (as at M&S), volumes of which actually rose in the short run.

- **Technological factors:** information technology (together with BPR (business process re-engineering)) plays a major role in helping companies to shed jobs, thus putting an increased and continuing squeeze on economic demand.

The above highlights how the apparently separate ingredients of PEST need to be examined to see how they might interact together to assess their overall impact.

Growth drivers

The next area of analysis is the main growth drivers within the market. The PEST factors will identify some of the key drivers of growth which are outside the industry, but in addition these within the market itself need to be examined.

Growth drivers which are inherent in the market can include a variety of things, for example:

- **Service innovation:** a new market (or segment) may be more attractive to customers than the existing one, either because the need is now delivered in a cheaper or better way. For example, telephone banking and telephone insurance offers customers either a cheaper or better service (or, arguably, both), than existing more expensive or inflexible providers.

- **Technology innovation:** a new technology (for instance, mobile telephones or personal computers) may enable the customer to satisfy previously unserved needs or ones which were at best inconveniently served in the past.
- **Increased learning about products or services:** there may be an increase in awareness among customers that the product or service exists, and how its benefits can be extracted. Once customers have learned more about these benefits, this is likely to increase the frequency of usage.
- **Price reductions:** as a market expands, growth can feed up on itself as companies gain economies of scale. The benefits of these economies are then passed on to the customer in the form of lower prices. These lower prices can then induce penetration of new customers and/or increase frequency of purchase. Or, a single competitor might break rank and reduce its prices, causing a surge in demand and increasing its own market share. For example, when *The Times* newspaper (in the UK) reduced its price to 30p it not only triggered a price war but a significant increase in the volume of the total market (but not the actual monetary value of (non-advertising) turnover, as turnover value is price multiplied by physical volume).
- **Scarcity of substitutes:** shortages of other means of satisfying needs can generate an (often unsustainable) increase in market or segment growth. For example, in times of economic boom the demand for external consultants frequently increases due to internal skill shortages within companies, not because they have anything particularly wonderful to offer.

So, how important are the growth drivers inherent in the market which are not already detected by the PEST factors? The answer is, they can be very important indeed. Growth can be generated by spontaneous increase in demand by customers or by industry innovation. Or the wider PEST factors can provide an environment conducive to growth. But even the PEST analysis may not always pick up the potential for growth to be driven by technology through innovation within the industry. The 'T' of the 'PEST' factors is normally aimed at detecting trends outside the particular industry.

Also, when using the 'S' (or 'social and demographic trends'), this does not always identify key market trends such as changes in buying criteria, and method and frequency of use.

Once all the key PEST factors and growth drivers within the market have been identified it is essential to evaluate their combined effect. This rarely means constructing a complex computer-based model. Instead a pictorial representation of the overall growth drivers (novel in the strategic literature) provides stimulus for debate. This is accomplished through vector analysis (where arrows are used to represent the strength of growth drivers) which are now explored in more depth.

Vector analysis is a way of mapping the impact of forces for development and growth in an industry. The length of the vector arrow represents the perceived strength of the force driving growth. (Later on a similar approach will be applied to evaluate the implementation difficulty of projects for achieving breakthrough growth – see Chapter 5.)

Figure 3.7 now analyses a market – management consultancy – which grew very rapidly in the late 1980s in the UK, and then went into a sudden and dramatic reverse. Management consultants expanded very rapidly during this period, with major firms growing often at compound growth rates of 25 per cent or more. Although management consultants should perhaps have known better, very few individuals with power within these firms openly questioned the sustainability of phenomenal growth rates which were extrapolated out into the future.

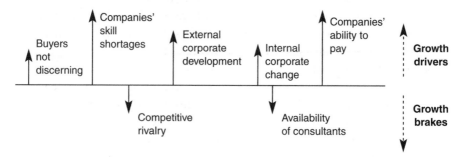

Fig. 3.7 Drivers or growth – UK management consulting market 1987–90

Figure 3.7 explores the key factors underpinning this growth. During the period of 1987–90 there was an often unquestioning use of consultants by big companies during skills shortages and when these companies were still trying to develop rapidly. Also, larger companies' ability to pay ever-increasing fees was still relatively strong. Around the late 1980s there were few blemishes to act as brakes on this heady rate of growth (for instance, rivalry which provided some check on the level of fees).

But if we now fast-forward to Figure 3.8, which shows the overall position during 1991–3, the situation is much bleaker. Although company restructuring and simplification is now a new growth driver, this is counter-balanced by buyers being more discerning, fierce competitive rivalry, weaker ability to pay and a tight financial climate. The results was lower fee levels, fewer jobs and a massive squeeze on the market. Few big firms came

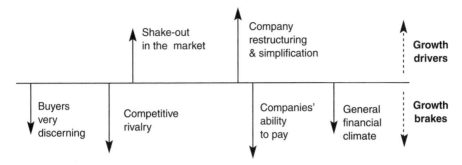

Fig. 3.8 Drivers of growth – UK management consulting market 1991–3

clean in public on the severity of the downsizing they undertook – not wishing to undermine their bargaining position.

So, was this precipitous turn of events predictable? I think most of it was, even if the timing and extent of the impact were still uncertain before the event. Indeed, I left the large consulting environment in late 1988 partly because I was deeply concerned about the sustainability of this growth trend.

Even by 1995 there has been only a slow return to growth in the consulting industry. Much of this growth has been achieved on the back of BPR (business process re-engineering – or perhaps from a consultant's point of view this means 'big and profitable review'). The overpowering lesson from this case study is that you can never afford to ignore the key growth drivers and especially that you should also be alert to the growth brakes. Growth brakes are the forces which throw growth into reverse. To identify the potential growth brakes you need to amplify the 'weak signals' concept from the environment (Ansoff, 1975). Weak signals are either incidents or patterns in environmental change which suggest a shift is about to occur externally or that some new development is about to take off.

The five competitive forces

The five competitive forces (Porter, 1980) this provides a very usable framework for analysing a company's immediate and future competitive environment. These five competitive forces comprise:

- entrants (the threat of);
- substitutes;
- buyer power (i.e. of customers);
- supplier power;
- competitive rivalry (between existing players).

Each one of these forces can be evaluated in two ways, particularly to explore:

- whether the force is favourable or unfavourable – in generating longer term profits in the industry; and
- its relative importance (in terms of impact on profit).

An unusual case – the burial industry

In analysing a perhaps unusual industry – that of undertaking (or, more explicitly, burials and cremations) – it can be seen that overall a relatively favourable picture emerges (see Figure 3.8). The European industry is ripe for strategic breakthrough, even though the total market volume is actually decreasing (as people are living longer and longer) – in the US the market is already transformed.

First, buyers have relatively low bargaining power. When someone dies it is usually an urgent process to sort out the funeral and other arrangements. Death is what sociologists have described as an 'unscheduled incident'. Further, the buyer is in the perhaps unusual position of paying for the burial indirectly – from the deceased's estate. The buyer (the deceased's relatives) may also be emotionally affected by the death. The buyer is thus unlikely to be in a state of mind conducive to driving a hard bargain, to shopping around or going for a lowest-cost burial. This might look conspicuous in front of other relatives. In short, this situation of low buyer power is of clear advantage to players in the undertaking industry.

As Jessica Mitford (a critic of the funeral industry for many years)[1] explains on UK Channel 4:

> 'The funeral transaction is unlike any other. If you buy a car or a house you discuss it with everybody, you shop around, and you consult. But if you have got a dead body in your living room then this puts a different complexion on things. You are likely to call the first undertaker who comes to mind.
>
> Once he comes in there and gets the body, that's the end of it as far as he is concerned. In other words, you are very unlikely to insist on someone else after that.
>
> The nature of the transaction is that you are probably in a fog of misery. You are not quite in your right mind and very susceptible in fact to all that the undertaker has to tell you, after all he is the expert.

This is compounded by the fact that when there is a death in the family then there is a lot of guilt feeling around – 'Oh dear, I wish I had been nicer when he was alive' – that kind of thing. And guilt feelings are very much what the undertaker counts on in selling his merchandise.

The fact is that people can be easily talked into something they don't need and cannot afford.'

Second, 'substitutes' to a conventional burial in modern society don't really exist (except of course the substitutes of going for cemetery versus crematorium options). The do-it-yourself burial is not socially acceptable. 'Substitutes' are therefore relatively unimportant. (In a number of other industries this is similarly the case, but when using the five forces tool managers spend a lot of time trying to brainstorm substitutes. However, there is a caveat here that in certain industries potentially important 'substitutes' can be easily glossed over because managers haven't thought about the industry from the customers' perspective and also deep enough about innovation possibilities.) But this may be largely due to ignorance. Jane Spottiswode (UK Channel 4), author of *Undertaken with Love*, tells about the do-it-yourself (DIY) experiment with her husband's body:

'Well, the only real difficulty was getting a coffin, because I started with local undertakers and, shock, horror, they said 'We only provide it as part of our full service'.

So then I tried the undertakers' suppliers, and the same thing happened. But then I found one, they thought it was a bit unusual. I got the coffin. It was chipboard and it was £36 plus VAT.

Friends of mine had a Volvo, and they didn't want me to pick it up in my Mini – it wasn't quite the thing; we put it in the loft until my husband died because we knew there was no way he would live – he had lung cancer.

When he died, after various tribulations we put him in the coffin and we took it and him to the crematorium. The funeral cost us just under £200 for everything.'

Apparently (according to Channel 4) in the UK you can bury a body in a back garden (and don't even need a coffin) – but you do need a death certificate (but check the legalities first). (This is what separates humans from Sandy and Hazel, the gerbils buried in my back garden.) In the UK there is now even a movement of DIY funerals – 'The Natural Death Centre' (*Sunday Times*, 8 January 1995, 'Style', p 10).

Third, entrants may not be attracted to the undertaking industry because of its traditionally gloomy image. On the other hand, real entry barriers may not be so high, particularly where a determined player enters by acquisition (as is now happening in the UK). Acquisitions may therefore enable entry and thereby shift the entry barrier indicator from being a 'favourable' force to one which is 'slightly less favourable'.

Howard Hodgson (a former UK undertaker – now millionaire and author of *How to Get Dead Rich*) reflects on how business was done in the industry 20 years ago.

'It was very much a cottage industry [in 1975], it was very much, other than the Co-Op, family, small. We needed to buy these [businesses] locally in order for us to have a strategy, which went from strength to strength. In fact, by 1990 we had established 546 outlets in the United Kingdom and were the largest funeral directors in the country.'

This entry/acquisition strategy yielded some very tangible economies of scale for Howard Hodgson's business. He continues:

'There were considerable economies of scale. The average family firm of funeral directors had to have a hearse, probably two limousines, and conduct five or six funerals a week. The capital equipment was used once a day. By acquiring firms in the area and rationalising, we were able to get one of these limousines to go out five or six times a day each.'

Besides Howard Hodgson, a major entrant is Service Corporation International (SCI) of the US. Bill Heiligbradt, president of SCI (a nearly US \$1 billion company worldwide) said on UK Channel 4:

'We have found [in Australia]... that people have chosen *to spend more on funerals. I would again emphasize the word* chosen, *it has been their choice.*

What we are here to do is to offer services and merchandise that make people feel better at a tough time in their lives. ... So the fact that our revenues have grown [per funeral] in Australia is because the Australian public desired it. In the UK that's our goal as well.'

Apparently (according to Channel 4) funeral prices since SCI entered the Australian market have increased by 40 per cent. Even where pre-paid funerals are involved, this can apparently increase industry profitability as the supplier reaps the fruit of receiving pre-paid investment funds. Estimates by the *Sunday Times* ('Style', 8 January 1995) of the value of just 25 per cent of funerals being pre-paid are put at £5 billion. This obviously suggests both a major threat and opportunity for investment institutions like insurance companies.

Fourth, suppliers may have some bargaining power (especially in restricting space for graves or even for cemetery plaques), but there appears nothing special in the supply of hardware like coffins, hearses or the provision of flowers. (The one exception is perhaps the availability of land for burials.) The overall verdict is therefore that 'suppliers' are favourable to industry profitability (as a force), but that this force is relatively unimportant.

Fifth, existing firms in the industry are currently relatively fragmented (few having significant market share, even locally against one another). Also, competitive behaviour is restrained given the cultural norms of the industry. Thus we would rate competitive rivalry overall as favourable, but as relatively important. So if rivalry were to increase significantly, this would have a big impact on the industry.

So, taking the five forces as a whole (see Figure 3.9), it can be seen that the industry is currently relatively favourable to making a good, longer term profit. This analysis suggests that:

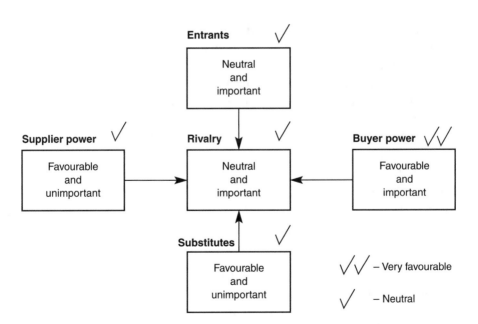

Fig. 3.9 The five competitive forces and the undertaking industry

- if already in the industry, longer term profit should be good (unless entrants move in and restructure the industry or if buyer power strengthens);
- if rated against other industries for identifying avenues for strategies for growth, it might be considered to be an (inherently) attractive one to enter;
- critical success factors such as building one's brand (to keep entrants out) and perhaps seeking a differentiation strategy can be readily identified.

The relative attractiveness of the undertaking industry has not escaped the attention of new players. Coincidentally, after I completed this case analysis I was struck by a feature entitled 'The New British Way of Death' appearing in *The Times* (20 November 1994). This feature contrasted the clinical and gloomy British approach to the death business with innovation in the industry in France.

Apparently it is now just four years since Michael Leclerc opened his first 'Supermarché de Mort' in Paris. He now has 60 supermarket franchises, 200 smaller shops and *one-third* of the French funeral business. In 1995 he is entering the UK – watch out existing funeral directors.

Michel Leclerc's business concept is to 'apply the technology of the food supermarket to the funeral industry'. In place of black, the Roc Leclerc colour scheme is blue and yellow, and in place of dim bulbs and heavy velvet curtains is strip lighting and stripped pine shelving. All the paraphernalia of death is on display, with a price tag. The main things we can offer', Mr Weller (the UK franchise manager) says, 'are choice, economy, and no hidden extras. We aim to charge between 20 and 30 per cent less than elsewhere but, above all, to offer the widest possible range, which our customers can view without the pressure of having a funeral director at their shoulder.'

Monsieur Michel Leclerc himself says on Channel 4:

'... we will try to reduce prices by between 40 and 50 per cent, because to me prices in England are very high, and I think we will quickly expand. I don't see what can stop us.'

As Jane Spottiswode (the Channel 4 expert on DIY funerals) says:

'Why don't Texas and MFI and all those firms that profess to be do-it-yourself experts stack flat-pack coffins; stick-it together yourself. Again I was laughed to scorn. I received quite a nice letter from Sainsbury's who thought it was a good idea, but not for them.'

As someone with a strategic (as opposed to a morbid) interest in this industry, I was intrigued to learn from *The Times* that:

- In principle, if one were able to secure a cheap burial site one could achieve a 'lowest cost' grave for 'as little as' £300 (including a cardboard coffin for £49.50). To this you would need to add the funeral service itself - still coming in at the cheapest at £645. More recently (*The Sunday Times*, 'Style', 8 January 1995) the lower cost burial options have been exalted as 'environmentally friendly', saving the burning of hundreds of thousands of coffins each year.
- Alternatively, you might opt for a more conventional and, by comparison, up market burial for over £4,000 (with an expensive oak coffin at around £2,000).
- Burial at sea is a novel proposition – this option saves the graveyard or cemetery cost, but requires 'boat hire with precise navigation equipment' (presumably to avoid the coffin turning up by mistake on a public beach) – a cost minimum of £3,000.

What emerges therefore from our industry analysis is a cosy industry structure ripe for innovation and restructuring, offering better quality at a much more acceptable price. To go one better than the Leclerc business concept, one might even imagine the possibility of a telephone-based funeral service or Funerals Direct PLC (perhaps called 'Death Direct' would be too unsavoury). This concept might offer the advantages of speed, simplicity, openness (about price) and flexibility.

One specific factor which could be changed is the bargaining power of customers. There is near-local monopoly or oligopoly of undertakers. The assumption is that bodies cannot really be moved around very far because of twin problems of refrigeration and speed (why do funeral vehicles never seem to exceed five to ten miles per hour?). But there is no physical reason why bodies cannot be transported quicker (if colder) to a central location prior to collection for the actual funeral. Even cost would not be a major issue if one had a national network with high market share (supplementing the 'Death Direct' concept above).

Using the five competitive forces

Before we leave this example, there are a few more general and serious points which need to be made.

1. When doing the five competitive forces you must *try* to put into the back of your mind which particular player you are. Otherwise the analysis of

the industry itself will become confused with your own particular position. (Your own competitive position is best addressed by doing a second
analysis to check out the critical success factors which emerge *vis-à-vis*
your business.)

2. You may need to do more than one analysis using the five forces,
depending on whether you have in effect one industry, or more than one
industry or market to analyse. For example, in the car market you need
to do separate (although related) analyses for the executive and smaller
volume car market. These two markets have quite differing characteristics (and inherent attractiveness).

3. You need to look at the competitive forces not in isolation but in terms
of how they interact with one another. For instance, buyers may seek
to enter the market (via backward integration). Or suppliers may also
seek entry (via forward integration). Equally, buyers may look wider
for sources of supply (if competitive rivalry is low), enticing new
entrants in. Finally, new substitutes might be sought where buyer
power is low.

4. When the industry changes significantly it is frequently not because of
one competitive force, but because of changes to two or possibly three
forces combining together. For example, in the UK supermarket industry in 1991–4 the 'hot triangle' of buyer power–entrants–competitive
rivalry was instrumental in changing the strategic behaviour of leading
companies (see Chapter 6 for a full case study on Tesco PLC).

5. Besides its use for strategic positioning of existing business, the five
competitive forces is an essential analysis for evaluating any new
strategic development. This is even if the 'market' or 'market segment' seems to be very similar to existing ones. Also, strategies for
growth can frequently entail changing the industry structure. For
example, this might involve introducing new substitutes or restructuring the industry through acquisition. Or industry change might
occur by innovation in cutting out players in the industry chain, or
by radically reducing costs (especially in mature and competitive
industries). For instance, telephone sales of motor insurance in the
UK in the early 1990s created a virtually new set of five competitive
forces, with initially low competitive rivalry (one main player) and
with weak substitutes.

6. Where managers apply the five competitive forces they frequently ignore
or fail to deal systematically with the relative importance of each force.
Figure 3.10 helps to avoid this problem by separating out 'unfavourable'
ratings of the five forces against their relative importance. This relative
importance will differ between industries and particular markets. Note

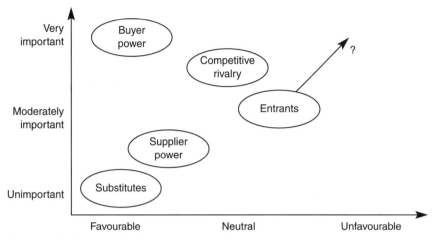

Fig. 3.10 Evaluating the five competitive forces

that in the undertaking industry most elements have 'favourable' ratings, but some of these are of lesser importance.

7. Porter's five forces are valuable for understanding your customer's industry. This can give significant edge to your marketing efforts, and to the design and delivery of products and service.

Industry dynamics can also play an important role. One of the criticisms that can be levelled at Porter's five forces analysis is that it appears as a static model. Although this was never intended by Porter, it needs to be demonstrated how the competitive forces can be used dynamically.

Figure 3.11 shows how the competitive forces can be used dynamically. The competitive forces need to be overlaid against:

- the economic cycle;
- the industry cycle.

Figure 3.11 was born during some inspired moments of reflection by a number of Scandinavian managers from SISU. SISU manufactures and markets trucks, tractors, logging and defence equipment, and other systems throughout the world. (SISU's home base is Finland.)

This picture shows an industry life cycle overlaid with the economic cycle. The effects of the economic cycle can be pronounced, as in the early 1990s recession. Note how the SISU managers show the five forces moving from favourable or neutral to adverse (circled as they move to the right). The picture produces almost a cartwheel effect. This closely paralleled the analysis of the UK management consultancy market earlier on in this chapter, and also the forthcoming case on Tesco in Chapter 6.

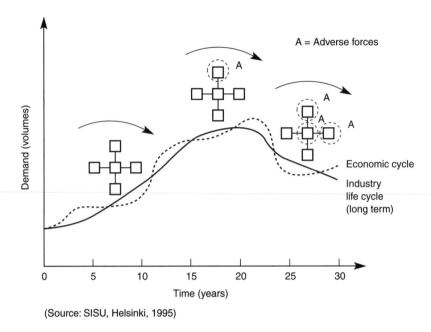

(Source: SISU, Helsinki, 1995)

Fig. 3.11 Using the competitive forces systematically

As one of the SISU managers put it:

'The real challenge is that senior managers need to hold in their mind not just the economic cycle, but also the competitive forces. They also need to be able to map the longer term industry cycle against the competitive forces – which do change. In our markets, because the effect of the economic cycle can be significant, we have to be able to think ahead and be very flexible to operational changes.'

The sixth competitive force – industry mindset

Our next step is to take a more novel and even richer look at the competitive forces. I have now been applying Porter's competitive forces for nearly ten years. Although the framework is very powerful I have always felt that there is some key missing ingredient. Because of its power it appears that no one has tried to develop Porter's framework further. Indeed, it is only relatively recently that a colleague at Cranfield (Bowman, 1992) sought to develop Porter's notion of 'generic strategies' (cost leadership, differentiation and focus) by charting movements over time in the mix of generic strategy. He also went behind the simple variables of 'value' and 'cost' into more specific trade-offs like perceived use value versus perceived price, and also producer effectiveness versus cost efficiency.

The missing ingredient in industry analysis is that of INDUSTRY MINDSET. 'Industry mindset' can be defined as:

The perceptions, expectations and assumptions about the competitive environment, the level of financial returns, and the factors critical for success in the industry.

The key ingredients of our definition are as follows.

- **Perceptions:** the ways in which current industry events are interpreted (or misinterpreted).
- **Expectations:** the broader beliefs about how the industry may develop. These expectations may be completely appropriate or widely appropriate.
- **Assumptions:** the specific beliefs about the key competitive parameters which drive financial performance in the industry. Assumptions about these key competitive parameters are frequently implicit and not thoroughly tested or debated.

Previous theory has focused mainly upon mindset from a within-company point of view, for example in Spender's idea of 'strategic recipes' or more recently Goold *et al*'s (1994a and b) idea of managers' 'mental maps'. The notion of 'industry mindset' goes much broader than this as it spans different competitors and other players in the game.

The industry mindset plays a major role in shaping industry change (as it has in the US motor industry), thus transforming Porter's five competitive forces model from a static into a much more dynamic model. Figure 3.12 reframes Porter's forces by:

- positioning industry mindset as the overarching, sixth force, the force which plays a profound role in shaping the other 'big five' forces;
- explaining how the other five forces interact with one another.

To illustrate the final point, buyer power is closely linked to substitutes (via companies deciding to do-it-yourself) and also to supplier power (via demand/supply imbalance). Also, entrants may restructure the industry, impacting on rivalry.

Or, suppliers themselves might enter the industry via downstream development.

Finally, substitutes and rivalry might together provoke fresh industry innovation. Few players with longer term stake in the industry will sit idly by and watch their market position significantly eroded by new sources of competition.

Figure 3.13 now shows more specifically how industry mindset can play a profound influence over industry dynamics. The prevailing industry mindset

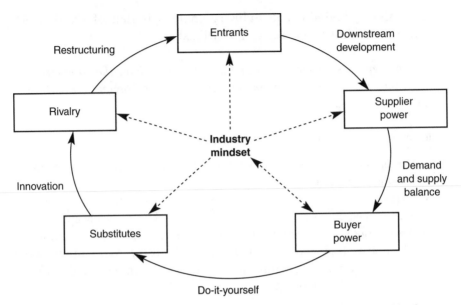

Note: the 'big six' competitive forces is a refinement of Michael Porter's five competitive forces (*Competitive Strategy*, Porter E.M., The Free Press, Macmillan, 1980).

Fig. 3.12 The 'big six' competitive forces

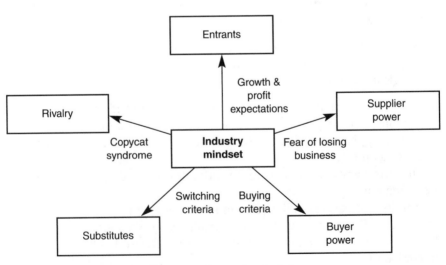

Fig. 3.13 The impact of industry mindset – the sixth force

may send signals to players adjacent the industry, attracting new entrants because of prevailing growth and profit expectations. (For instance, going back to the undertaking example, the cosy environment has now attracted new entrants, who have entered by acquisition.)

Also, rivalry is intensified by the 'copycat syndrome' – particularly when there are relatively uniform perceptions of what recipes currently make money. The copycat syndrome is often manifest in tactical pricing, culminating in a price war, as seen earlier in the UK newspaper market example.

The industry mindset may also have an impact on the role of buyer power and also upon substitutes. This impact can occur by influencing buying criteria and also the switching criteria of buyers. Buyers may have narrow perceptions about what substitutes are available and inaccurate expectations about how new substitutes will perform. They may also make assumptions, for instance, that their purchase will not result in rapid obsolescence.

For example, in the mobile telephone market of the early to mid 1990s, first-time customers had poorly defined buying criteria initially. They had even less well defined switching criteria. Having made their first mobile telephone purchase, within a matter of months they learnt of the full cost burdens, the limitations of the hardware (and the particular system it is reliant on). Perhaps within months (or even weeks) the customer might become aware that substitute systems (as well as the actual telephone itself) exist. In a relatively short period the buyers' switching criteria are likely to crystallize, based on their learning about the opportunities and often severe limitations of the product. The naivety of buyers' criteria is illustrated by a personal experience. Tempted by a 'free connection deal' I was unaware of the £50 disconnection fee I was asked to pay to a well-known supplier to get rid of hardware which did not meet official performance standards. (My eight-year-old son kindly offered to dispose of the handset into our local River Cam.)

This example highlights how easily the five competitive forces analysis might easily fail to identify a key driver of industry change where the five forces is analysed as a quick snapshot.

Finally, industry mindset plays a key influence over the power of suppliers through the fear factor. As anyone who has run a business knows, the fear factor of not securing the business plays a key role in undermining supplier power. When using the five competitive forces model it is remarkable how rarely 'supplier power' is credited with much competitive significance. This is probable due to the erosion of this power by the fear factor.

By putting 'industry mindset' at the centre of the framework, you might easily fall into the trap of ignoring other interactions between the forces. To avoid this trap focus on each of the five 'hardware' elements of industry structure (as per Porter) in turn, shown in Figures 3.14 to 3.18.

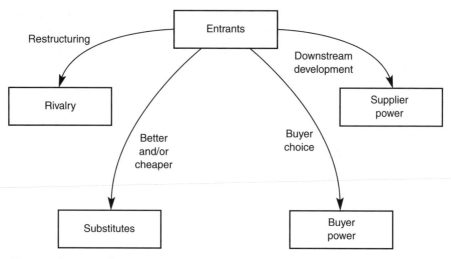

Fig. 3.14 Impact of entrants

Certain interactions between the five forces have already been explained, so I focus now on the new elements.

- **Entrants:** these may introduce better and/or cheaper substitutes and may broaden buyer choice, giving them more bargaining power (Figure 3.14).
- **Rivalry:** intensifying rivalry may either squeeze suppliers' prices or may encourage closer collaboration via partnerships in order either to facilitate differentiation or low cost strategies (Figure 3.15).
- **Substitutes:** these might take existing suppliers out of play. This underlines the importance of thinking about substitutes both within your own part of the industry chain, but also either up or down the chain (Figure 3.16).
- **Buyer power:** this might intensify rivalry through buyers increasing the extent to which they shop around. Also, buyers might be tempted into developing upstream in the industry chain by entry strategies (Figure 3.17).
- **Supplier power:** here the overall demand/supply balance is a very important factor in adding to, or subtracting from, the negotiating power of suppliers (see Figure 3.18).

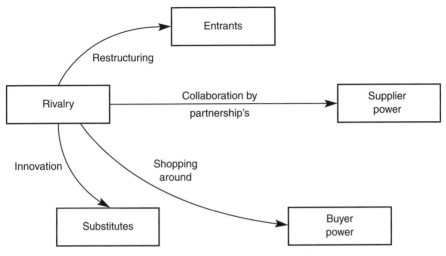

Fig. 3.15 Impact of rivalry

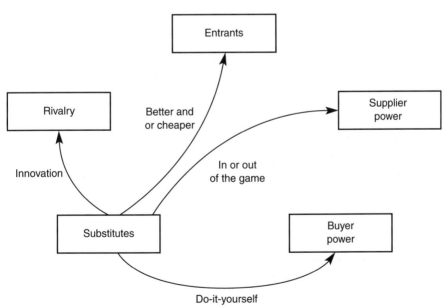

Fig. 3.16 The impact of substitutes

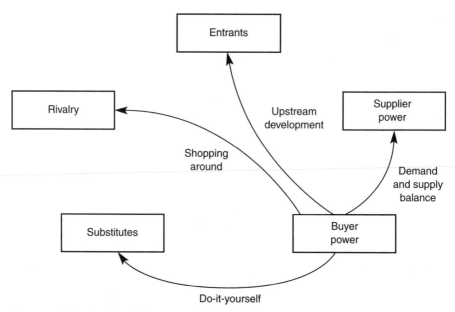

Fig. 3.17 The impact of buyer power

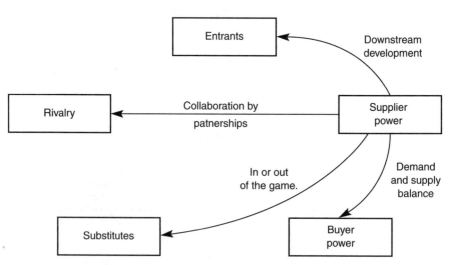

Fig. 3.18 Impact of supplier power

Short exercise

How would you characterize the mindset of your own industry, particularly of the dominant players, rogue players and of new entrants? How is your own company's mindset similar or different to that of the industry at large? To what extent do any of these differences give you psychological advantage?

STRATEGIC POSITIONING AND DEVELOPMENT

Having now evaluated the PEST factors, the growth drivers inherent in the market and the (now six) competitive forces, it is now time to set about evaluating total market attractiveness (or 'TMA').

The GE (grow-earnings) Grid

Total market attractiveness gives an overview of whether a particular market (or segment) offers longer term financial returns on a par with, greater than or less than other industries. These 'other industries' are ones which either you are already in or might conceivably enter. Wider still, you can make comparisons with dissimilar industries which a key factor of production – finance for investment – could be in.

The best way to distinguish the total attractiveness of the competitive environment from your own competitive position is as follows. Imagine the strategy development director of Venus PLC landing on earth for the first time in his or her (its?) spaceship with £100 million in freshly minted £50 notes to invest. What industries does he/she/it invest in? He would possibly avoid many declining industries downsizing because of economic constraints, their ecological pressures and where there is relatively fierce competitive rivalry (for example, coal mining). He might be more interested in the home entertainment, communications and computing market – an emerging, possibly fast-growing industry with perhaps more relaxed (currently) competitive rivalry. By testing out total market attractiveness he would perhaps be able to screen out investment opportunities even before considering what kind of competitive strengths he might be able to attain in a new business venture.

Figure 3.19 allows the separation of two variables of total market attractiveness from competitive position. The vertical, left, axis depicts 'high', 'medium' or 'low', total market attractiveness. The horizontal axis picks out 'strong', 'average' or 'weak' competitive positions. Once known as the GE grid (named after General Electric of the US, where the grid was developed), this tool enables a multitude of factors to be compared

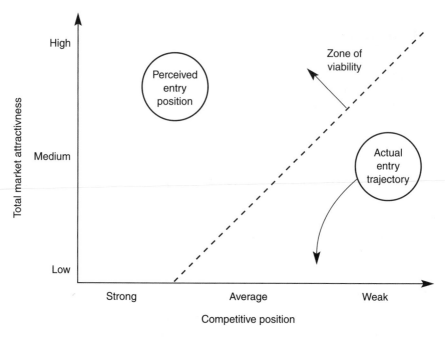

Fig. 3.19 Mapping market entry strategies

simultaneously. The GE grid is helpful for strategies for growth, particularly because the quantitative growth rate is heavily counterbalanced by looking at the qualitative aspects of the market place.

An easier way of remembering the 'GE grid' is to call it the 'grow-earnings' grid. The GE grid enables you to:

- position an existing business, having analysed its TMA and competitive position;
- compare it with other business units;
- evaluate new business opportunities;
- reposition a business (from right to left on the GE grid, or even (by shifting the business' market focus) diagonally north-west), in a turnaround strategy, or by continuous improvement;
- challenge the adequacy of investment to achieve such a repositioning (both long-term investment and revenue costs with longer term benefits);
- compare your positioning with other key competitors operating in the same or differing market segments.

The GE grid thus enables you to distinguish between possible breakthroughs in strategies for growth from likely breakdowns. (Pioneer UK even named it the 'great expectations grid.') Besides TMA, to position a business effectively on the GE grid you also need to take some view of its competitive position. The following ten key criteria will usually suffice (as a checklist).

1. Brand, image and reputation.
2. Simplicity of product/market focus, or alternatively a relevant and broad offering.
3. Relative market (or niche) share.
4. Product and service performance.
5. Distribution channels.
6. Cost base.
7. Responsiveness (but this doesn't mean reactiveness).
8. Technical and non-technical competencies.
9. Financial strength.
10. Management skills.

Profiling of competitive strength

The above factors can be scored as 'strong, average or weak' or alternatively as a 1–5 point scale (see once again Figure 3.5). Also, the relative importance of the factors can be assessed by weighting some factors as being more important than others. This analysis needs to be done relative to one or more key competitors, otherwise it is prone to subjectivity.

As an example of competitive strengths, a major international hotel chain identified the following dimensions:

- brand name and service reputation;
- locations;
- booking systems and services;
- reception service;
- ancillary facilities;
- room quality;
- food (and beverages) quality;
- cost base;
- personalized customer service.

Below are some useful pointers to adding a more objective bite to the analysis.

- **For aspects of perceived superior value:** test out whether particular customers or market segments do actually perceive you as superior to a particular competitor.
- **For actual value (of product or service):** disaggregate the dimensions of this value and compare line-for-line with a key competitor.
- **For cost base:** estimate either measurable differences in cost or proxies for cost (including cost drivers and likely cost behaviour – see Chapter 9).

But a word of warning in the case of the GE grid should be added here. It is important that detailed analysis doesn't become an end in itself. Often a

quick and dirty assessment of business position is as good as a sophisticated analysis based on carefully weighted scores.

However, in the case where scores are used, it may be quite revealing
when managers find it a major struggle to make judgements about the
various business areas they are in because of lack of data and very imperfect knowledge.

A very important use of the GE grid is to test out the realism of entry
strategies. A key rule is that 'if you enter a new market then you invariably
enter it from the right of the GE grid'.

If you know relatively little about the external position of a business
(TMA, PEST, growth drivers, competitive forces) then you may also (in the
worst case) fundamentally misjudge not merely competitive strength, but
also the total market attractiveness.

In Figure 3.19 this is exactly what happens. A company in a service
industry and with a strong brand name integrates forward into a high
street distribution channel. Its brand name, however, does not give it particular competitive strength. Also, it has fundamentally misjudged the
TMA due to:

- misunderstanding the factors driving market growth from within the
  market;
- overlooking key PEST factors;
- being bullish about competitive conditions.

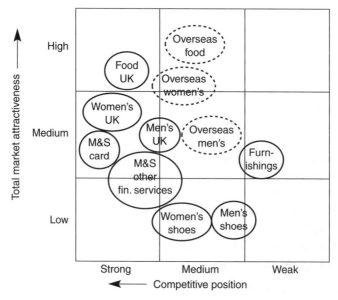

Fig. 3.20 GE grid – approximate current positioning of M&S businesses

The result was predictably that the company failed to make money, with subsequent closure and divestment two years after entry.

To demonstrate the use of the GE grid, let us briefly return to Marks & Spencer's portfolio of businesses (see Figure 3.20).

At M&S, women's and men's shoes are not (relatively) strong in terms of competitive position, and they are also found to be in relatively crowded and competitive markets. Furnishings are positioned as even weaker than shoes. However, furnishings is perhaps a slightly more inherently attractive market than shoes (in the UK the shoe market is a very cluttered one).

Having experimented with the GE grid we may now wish to relabel it to make it more user-friendly and easily memorable. This is particularly important as the GE grid has nine possibilities (and not just four, as in other positioning matrices).

Making the GE grid manager-friendly

Figure 3.21 nicely relabels the GE grid to become more manager-friendly. Starting at the north-west point, business units with high total market attractiveness and strong competitive position are called 'Big Bang' to suggest that they are likely to throw off a lot of cash. Businesses with medium

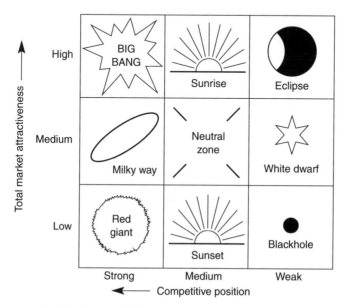

Fig. 3.21 Relabelling the GE grid

total market attractiveness and strong position are still likely to generate considerable cash (and earnings). While moving south, a strong position in a low market attractiveness area is more likely to struggle to produce a good profits and cash stream.

Moving to the middle of the GE grid, an average position in a highly attractive market may again be very well rewarded. But this 'Sunrise' position may easily slip in terms of competition position, becoming an 'Eclipse' or move into the middle, Neutral Zone.

The 'Eclipse' is an interesting business position: here a business unit might move out of the dark into a Sunrise position. Or, it might be about to fall off the edge of the grid to the right.

At the bottom of the grid, a Sunset business (average competitive position in a market with low attractiveness) will probably struggle to make adequate profit and be hard pushed to generate much cash. We call this the 'Red Giant' because it is often a substantial business but one which has not got much potential for strategic development (except through incremental development or by break-out into more attractive niches elsewhere).

Equally, a weak position in a medium attractive market is also unlikely to generate reasonable financial returns (the 'White Dwarf' – this is so named because it is a burnt-out star).

A weaker position in a low attractiveness market will invariably lead to financial losses and the need for continual financing. This is called the 'Black Hole' of the GE grid. An example of a black hole business might be Rumbelows, the former UK electrical retail chain closed down in 1995 by Thorn EMI.

A special danger is where a company is seeking to diversify and management thinks that it will be able to enter the market in the 'Big Bang' or 'Sunrise' cell of the GE matrix, but actually enters in the 'Black Hole' position. Because of lags in recognizing this problem it may be some time before it is reflected in financial results and its root causes are diagnosed, therefore leading to increased, rather than reduced, commitment to this strategic development move.

Further, there are some important migration paths which business units may go through. For example (see Figure 3.22), a business might begin with an average position in an inherently attractive business, then achieve dominance (a 'Big Bang' position) before slipping back to a harvest position. Or, from 'Big Bang', deterioration might set in, moving the business through the Neutral zone towards 'Sunset'. NEXT, the fashion business in the UK, went through this evolutionary path during the 1980s. Or, you may find (as in the telephone insurance industry) entry into a Milky Way position/Big Bang, then fading into a Red Giant

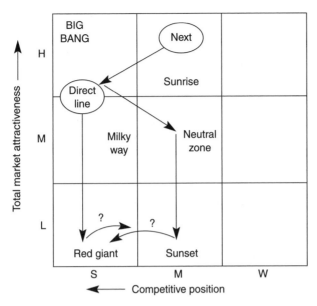

Fig. 3.22 Mapping strategic attractiveness using the GE grid

(insurance company Direct Line's actual position at the end of 1994). See again Figure 3.22.

This suggests it is frequently possible to conjecture, given where a particular business is now, where its likely trajectory will be. This may help suggest options for avoiding default trajectories.

Differentiation, cost leadership and focus strategies

It is now time to take a look at the generic routes for strategic development – differentiation, cost leadership and focus strategies. Each of these routes can offer a viable route for breakthrough strategies for growth. These generic routes derive from Porter (1985). Porter suggests that differing generic strategies (or 'competitive styles') may be available across industries. Notably, a company may compete primarily with a differentiated value that it offers its customers, or on the basis of driving its costs down to have low (and possibly the lowest) cost levels in the industry. Porter suggests that, with very few exceptions, differentiation and cost leadership of strategies are mutually exclusive. He argues that if you do try to have a mixture of both strategies – and particularly if you try to cover a broad range of products while also emphasizing a few key products (a 'focus' strategy) – then you fall between all the various strategic stools. Porter calls this lack of choice, graphically, 'stuck in the middle'.

What he does not say, however, is that if you differentiate then costs do not matter – because they still do. Nor does he say that if you pursue cost leadership then you do not deliver a level of value or quality comparable to industry standards – again, you do.

Porter's typology appears to work best where the strategic terrain is uneven, and where differences in value added and cost levels between key players are both significant and readily measurable. For instance, if we look back at our extensive analysis of Marks & Spencer, in the mid 1980s M&S foods was clearly a differentiated player relative to many of the other supermarket chains. But by the mid 1990s this distinction had become more difficult to make. Waitrose, Safeway, Tesco and Sainsbury had all launched their convenience foods seeking to imitate M&S – with varying but sometimes tangible success.

The niche convenience food industry is not an unusual exception. In many industries the notion that these are relatively simple routes to competitive edge simply does not apply in management practice. But Porter never actually said that generic strategies were both necessary and sufficient ingredients for competitive strategy. Increasingly managers need to seek not so much single sources of core advantage but multiple and reinforcing sources. The successful company needs to build a system of competitive advantage, and one that is continually renewing itself.

To some extent, therefore, management thinking has moved on from Porter. Practitioners and theorists realize that the ideal strategies of Porter are often of no real assistance in evolving business-specific sources of competitive advantage.

Bowman (1992) distinguished between perceived use value and perceived price, and also between producer efficiency and unit costs. This perhaps offers a more practical route towards evaluating product/market strategies.

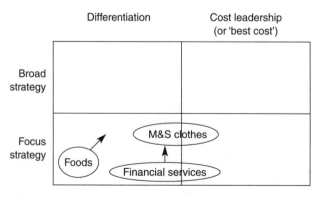

Fig. 3.23 Porter's generic strategies applied to Marks & Spencers

As an illustration of the generic strategies, Figure 3.23 plots M&S's business units on Porter's matrix of generic strategies. Note that M&S has not adopted a 'broad strategy'. We define a broad strategy as one which:

(a) covers a great diversity of customer needs and market segments; or
(b) covers a wide and perhaps complex range of products and services; or
(c) covers both (a) and (b).

M&S has a relatively simple product line across its businesses and also has a clear (although varying) customer focus.

For instance, M&S foods are clearly targeted as a premium buy while clothing is much more focused on economy and on excellent value for money. Interestingly, M&S clothing is one of those rare examples where one can find, simultaneously, a relatively tension-free blend of differentiation and cost leadership. Porter himself makes exception for this and M&S falls neatly into these exceptional circumstances as the company:

- has relatively high market share, achieved partly by differentiation (relatively to similar players in the same group or 'strategic group'), and partly by a virtuous combination of lower costs and superior value for money;
- achieves cost leadership in certain product lines by economies of scale (gained through a combined market share *and* focus strategy) and also by exercising its power over suppliers;
- M&S's dual attention to quality and cost. The quality focus helps to (a) add value by reducing lifecycle costs of clothing (does M&S underwear ever wear out?), and by (b) also reducing costs of returns etc.

In Figure 3.23 we also see M&S financial services following a parallel pattern of a dual generic strategy to clothing, but with narrower focus.

Using the generic strategies in practice

Porter's grid of the generic strategies can be of great use in identifying breakthrough strategies for growth from a number of angles, as follows.

- Highlighting strategic choices or dilemmas in how a particular business unit competes.
- Raising issues about the homogeneity of strategy across the corporate frontier – if some businesses are strongly cost leaders and others are trying equally hard to differentiate then you may easily end up with corporate stratophrenia, or with some business units being managed inappropriately.

- The choice of differentiation versus focus strategy has implications for defining critical success factors. It also impacts on investment and cost programmes, and attempts to shift organizational culture and develop skills.
- With a broadly based strategy it is harder to identify where value is being created or destroyed in the business as a result of the many interdependencies existing. (For more on this point see Chapter 4.)

Porter's generic strategies contribute significantly in helping to gain greater clarity and simplicity in strategic development choices. The grid can be very useful simply in mapping the top management team's perceptions of where they are currently positioned, and how they are trying to reposition businesses. As Bowman (1992) found, different individuals in the same team can have very diverse notions of both existing position and intended development.

Seeking sustainable advantage

Although Porter's disciples (e.g. Ghemawat, 1991) emphasized sustainability of competitive advantage, this can again suggest that the key task is to protect competitive advantage once this has been gained. The danger is that competitive advantage is regarded as a 'thing' that you create and then maintain or develop. Many sources of competitive advantage are, however, less tangible. They are continually being recreated, frequently on a daily basis. In particular, sources of advantage such as.

- building corporate image;
- responsiveness to customer demands externally;
- internal responsiveness;
- problem diagnosis and solving – whether this is tactical or strategic;
- capturing and evaluating, and exploiting new business opportunity;

are ongoing processes, and need to be supported through strategic learning.

These processes are becoming increasingly important relative to more tangible sources of advantage: e.g. assets; market share; products. This shift from tangible towards less tangible sources of competitive advantage occurs as the service element in value added by the business goes up, and as businesses become more complex and interdependent.

In the long run, softer sources of competitive advantage may account for the majority of variance in the performance of companies in the same sector. This is not to say that the more tangible sources of competitive advantage are unimportant, they clearly are; but the software of competitive advantage is becoming primary in many cases. Tangible sources of competitive advantage allow you access to the pitch in a meaningful way, but the 'competitive game' is increasingly decided by the softer sources of advantage – especially in the long run.

A further useful dimension is that of time-based competitive advantage. Responsiveness and flexibility are clearly increasingly important factors for the successful organization. The following illustrates some important ways in which time (or speed) plays a major influence in shaping competitive advantage and offers new ways of configuring breakthrough. Speed is important in:

- reducing the length of time taken to develop and launch a new product or service;
- achieving faster yet smoother integration of new acquisitions;
- securing quicker turnaround time of customer enquiries and confirmation of transactions;
- accelerating major change programmes through the use of task forces and by project management;
- speeding up the business planning cycle without undermining the quality of decision-making.

Speeding activities up without detriment to quality, and without increasing costs demands much more effective learning and feedback in the management process. Without continual and open learning, accelerating processes may result in costly errors.

Time-based competitive advantage has close resemblances to some key themes within project management. Project management tells us that quality, cost and time are three variables which need to be continually traded-off against each other. To illustrate this, where there is continual attention to quality cost may be underemphasized. Where a process is accelerated it is often thought that costs will increase due to problems associated with activity compression. However, costs can often be reduced by accelerating activity. In addition, customer value can be increased, speeding its delivery.

The organization which is able to deliver a more responsive service may, in turn, reduce customers' costs or risks. This benefit might be converted either into premium pricing or into greater volumes. Alternatively, a more responsive service may reduce the tendency for customers to switch to other suppliers.

Moving up strategically – the STAIR strategy health test

To bring together the strategic analysis it is useful to apply the final tool – STAIR analysis – which will be illustrated later in the BMW and Rover case (Chapter 8).

STAIR (see Figure 3.24) stands for:

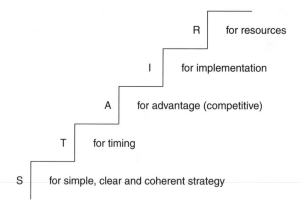

Fig. 3.24 The STAIR strategy health–check

- S for simple, clear and coherent strategy;
- T for good timing;
- A for advantage (external and internal);
- I for implementation (capability);
- R for resources (appropriateness and sufficiency).

STAIR analysis can be applied in a number of contexts. First, it can be used to evaluate a new breakthrough strategy for growth. This can include both acquisitive and organic development. Second, it can be applied to an existing strategy where some concerns exist. Third, it can be used as a way of learning from past strategic development whether this was success or failure.

The STAIR tool can be used as a quick test on a strategy. With practice, a manager can, in just a few minutes, explore whether a strategy for growth is likely to be robust. Or, to get more ownership by a management team, one might go more systematically through each of the five criteria. One way of focusing the challenge is to give yourself a score – between 0 and 100 per cent – for each of the five STAIR criteria. For instance, in one company (the fictitious WOK International), which undertook a strategic review in the early 1990s, the STAIR test gave the scores shown in Table 3.1.

If one were to compile a lenient score for this strategic development, this produces (as an average) a score of 40 per cent. This was significantly below the 50 per cent 'pass mark' which could be regarded as the absolute minimum level of acceptability. One would probably aim for at least 60 per cent.

A more robust way of scoring (especially if a strong reality shock is needed) would be to multiply the five percentages together. The result in this case is less than 1 per cent! WOK's strategy for growth (as it was then defined) was never realized, suggesting that this more robust test was very appropriate.

Table 3.1 An illustration of STAIR-WOK case study

Criteria	Score	Comment
Simple and clear strategy	60%	Although WOK's strategy was well thought through, it was still complex
Timing	30%	The recession was just about to impact on WOK's markets
Advantage (internal and external)	50%	WOK's competitive advantage was variable
Implementation (capability)	40%	Some key skills were missing or scarce in WOK
Resources	20%	There was actually little hope of resources from the wider group

Another approach is to see the STAIR test as a series of hurdles. If any of the five criteria give a low or zero percentage score (for instance, 20 per cent or less), then the strategy immediately fails. (As one group of managers put it to me: if you get a low or zero mark then one of the steps in the STAIR is missing – so you immediately fall down them.)

The STAIR test is unique in that it challenges the most taken-for-granted elements of strategies for growth. So often the timing issue is never really thought through. Or, it is simply assumed that ample implementation capability exists. But, as will be seen in Chapter 5, the implementation capability is frequently a mirage.

Finally, it is often naively assumed (as in WOK International) that adequate resource – especially financial resource – exists. It may not.

Highlighting strategic disease – the downward STAIR analysis

To round off the STAIR tool, it is also possible to probe using its mirror image (see Figure 3.25) of the downward stair. This downward stair poses some further challenges. Here STAIR means:

- S for simplistic (and superficial) strategy;
- T for temporary and tactical;
- A for actively resisted (either internally or externally);
- I for impractical;
- R for (unduly) risky.

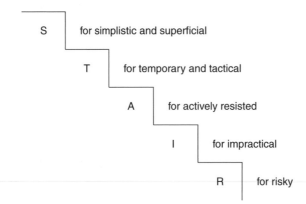

Fig. 3.25 The 'downward' STAIR strategy health–check

Obviously, if you score this from 0 to 100 per cent (where 100 per cent is 'extremely high' then a high downward STAIR score is a very strong indicator of probable failure. The downward STAIR test is of obvious relevance in weeding out unwise and over-optimistic strategies for growth.

A simplistic strategy is one which is so broad-brush that it doesn't really grapple with the key issues. This is typically the result of superficial analysis. Very frequently the effort is only applied temporarily and without sustained commitment – programmes are often short-term and disconnected (tactical).

The attempts by the UK electrical group Comet (part of Kingfisher Group) to reposition itself in 1994 illustrates these classic traps. Comet attempted to shift its image from a 'low price, low service' towards a 'moderate price, reasonable service'. But this plan did not take into account both the difficulty externally of shifting Comet's image and internally in changing the mindset towards a service culture. Also, efforts to change were not applied for long enough to be effective and by early 1995 Comet reverted to its old competitive style (that is, temporary and tactical). (Comet is somewhat reminiscent of K Mart in the US.)

Also, the growth strategy might be actively resisted by either internal stakeholders or, externally, by customers, competitors, regulators etc.

Finally, the strategy might be either (or both) impractical or unduly risky. One suspects that although Comet's plan was visionary it was not really very practical. It involved not merely changing store layouts, retraining and better systems, but also changes in working routines and rituals.

To give a vivid illustration of the difficulty of changing routines and rituals, in early 1995 a visitor to a Comet store observed a young couple who had ordered a hi-fi set from Comet not just once but four times. Each time they came in to collect their order they were told: 'I am sorry, someone has obviously sold it. You see, when it comes in it goes into the showroom, and another customer sees it and buys it.' This was the fourth hi-fi system that they had come in to collect. Apparently they had set their heart on that particular model which they needed for a family disco that night.

In early 1995 Comet reported a fall in relative market share of over 10 per cent in one year, along with disappointing financial results. Kingfisher Group embarked on fresh attempts at a turnaround.

SUMMARY AND CONCLUSION

Strategic analysis is an essential ingredient in breakthrough strategies for growth. The strategic analysis toolkit (if used selectively) can help identify and evaluate opportunities both within and outside the current domain of corporate activity.

The first step is to gain a more deepened objective understanding of the market (or industry) structure, and how it is changing and the underlying dynamics. Once a realistic assessment of competitive position has been made it is then possible to target and cost out how strategic repositioning may be achieved. Where it is intended to build a new business from scratch then again the investment costs and effort needed can be established much more realistically.

The generic strategies (Porter, 1985) are of some help in ensuring consistency and clarity in how strategic development is managed. But even more useful is the onion model of competitive advantage described in Chapter 2. This provides an important mirror with which to check your assumed 'sustainable advantage' against. Otherwise your 'breakthrough' strategic development is likely to result in breakdown.

Finally, Figure 3.26 summarizes the tools and their uses.

Tool	Use
Gap analysis	* Setting stretching strategic objectives * Implementation planning and measurement
SWOT analysis	* Brainstorming * Issue analysis * Presenting strategic position
PEST analysis	* Analysing industry environment * Scenario analysis * Generating critical success factors * Input to GE grid
Growth drivers	* Industry analysis and change * Analysing product/market opportunity * Input to GE grid
Five competitive forces	* Analysing competitive environment * Input to GE grid (vertically) * Generating critical success factors
Industry mindset	* Predicting industry change and competitor response * Understanding the other five competitive forces
GE grid	* Business positioning (existing) * New opportunity – evaluation * Understanding investment requirement * Appraising possible divestment
Profiling competitive strength	* Input to GE grid positioning * Input to onion model of competitive advantage (Chapter 2)
Onion model (of competitive advantage)	* Input to GE grid * Understanding sustainable competitive advantage * Exploring competitive disadvantage
Differentiation, cost leadership, focus strategies	* Evaluating existing business strategy * Appraising new business opportunities * Testing for sustainability
STAIR analysis	* Quick strategy health-check * Appraisal of strategic options * Evaluating specific areas of opportunity * Evaluating implementation strategies

Note: all of these tools are equally relevant to acquisitions, particularly the GE grid, onion model, and STAIR test.

Fig. 3.26 Strategic tools

ACTION CHECKLIST

- What is the overall gap between where your business is (in terms of sales, profits, cash flow and competitive position) versus where you want it to be?

- From the SWOT analysis of your own business, what growth opportunities exist where you could achieve and sustain genuine strategic advantage?

- Which PEST factors could conspire to frustrate your strategies for growth, and how and when might these crystallize?

- What key growth drivers underpin your assumptions and are these likely to be sustained, and why?

- Does or will analysing the competitive forces suggest that growth opportunities will or will not be accompanied by increasing competitive pressure, and reducing margins and volumes?

- What do the competitive forces suggest your critical success factors are (for instance, differentiation, cost base, customer focus, product or service characteristics)? (Note, don't create too many critical success factors, and especially avoid too many internal ones – which threaten to become 'critical success factories'.)

- How might the 'industry mindset' affect the other competitive forces impacting on the strategic opportunity?

- What does the 'grow-earnings' (GE) grid suggest about where existing businesses are positioned (and could be successfully grown) and also emerging businesses?

- What does the GE grid suggest about likely profitability?

- Which of the generic strategies (differentiation, cost leadership, focus) do strategies for growth capitalize on, and how easily and quickly can these be effectively copied?

- Overall, how do strategies for growth shape up when exposed to the STAIR test?

---

[1] 'Over my Dead Body' was produced by RDF Productions for Channel Four Television Corporation

*'Finance should never be seen
as being the enemy of strategy,
but as its handmaiden'*

4

STRATEGIES FOR GROWTH AND SHAREHOLDER VALUE

INTRODUCTION

Financial analysis traditionally occupies a central role in managing strategies for growth in nearly all companies. Yet this traditional role is often targeted at easier to quantify, internal (and sometimes short-term) variables.

Finance has not always had the best name among non-financial managers. As financial analysis is closely connected to corporate controls and measures there appears to be an inevitable tendency to see it as being in a policing, rather than in a more creative and exploratory, breakthrough role.

But over the past decade a new way of looking at the role of financial analysis in strategic development has increasingly come to the fore. Writers like Rappaport (1986), Reimann (1990), Copeland *et al* (1990), Ellis and Williams (1993), McTaggart *et al* (1994), Mills (1994) and Grundy (1992b, 1993b) have sought to reposition financial analysis alongside strategic analysis at the heart of the strategic development process. In the UK, companies like Abbey National, BP, Lloyds Bank, ICI and National Power have all benefited from applying value management to strategies for growth, often as a check on strategic analysis. (In the US, Emerson Electric, Wal-Mart and Coca-Cola are enthusiasts.)

This wave of thinking has been variably called 'shareholder value management', 'value-based management' or 'managing for value'. These more pure (financial) value approaches tend to stress the quantification of financial value, based on an overlay of strategic value. The problem with calling the process 'shareholder value management' also over-emphasizes the management of shareholder's value and the dividend stream. I prefer the term 'strategic value management' because this stresses the following.

- That strategy and value analysis are equal partners and that one should not dominate the other. They are especially complementary in evaluating strategic development decisions such as acquisitions, joint ventures, investment in new markets, products and distribution.

- Both strategic and value analysis can be used to help creatively shape strategic development – this task is not solely or primarily that of strategic analysis.
- The need to avoid the deterministic and simplistic notion that all the value of strategic development projects can be readily and mechanistically captured in the financial numbers.

Expanding on the second above point, first, value analysis can be based to trigger strategic questions about existing or new businesses which in turn lead to breakthrough ideas. It can be invoked early on in the thinking process about options for strategic development, and not merely downstream at the business case stage. It may also be used to perform cross-company, cross-industry and cross-market niche comparisons of relative profitability. It provides a reality check on corporate growth programmes subjected to a rare qualitative, strategic analysis.

Turning next to the point about quantifying the value of a strategy, what strategic value management does not say is that relatively uncertain and contingent value can be always translated into meaningful financials. There may be exceptional circumstances where this can be misleading or inappropriate (given an organization's controls and financial recipes). For example, when Rolls-Royce Aeroengines invests in a new engine it may be extremely difficult to forecast demand with any real degree of precision five to ten years out. Thus alternative approaches to a single series of forecasts needs to be found.

However, there is plenty of evidence (Grundy, 1992b) that in many situations value can be financially appraised, providing the conditions under which it may arise or be destroyed are thought through strategically. Also, value may need to be carefully tested through scenario analysis, for example as it has at Shell and at British Telecom.

The rest of this chapter now examines:

- the traditional role of financial and strategic analysis;
- a process for strategic value management;
- analysis tools for strategic value management;
- applying strategic value management to special cases;
- conclusion.

Specific tools and concepts which are introduced include:

- value drivers;
- discounted cash flow;

- the strategic project set;
- growth drivers;
- importance/uncertainty grid (for evaluating assumptions);
- the base case (without the investment);
- alignment (of the value system);
- interdependencies;
- targeting intangibles;
- protective value;
- degrees of competitive and financial advantage;
- the business case;
- contingent value.

CAN FINANCE AND STRATEGY BE FRIENDS?

This section first looks at the key differences between strategic and financial analysis, with a case illustration and then a quick review of lasting theory. Focus will then be turned on the key shifts involved in making strategic value management a reality.

Some key differences between strategic and financial analysis

Strategic analysis has been typically concerned with more qualitative analysis leaving all the quantitative analysis as the demon of finance. Figure 4.1 summarizes the key differences.

Strategic analysis...	Financial analysis...
• Captures a wide range of variables – both external and internal	• Focuses on a narrower range of variables – primarily internal
• Evaluates tangible and less tangible areas of value	• Is primarily concerned with tangible areas of value
• Involves mainly qualitative measures	• Involves more quantitative measures
• Has longer term horizons	• Has a bias towards shorter term (with some exceptions)
• Is about creative thinking	• Is more about the control process
• Deals with broader uncertainties	• Employs techniques for measuring specific risks

Fig. 4.1 Contrasting strategic and financial analysis

But financial analysis can be linked very closely with external analysis, for instance by tracing financial variables back to their underlying (and often external) value drivers. (Value drivers are the direct or indirect, internal or external factors which determine the economic value added by a business.) Also, financial analysis can be used (as will be seen later on in the chapter) to help gain a clear focus on intangibles.

Further, there is no fundamental reason why financial analysis cannot be long term, indeed applying discounted cash flow (DCF) financial analysis is the most natural way of evaluating a longer term strategy. For example, some companies (like BP) have used DCF for many years now to value their business strategies (and not just at the project level). Further, if the most appropriate, strategically driven analysis of uncertainties and risks is applied, then financial analysis can be used to illustrate the effect of a number of critical and external value drivers. (This helps avoid 'DCF' becoming, in effect, 'deliberately confusing figures'.)

Case study: Rolls-Royce Aeroengines

Rolls-Royce Aeroengines supplies the aeroengines for both civil and military aircraft. The combined group (including its engineering division) has a turnover of over £3 billion. Rolls-Royce is a world player in a very tough and competitive market, competing against General Electric (GE) in the US.

Over recent years Rolls-Royce Aeroengines has invested considerable sums in developing its engine range, particularly the Trent engine. A key dilemma which Rolls-Royce faces is how to appraise these strategic investment decisions. Should it, as most of the conventional corporate finance books suggest, approach this by appraising each engine as an incremental stream of cash flows based on a discrete project?

In reality, it is not quite so easy to do this neat and clean exercise because the sales of one product can be interdependent with the sales of another. This is because the customer may (through building up a longer term relationship) seek to buy more than one type of aeroengine – for different applications.

In addition, there may well be important linkages of an internal operational nature which enable considerable efficiency savings through doing a set of projects, and not just one.

Where these interdependencies are very complex, close and hard to unravel, it would seem more appropriate to evaluate the set of projects (or products) rather than the individual one.

Although this insight may come to a strategist as being relatively obvious, it is certainly not so obvious from a review of most financial theory.

The Rolls-Royce Aeroengines case stresses the need to evaluate strategic development decisions at the most appropriate level. Because the planners at this company still viewed individual projects as being the units of analysis they ended up trying to appraise something whose value in large part resided elsewhere – in making a contribution to a higher level, strategic effect. No doubt the planners felt that to invest in a product you needed to justify it individually with financial numbers. Arguably, those products were so independent that product groupings at a more strategic level were the only meaningful units of financial analysis.

The Rolls-Royce Aeroengines case highlights graphically that when the numbers don't make sense, strategic thinking and analysis can often suggest a possible solution. Before examining how strategic and financial analysis can be integrated in a single framework of strategic value management, here is a quick review of existing theory.

Existing theory

Some years ago Barwise, Marsh *et al* (1987, 1989), in a major London Business School study suggested that there are three possible major ingredients when investing in strategic development – strategic, operational and financial appraisal. In particular, the links between strategic and financial appraisal seemed to be most complex and least well understood by managers (a finding echoed by a recent study of strategic investment decisions by Carr, *et al*, 1994).

Existing theory suggests a number of factors inhibiting the linkage of strategic and financial appraisal, through the following.

- **The concepts themselves:** strategic appraisal typically attempts to understand how a business unit fits in totality within its external environment. By contrast, financial theory typically focuses on measuring the inherent value of a specific decision or project, often in relative abstraction from its wider context.
- **Management behaviour:** strategic and organizational theories also suggest that organizational decision-making is a fluid, iterative and messy process (sometimes described as being made through a 'garbage can model'). Managers make decisions based on incomplete and fragmentary views, and may miss some of the wider and longer term implications of the decision. By contrast, financial theory suggests that appraisal should be well structured, coherent and deductive, regardless of organizational context.
- **Management processes:** strategic thinking is associated with planning processes and systems. By contrast, financial thinking is associated with

the measurement of the most likely future performance and also with the setting up of parallel controls to track plans (often short term).

- **Decision systems:** strategic development decisions involving long-term financial commitment may be exposed to different mixes of systems – for example, strategic plans, business plans, budgets, acquisition cases and capital investment cases. This multiplicity of systems may, therefore, lead to major fragmentation of views in decision-making.

Strategic theorists highlight that although financial theory emphasized the technical aspects of appraisal, softer issues such as less tangibles, the analysis of interdependencies and uncertainty were seen as being of more importance to managers. It is as if the Pareto (80:20) rule needs to be reversed – financial theory appeared to be spending 80 per cent of its time dealing with only 20 per cent of the issues which were most relevant to the value of strategic development.

Second, managers (and in some cases theoreticians, too) overemphasized investment in discrete, incremental projects. 'Incremental projects' are those which can be justified as stand-alone, but which may distract from the core strategy. But, most interesting of all, strategic theorists argue that the investment vehicle should be seen as the business strategy itself. Many of the problems managers encountered might therefore be attributable to the level at which they defined the unit of analysis of the decisions.

Third, shareholder value theorists suggest that business strategies themselves can be valued using discounted cash flow. Coupled with the second point above (defining the unit of analysis), this suggested that it might be more appropriate to work down from the business strategy (or sub-strategy) as being the primary unit of analysis. Clearly, this working down from valuing top-level strategy could only be done effectively provided that adequate strategic analysis and vision had been applied at the top level in the first place.

Fourth, the strategic decision-making theorists suggest that managing the process effectively is itself a major problem. Where the decisions are made incrementally by focusing on discrete investment projects this can prevent a holistic view of the strategy and of its value.

Fifth, uncertainty itself is highlighted as a separate and very important issue. Uncertainty invites the use of scenarios focusing on specific decisions (as opposed to more global scenarios). (A scenario here is a mutually consistent view of the future.) Not only might these scenarios invite more probing of internal assumptions but also of the external assumptions and of the key interdependencies between those assumptions.

The above review has a number of implications for evolving a more effective and integrated process of strategic value management.

Strategic value management – the key shifts

Based on our quick review of theory, strategic value management needs to involve a fundamental shift in the mind set of managers involved in strategic development, particularly in:

- moving from a policing role to a more creative role in shaping strategy;
- changing from a more purely control role to one which is to do with corporate learning;
- evolving from taking business assumptions as given (subject to sensitivity analysis) to adopting a probing, questioning role (and of the right things);
- assuming that if value exists then it must be quantifiable – and readily so, and with a good degree of precision, to being sensitive to zones where value is inherently difficult to quantify;
- developing from a primary concern with the internal, easier-to-quantify assumptions, to softer, frequently external and harder-to-quantify assumptions;
- moving from an involvement relatively late on in the decision process (post option formulation) through to a role much earlier in the process.

But the real debate only starts here – just how can a manageable process be structured?

MANAGING VALUE STRATEGICALLY

Any strategic development decision can be managed through the following process (see Figure 4.2).

- **Definition:** define the scope and focus of the strategic development project, including its strategic objectives and context.
- **Options:** explore critical options for the decision and also any options which it forecloses.
- **Target and collect data:** target data required having done a first-cut review of the kind of external and internal assumptions, which will need to be made about key value drivers.
- **Assumptions:** collect and evaluate data through formulating the external and internal assumptions. Test these assumptions, and revisit the key options and work up contingency plans.
- **Business case:** present the business case and, where feasible, refine the programme to add more value at less cost and at lowest risk.
- **Controls:** translate the business case into monitoring measures and controls.

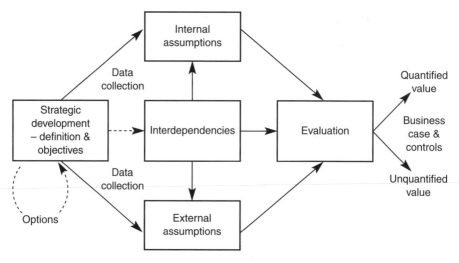

Fig. 4.2 Managing corporate value

These six stages are equally applicable to the large versus the small company. The level of formality will differ, but the fundamental process should not. This process very much involves continuous learning and reshaping, rather than seeing the investment project as a 'given'.

The style of appraisal adopted within the process is very important, especially to balance constructive contention against positive support. It is particularly important that during formal reviews of the business case top managers do not view the case as primarily something to shoot at or find holes in, but one where they can add value by suggesting ideas for positive improvement.

The following case example (called Superman PLC for convenience) highlights the reality of the strategy development process. This is based on an experience I had some years ago in line management when I was involved in trying to put more process into a company's growth strategies.

Case study: Superman PLC

Superman PLC was seeking to diversify into a new form of materials technology as a breakthrough in strategic development. I was the acting head of finance and planning for the new technology division, Interchem. Its product stream will be called 'Supersteel' (both the name and nature of its business are heavily disguised).

Superman's strategic development programme was managed as follows.

- **Definition:** to develop an international Supersteel genes business in the US and in Europe, with a sufficient market presence and platform to exploit new biotechnologies.
- **Options:** to explore the mix between organic and acquisitive developments, the role and type of strategic alliances, and the particular product/market, geographic and distribution focus.
- **Data:** to collect not merely data about existing markets but also about evolving market trends and competitor intent (including possible future entrants).
- **Assumptions:** to be in a position to derive specific and explicit assumptions not merely about the existing Supergenes market but also about the evaluation, market growth and market structure, the relative strength of key players and the competitive position of Interchem (fictitious name) in this new arena. How did Interchem's key strategies stack up against this unfolding scenario and how robust would these strategies be, not merely in the present but in the potential future environment?
- **Business case:** given these plans and the strategic context, what potential value could be generated from the growth strategy? How could this value be enhanced by reshaping or rephasing the strategic development programme?
- **Controls:** the existing controls laid out both financial and strategic milestones for tackling strategies for growth. Yet there remained unresolved issues about aligning the various controls. This was especially because the strategic milestones laid down targets to grow the business which might conflict with the even more important need to deliver shareholder value.

The above lists the deliberate process which I (and some members of the management team) sought to introduce. What was particularly memorable, however, was the resistance towards using a more structured process to guide decision-making. This seemed to cut across the perceived need for sheer speed of development. There was also a major thrust to make some visible moves which would suggest the division was on track to meet its strategic milestones.

This highlights the problems of controlling the strategic development horses when the reins are broken. This particular division did not prosper well over the next few years (it would be fair to say that a major strategic retreat began after it became apparent that the financial numbers were never going to look good – after several years).

Not only do we have to manage the analysis tools and processes, but also the mindset of the organization and its key stakeholders (see Chapter 5).

TOOLS FOR STRATEGIC VALUE MANAGEMENT

This section follows each one of the stages in the earlier strategic development process. First, if we examine the definition of the decision (or programme) more clearly we soon realize there are many problems in defining the unit of analysis. Is it a particular strategic development project or a more broadly based programme? Where there are many and complex interdependencies it is frequently easier and better to evaluate the financials at the level of a set of projects ('the strategic project set') (see Figure 4.1). Indeed, in some instances it may be best to evaluate the total strategy to establish where one or more key areas of breakthrough can come from.

Not only is it an issue as to what level of analysis should be conducted, timing is equally an issue. Often the commitment to a strategy for growth comes well before, for instance, major investment. The business case thus comes really too late, and then has to struggle to defend a strategy already beginning to disappoint. (See Carr, Tomkins and Bayliss's case studies, 1994.)

Illustration from a supermarket chain

During my regular shopping at a major supermarket (which I will call Saveco), I noticed a small difficulty. The trolleys which I chose at the trolley rank invariably seemed to develop problems when I entered the store. While they worked perfectly well in the car park, as soon as I got on to a smoother surface they careered generally over to one side rather than keep in a straight line. As I tend to move quite quickly this became a problem for other customers as well as for me.

After this had happened a number of times I approached an unsuspecting Saveco manager to enquire whether this was a generic problem, whether Saveco had recognised it and, if so, was it going to do anything about it?

The Saveco manager was very helpful and open about the situation. He told me:

'We are well aware of the problem and are pressing hard to have replacements. But you have to understand it isn't cheap – each one of these trolleys costs £70 each. It is very expensive to refit a whole fleet but we are tackling this problem now, particularly as it is very important to our customers.'

On the way back to the car I did a quick scan of the trolley parks. I estimated that if Saveco had, say, 700 trolleys per store and, say, 500 stores, the cost of replacing the fleet would be:

£70 × 700 units × 500 stores = £25 million!

The scale of investment might clearly be a big negative for Saveco's finance department, who would have a great struggle looking for a financial payback. However, this problem arises only because the project is being considered at the wrong level of analysis. The value of trolleys which go straight is dependent upon the contribution this makes to Saveco's overall customer service strategy. In financial analysis terms, to dissect the business system is to murder value.

One of the pieces of data I would look for (if I worked at Saveco) would be how important this problem was to customers and what would they pay (notionally) to avoid it?

My second thought was that, wasn't there a way of getting better and cheaper trolleys – if you sought out a new source of supply perhaps you could get the costs down to say £60, and the durability and performance up.

Options

Invariably there are a number of differing options for strategic development, for instance:

- in deciding the mix of organic and acquisitive development;
- in determining the speed of development;
- in deciding to what extent it is worth while piloting development prior to making a bigger commitment (usually it is);
- whether to delay commitment until there is a sufficiently strong implementation capability, enough resource, and the right timing;
- whether to pursue a number of product/market routes to development simultaneously (and thus perhaps spreading resources too thinly), or doing one major development at a time, and more thoroughly;
- thinking through whether the key objectives for growth and for value can be fulfilled at lower cost or with more flexibility through an alternative option.

Data collection

It is not a good idea at all just to go out and collect data to support a strategic development decision. Such activities are likely to result in overcollection of the wrong data.

Case study: Lion Assurance Co.

A consultant ran a strategic development workshop for a financial services company – Lion Assurance Co. Two teams of managers were tasked to identify and evaluate an area for strategic breakthrough.

They set out on a mammoth data collection exercise and returned four weeks later with two piles of market data. This was despite being asked first of all to list the assumptions which they would ultimately need to make and then target data sources. When the consultant saw this he was forced to conjecture: 'I wonder where in those two vast piles we will find the raw data to support the key assumptions (external and internal) to support the value drivers? Perhaps we could simplify things a lot by just setting alight both piles – data is such a nuisance because you feel you have to analyse it all.'

A much more effective process is to begin by managing the key value and cost drivers underlying a particular strategy for growth. Once this has been done, a shopping list of the dozen or so key assumptions should be created. This, and this alone, should provide the focus for collecting external and internal data.

Short exercise

For one potential strategy for growth:

- What are the likely variables which will actually drive value (externally as well as internally)?
- Given this, what sources of data (obvious and less obvious) could you use to get a really good feel for the viability of growth which adds value?
- How can you collect data quickly and cheaply?

EVALUATING THE ASSUMPTIONS

Defining the assumptions requires considerable debate and challenge to provide a realistic basis for a business case. In particular, high growth-oriented strategies can actually destroy, rather than create, shareholder value.

Example

A large organization was trying to value its investment in R&D (research and development). The financial analyst produced a figure for NPV in excess of £0.5bn, with an investment outlay of only about £65m. The finance director (who was completing an MBA at the time) asked: 'What is driving this wonderful NPV – why have you assumed such a rapidly grow ing market with no new entrants? And why do prices not fall, as the customers do have high bargaining power and may bargain away at least half the value created by the new and better technology?'

Managers are often inclined to invest in growth activities because they perceive that growth and value are integral, but they are not. For instance, the head of strategic planning at a major petrochemical company explains:

'I was sitting with a senior manager and we were looking at a model of his business which represented his future profitability and cash flows from operations and key assumptions about the market. The manager explained that it was easy to generate additional value through business growth as profitability was increased.

But we then played a 'what-if' scenario which increased the growth rate of part of the business using a cash flow model of the business's operations. The manager was shocked when the NPV of the business strategy actually went down.

This was because the 'growth' was not 'profitable growth' in value-based terms: although it was apparently profitable on an accounting basis, once an allowance for the time value of money had been made and particularly adjustment for additional working capital, it was not. This taught us a lot about the business as it not only raised questions about incremental value creation but also about the quality of opportunity facing this business and its competitive position.'

Not only do the sources of growth (or more technically the 'growth-drivers') need to be thought through market segment by market segment, but also the longer term value of growth. Taking another example, in the retail DIY market during the late 1980s and early 1990s, companies got both of these things wrong (see below).

Further example

The UK DIY market in the late 1980s expanded because of a number of key growth-drivers. First, the economy was booming and generated a high amount of discretionary consumer spending. Second, the housing market was both booming and active, with a large number of purchases each year, resulting in a demand for DIY following each house move. (With a booming economy it is also hard and expensive to buy-in tradespeople.) Third, it was possible to add the cost of DIY improvements to either mortgages or to consumer credit.

Growth in the sector saw a large number of out-of-town stores opening and new entrants offering opportunities for strategic breakthrough which proved not to be sustainable. By about 1990–1 the key growth-drivers had been put into reverse, demand softened, and the key players embarked on a self-defeating price war to expand and hold on to market share. In the course of this price war, significant shareholder value was destroyed by that key value drive – competitive rivalry – for several of the key combatants.

Summary questions in testing the external assumptions for a strategic development project are therefore as follows.

Questions on the competitive environment

1. How does the value of the opportunity depend on the company's external environment (directly or indirectly)?
2. Where the opportunity depends upon market demand, what competitive assumptions are made upon which volumes, prices and margins are based?
3. Why is the assumed competitive position believed to be sustainable during the middle and latter part of the life cycle of the opportunity?
4. What new competitive conditions may occur, and how might these impact on the value of the opportunity (e.g. substitutes, new entrants, industry restructuring)?
5. More particularly, how might specific competitors be either addressing the same opportunity already or be able to respond quickly?

Questions on customers and market trends

1. How do customers perceive the relative value of any end product or service upon which the opportunity depends? (Consider perceived image, cost savings, risk levels.)
2. How powerful are customers relative to the company and to what extent is the additional value created harvested by customers versus the company?
3. Upon what life cycle characteristics does the market opportunity depend (product or technology life cycles, industry life cycles, economic life cycles)?
4. How might these life cycles affect impact, not merely the quantity of demand but also its quality? What might shorten the life cycle of the opportunity?
5. What other regulatory factors might impact on the value of the opportunity?
6. If the value of the opportunity is dependent upon market growth, what are the factors which will sustain growth and under what circumstances may these cease to operate, and with what effect?

7. Have the growth rate and the projections of margins taken into account individual assumptions for each segment of the market, each distribution channel, and each major type of customer, etc?
8. What underlying market shares are assumed and on what basis have these 'markets' been defined?
9. What key trends may cause customer demand to shift over the period of the opportunity?

Turning to the internal assumptions, one of the most important assumptions underlying many business cases (which is rarely exposed) is the commitment of senior management. This can be both within the business and, where appropriate, at group level. In many cases internal commitment has been more uncertain than many of the external assumptions. This has been identified using stakeholder analysis (expanded on in Chapter 5) which asks simply: 'Which are the really key stakeholders in this project; who has high influence and who has a favourable attitude, a neutral attitude or is against the project?'

To test the internal assumptions of a strategic development project, it is suggested that the following questions are therefore asked, dealing with investment, costs and implementation assumptions.

Investment assumptions

1. What capacity levels are assumed and are these assessed in relation to the operating cycle over a whole annual period?
2. What unforeseen areas of investment may be required either of a future or indirect nature (e.g. expansion of office space) not currently included in 'incremental' cash flows?

Cost assumptions

1. How have 'incremental costs' been defined, and how do cost apportionments incorporate a 'fair' allowance for direct and indirect resources absorbed by the activity?
2. What further technical breakthroughs are assumed in order to support assumed levels of productivity?
3. What are the likely effects of reducing unit cost through gaining assumed economies of scale? Also, to what extent are unit costs increased if volumes are significantly less than 'most likely' assumptions?
4. Are unit costs likely to increase considerably as output reaches near capacity levels?

Implementation assumptions

1. Are time scales for implementation realistic?
2. Are there adequate operational resources to implement the project, especially where this relies upon scarce management and technical skills?
3. Is the area of opportunity one where the organization (and key individuals) has both the capability, the commitment and, where relevant, the appropriate culture to make it a success?

There are two useful checks on external and internal assumptions. First, is there a good balance between external and internal? A rough check is to use the acronym 'FORCE':

- financial;
- operational;
- resources;
- competitive;
- environmental.

Where 80 per cent of the assumptions are financial, operational or resource based there is a very good chance that some of the key external value-drivers have been under-explored (the competitive and environmental).

A second way of now testing the external and internal assumptions is by using a qualitative 'importance/uncertainty grid' (see Figure 4.3). Using this grid, managers plot key assumptions driving the value of the strategic investment decision. These can be external and internal, soft and hard assumptions, for instance:

- demand growth rate in key market segments will materialize;
- the impact of potential regulatory change will not be great;
- competitive rivalry – between existing players – will not intensify;
- new competitor entrants will not occur;
- customer buying intent will crystallize;
- a premium price will be achievable;
- cost levels are competitive;
- capacity levels are adequate;
- the implementation plan is feasible;
- adequate skills are available;
- the key stakeholders are committed.

Having selected a sub-set of these assumptions, these are now prioritized by using the grid (which can be a 'flip-chart', a white board, or a piece of paper). Once assumptions are carefully and skilfully defined, it is possible to debate the relative importance and uncertainty of these various assumptions (using a flip-chart, the assumptions can be easily moved around using post-it notes).

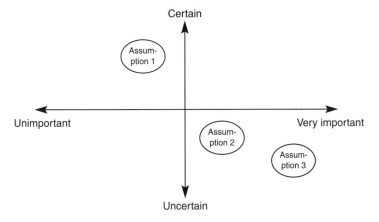

Fig. 4.3 The uncertainty/importance grid

At the beginning of the investment appraisal, key assumptions are likely to be mapped in the due north and north-east quadrants. Upon testing it is quite common to find one or more assumptions moving over to the danger zone in the south-east.

The uncertainty and importance grid is a vital tool for evaluating assumptions prior to undertaking key financial sensitivities. This tool helps focus these sensitivities towards the critical uncertainties (for example, to new competitor entry).

This method was pioneered in scenario planning but is even more relevant and useful in the field of evaluating strategies for growth. In fact, one of the most under-utilized applications of scenario planning is that of appraising particular projects. Scenarios are especially useful for getting a better handle both on contingent value and on protective value (see Appendix II). Chapter 5 will show that the importance/uncertainty grid is very useful in evaluating implementation strategies).

Short exercise

For a past strategy for growth which your company undertook:

- Using Figure 4.3, what were the perceived positionings of key external and internal assumptions prior to implementation?
- During or after implementation, how did these assumptions actually crystallize (again using Figure 4.3)?
- To what extent could these assumptions have been explored more deeply before the event (as opposed to with hindsight)?
- Do you think this might have made any difference to the decision and, if not, why not? (for example, due to politics).

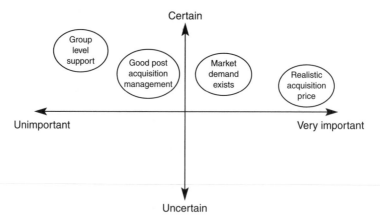

Fig. 4.4 Gleamtron's 'raw' uncertainty – importance grid

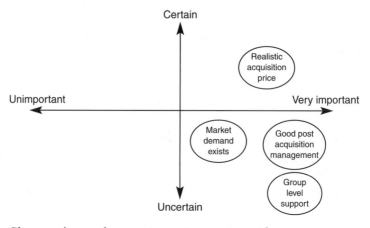

Fig. 4.5 Gleamtron's tested uncertainty – importance grid

Figures 4.4 and 4.5 give a graphic account of how the importance/uncertainty grid can be used. A UK-based high technology company, Gleamtron, was thinking about developing a new technology for improving the effectiveness of its processing operation. Gleamtron identified a company in continental Europe which appeared to have the appropriate technology. Exploiting the technology to its full however would require some changes to the end product and involve a substantially different geographic market.

The general manager of Gleamtron did a first-cut assessment of the key assumptions in Figure 4.4. These suggested that the project, though somewhat risky overall, was certainly a plausible area of strategic development. The assumption map was then tested out as follows by a consultant:

'I am not sure at all about your map. This is clearly a very significant, if not major, diversification for the company across many if not all the dimensions of strategic development. First you have a quite new technology involved. Then you have adjustment to product and markets (relative to current business). Finally you would need to make a cross-border acquisition – I suggest you have a rethink.'

The general manager then had another go at the assumption map and, within about three and a half minutes, came back with the revised picture, as per Figure 4.5.

Figure 4.5 showed in a dramatic fashion how potentially dangerous and difficult this venture actually was. This map highlights particularly:

- market-related uncertainties;
- potential problems associated with a cross-border acquisition;
- implementation difficulties generally;
- problems in securing support at group level.

The latter issue was particularly revealing. On reflection, the general manager identified that far from being supportive to this venture, group-level management would have been extremely averse to it.

Unfortunately, where business cases to support investment in growth strategies within a group are under scrutiny this fosters the opposite of what really needs to happen. As Goold *et al* (1994) explain, all too frequently the financial data are used to avoid managers querying the key uncertainties which are actually being suppressed.

Before we leave the topic of assumptions we also need to explore the 'do-nothing' or base case option.

The base case is what might happen without the investment decision. Traditional financial theory teaches us to evaluate incremental cash flows – 'incremental' meaning the difference between net cash flows, both with and without the investment project. For illustration, the head of corporate planning (himself a chartered accountant) of Rolls-Royce Aeroengines, Simon Hart, tells us:

'Actually, I think that most of our assumptions are that if we do nothing, then nothing will happen.

If we went into the market with a radically improved engine – with vastly improved fuel consumption ... then the guy who bought our competitor's [inferior] engine would fail in the market place just through the difference between performance.

> *The argument comes down to, if you don't do this, you won't be in the game in so many years' time. And the accountant would ... he doesn't know how to evaluate it.'*

The problem with the base case is that of predicting the rate or pace of decline. This is inherently difficult to predict. Some managers may then try to shield financially suspect projects behind the argument that unless the project is implemented, the strategic and financial health of the business will be irreparably damaged. See Figure 4.6 for a classic illustration of a declining base case.

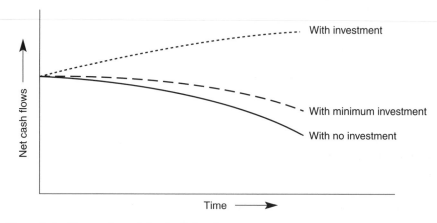

Fig. 4.6 An illustration of the declining base case

The two cases of the engineering group and the chain of pubs (see below) highlight the need to explore a number of key questions surrounding the base case. This is needed both to explore how vulnerable the business is under a 'do nothing' or 'do minimum' scenario, and to understand what can be done about it to achieve strategic objectives at lowest (realistic) cost.

Example

Managers in a chain of pubs sought significant investment to refurbish their chain of outlets. The finance manager within group head office who reviewed their business case reflects on this:

> *'These managers said, we need to take the difference between a static view of current revenues and our assumed decline. Now that got them into much trouble, terrible trouble [his tone now getting very serious] because it was very easy for us to say that therefore anything you can do will make money, so the incremental analysis was very dangerous from a purely financial point of view.'*

The managers in the pub chain may have been right to have identified a possible decline in trade with no further investment. However, they may not have come up with the most effective option for dealing with this threat. To begin with, what other investment options might have achieved the objective of maintaining the business at less cost? What other changes in operating routines and marketing might have been considered? (for instance, there might have been a proposal to have jazz bands twice a week; or turn the lights down so that poor decor was not apparent or becomes a perceived benefit – resulting in a better atmosphere). Even the 'harvest option' of 'do minimum' might have a higher NPV than a heroic investment to refurbish the chain of pubs in the face of sinking demand.

Summary questions in defining the base case are as follows.

1. Where the 'base case' assumes improving external conditions, what key competitive assumptions is this based on? How may these change?
2. Where the 'base case' suggests the business is in decline, then what are the key competitive assumptions upon which this is based?
3. In a 'declining base case', what could be done to reduce or halt the decline without requiring new investment (e.g. improvement via operational change)?
4. What degree of uncertainty surrounds the pace of decline of the 'base case'?
5. Where the 'base case' for the business unit overall is difficult to define or predict, what is the approximate value of a 'protective' nature which managers put on the decision's defensive benefits?
6. Does the degree of decline of the base case suggest that the business unit overall should be fundamentally reappraised?

The two other key problem areas are those of interdependencies and also intangibles.

Dealing first with intangibles, strategic development decisions add value only insofar as they are part of a 'corporate value system'. The corporate value system is the set of processes within the areas of business which add value through mutual alignment, and by alignment with the external, competitive system. Interdependencies thus need to be explored because they are essential in understanding how the business operates as a total competitive and financial system.

Interdependencies exist in a variety of forms. Some interdependencies are external and reflect the impact of one external assumption on one another. For example, a resurgence of economic growth may increase the size of a particular market and also attract in new entrants.

Many of the internal assumptions depend upon external variables, giving rise to more interdependencies. (For instance, competitive rivalry may lead to a high incidence of price discounting and thus to lower margins.)

But many of the more interesting interdependencies are those within the business strategy. For instance, one product may benefit or suffer due to the introduction of a new product. FMCG (fast-moving consumer goods) companies realize this and also supermarket chains opening superstores – these companies are acutely aware of cannibalization effects. But this is not so commonly appreciated in many other industries.

The analysis of interdependencies should follow on from the analysis and testing of the external and internal assumptions. Where the decision process is less formal this analysis should be integral with the evaluation of assumptions.

Below is a summary of key questions for exploring interdependencies.

1. What are the key interdependencies between external assumptions (e.g. between regulatory change and market growth and structure; between economic slowdown and competitive rivalry etc.)?
2. What are the key interdependencies between internal assumptions (e.g. between sales of one product cannibalizing sales of another product, and between sales of a new product 'piggy-backing' off an existing product)?
3. What are the key interdependencies between external and internal assumptions (e.g. between assumed intensity of competitive rivalry and price discounting, between perceptions of company image and actual service quality etc.)?
4. What key policy interdependencies exist (e.g. with corporate intent), and how may the intent of specific internal and external stakeholders be shaped?

Intangibles are one of the main curses of strategic development decisions. But it doesn't have to be that way. Returning to what a manager at Rolls-Royce Aeroengines had to say about intangibles:

> '*Isn't the principle of these intangible benefits that, one day in the far distant future, they will actually materialize?*
> *It's a strange system where you don't try to quantify the benefits, otherwise you are hard-pressed to justify why you are doing it.*'

For many managers, intangibles have become the 'no go' zone of financial analysis. Although these are areas of value extremely difficult to quantify in financial terms (and perhaps impossible to quantify with precision), there are invariable ways of defining intangibles better. This can be done by looking at the project from different perspectives.

- **Competitive:** impact on customer perceptions of value or in measurable improvement *vis-à-vis* competitors.
- **Operational:** performance improvement or flexibility of operations.

- **Organizational:** impact on morale and, indirectly, on motivation.
- **Opportunity generation:** the opportunity which might be opened up or explored as a result of the investment project.

The first step with intangibles is to ask 'Why is the value thought to be of an intangible nature?' This may be for the following reasons.

- The benefit accrues to the customer rather than directly to the company. However, there may also be indirect benefits to the company via reducing the customer switching its source of supply, or through increased orders (and volume), or through increased prices, or through protection against discounts. For example, when Hewlett Packard tried to appraise the value of attaining a particular quality award, it found that most of the value came relatively indirectly and could not be harvested in a simple or direct way.
- The benefit may be of a future and essentially contingent nature. This may be contingent because a future state of the world is required to crystallize a market – this may require alignment of a credible product offering, customers recognizing the need exists, potential demand actually crystallizing. Even in this situation, your particular company needs to be credible as a supplier to generate value. For instance, at Rolls-Royce Aeroengines, value was contingent until the customer, the airframe and a credible engine all lined up.
- The benefit accrues via a number of internal interdependencies with other areas of the business, or these may occur because the investment project is essentially part of the 'business' infrastructure.
- The benefit comes due to the project being essentially protective or defensive in nature. For example, at Post Office Counters in the UK, most of the benefits of the investment programme were seen as of a protective nature. It was thought that unless Post Office Counters business invested in more modern automation, it would simply not be able to compete in terms of speed and price against competitors and substitutes. Also, the declining base case is difficult to define, or the protection is against some unlikely but high-impact event.

A process for dealing with intangibles is therefore:

- to identify why the value is of an intangible nature;
- to seek possible alternative measures to help target and provide indicators of alternative measures to those of purely financial value (see Figure 4.7);
- through management consensus, to compare what value managers are prepared to put on the area of intangible value.

Types of intangibles	Related to other appraisal problems	Possible focus for measurement
Product image	Customer value	Customer views of product
Reduced customer product and service	Customer value	Customer views of costs and risks
Customer loyalty	Customer value	Estimated revenue and likelihood of switching
Protection of business	Protective investment	Monitoring incidence of existing loss of business
Spin-off opportunity	Contingent value and interdependency	Specify conditions under which opportunity arises and is harvested
Flexibility	External and internal interdependency	Specify conditions under which flexibility will add value
Cost savings elsewhere	Internal interdependency	Before and after measurement of cost drivers and of impact
Alignment of external and factors	External and internal interdependency	Specification of conditions under which alignment may occur and probable value

Fig. 4.7 Types of intangibles and possible measures

A summary of key questions for evaluating intangibles is therefore as follows.

1. Does much of the value of the opportunity depend on less tangible factors?
2. If so, are these factors measurable at some future point in time in financial terms, or not?

3. Where these are difficult to quantify financially, even at some future date, are there other ways of quantifying or assessing whether benefits have been realized (e.g. in market-based or operational measures)?

4. If so, is there an 'appropriate worth' that managers would be prepared to pay for these (or alternatively, if they had them, what would they pay to retain them – i.e. what is their 'deprival value')?

5. Are these benefits difficult to evaluate because they are, in effect, consumed externally (e.g. by customers)? If so, are these capable of being harvested by extra prices, or by avoiding price reduction, or avoiding a loss of volume which might otherwise occur?

6. Have all areas of less tangible costs been included in the appraisal (for example, does going ahead with the project result in difficult-to-quantify distraction costs as the business becomes increasingly complex)?

7. Where no formal value is put on intangibles, how is it proposed to reflect this value in the decision process, especially where there are tight financial constraints in place?

8. How will the less tangible factors be subsequently measured (e.g. by measuring service levels, customer perceptions, employee perceptions etc.)?

9. Under what specific circumstances will assumed 'synergies' be harvested and how can this be measured?

10. Has future and 'contingent' opportunity which may spin off from the project been included, and, if so, how?

11. Also, might the project foreclose other opportunities of significant value and what is therefore the contingent value lost by the opportunity?

Many strategies for growth are justified on the back of intangibles (at least in part), so it is particularly necessary to ensure that they are thought through and probed as rigorously as possible.

Integrative case: Alton Towers and the zebra factor

The following case records a conversation at a conference (for accountants) on the topic of linking strategy and value. At the coffee break, one accountant rushed up to one of the speakers to ask a burning question about a proposed area for breakthrough. He said:

'I'm the accountant for a stately home which is open to the public. The owner has a small zoo and has asked me to financially evaluate a new project – to add a zebra feature. The question is this: how do I set about doing the incremental cash flows?'

The accountant had fallen into the classic trap of trying to do the numbers before thinking through the strategy and impact on both competitive position and the operational effects. The speaker responded:

> *'First, it seems to me that you have not really defined the problem or opportunity. Why do you need a zebra feature? Is it because visitors have said things like "What a nice little zoo – the crocodiles, the llamas, the monkeys, but where on earth was the zebra?" – and go away patently disappointed?*
>
> *Or was this just thought of as a nice-to-do? Or was it part of a bigger grand plan (effectively a strategic project set) to reposition the estate as a kind of mini-Longleat (a safari park bristling with zebras and lions) or even a Chessington World of Adventures (with lots of animals hanging around, looking rather redundant, while the visitors go on some scary theme park rides and water chutes)?*
>
> *I think this is an example of where you need to think through the project in terms of its degrees of competitive and financial advantage.*
>
> *Basically, a single lonely zebra is not likely to do an awful lot for the estate. It will add to costs whilst not necessarily adding to customer satisfaction. In turn, this means you will not be able to justify any assumed benefits by way of increased volume of visitors or any price increase.*
>
> *But if you were to push the project up the slope of competitive advantage quite considerably* (see Figure 4.8) *by say:*
>
> – *adding a whole new jungle feature;*
> – *and a mini train to take visitors around it (without fear of being gobbled or pawed by the lions);*
> – *advertising this as a unique 'stay alive – but in the jungle' feature;*
>
> *then there is just a hope of either getting more visitors throughput or increasing prices, or both.'*

The zebra example highlights how managers often fail to grapple with uncertainties, intangibles and interdependencies because they don't apply sufficient strategic thinking about the particular project. This strategic thinking can and must be sharpened up by close-in financial analysis.

Notice, too, that most strategic development projects do not produce financial benefits in a linear way. Figure 4.8 shows net financial benefits increasing almost negligibly at first until a quantum level is reached. It is only when this happens that the real returns are recouped.

The financial benefits typically arise therefore through a series of curved steps or levels.

But, what about Alton Towers, which is arguably the UK's most developed theme park and the only one credibly claiming 'world-class' status (a kind of mini Disney park). Supposing you are the accountant of Alton

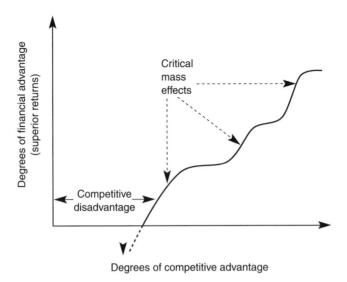

Fig. 4.8 Degrees of financial and competitive advantage

Towers and are asked to present a business case for a new feature – the Nemesis. This ride has to be seen to be believed – it is truly a breakthrough feature which has repositioned Alton Towers in the popular imagination.

Some brief facts on the Nemesis project are as follows.

- This will be incorporated within an existing theme area of the park – 'The Forbidden Valley' – where Alton Towers already has a number of very exciting, if nasty, rides.
- Other main theme areas are: the Gloomy Wood; Katanga Canyon; Festival Park; the Gardens; the Towers; Tower Street; the Land of Make Believe; and Fantasy World.
- The Nemesis ride lasts for around a minute, during which time the victims will loop the loop several times, rush through a canyon at great speed (almost hitting a smoking bus) and then come to an abrupt halt.

My daughter (who is currently 11) would like to add a little to this case study:

'I wasn't sure that I would actually go on it – the hour and a half queue gives you lots of opportunity to have doubts ... You don't really see any-thing – the world just spins around as you feel you are coming out of your seat ... especially if you are small, like me. It feels like seconds but it gives a lasting memory ... you feel really ill – sick with excitement.'

The unique selling proposition of the Nemesis project is thus fear. This is maximized by having riders dangling their legs from their seats in thin air.

There will be no physical security as is found, say, in sitting in a runaway train or a normal ride.

The benefits of the Nemesis project (which is going to be really quite expensive considering the huge engineering works) are:

- it will measurably increase the flood of visitors to the park eager to try the Nemesis experience;
- it will, at the same time, add to capacity by distracting visitors from other more tame experiences which are quite busy.

The actual results of Nemesis exceeded Alton Towers's expectations. In the first spring of Nemesis other areas of the park became eerily quiet as visitors queued for between one and three hours to go on the ride. Really lucky visitors actually went on it three times in one day. In fact the ride was almost too successful in its first year, virtually unbalancing the flow of visitors through the park.

This attraction is thus likely to have resulted in measurable incremental flow of visitors to the park. It would certainly have done much to prevent any erosion of trade that might otherwise have occurred (the declining base case). It was also of major intangible benefit, helping build the Alton Towers name outside its traditional core market (most UK managers have by now heard of the ride and some have even thought about going on it as the ultimate experience in turbulence).

But there are other issues too. I discreetly asked at the end of the 1994 season what new and bigger ride was in for 1995. The answer was that only one of the older rides was being replaced. I felt let down. Over the last three years there has always been a new ride to resuscitate interest and demand. With any successful strategy for growth, you always need to ask what the encore could be.

So, will Alton Towers now milk the Nemesis ride? Maybe it has to, given the sheer cost of development. But one of the downsides of the project is clearly its bulkiness. We are very much looking forward to new experiences in 1996...

The Alton Towers case highlights once again the need to think through:

- the way in which value is created as part of a system of business activities;
- the internal and external interdependencies (both now and future);
- the importance of building, and then harvesting, intangibles;
- the need to juggle with competitive, operational and financial advantages through time in strategic development;
- the importance of separating out (like the Zebra feature case) different 'states of the world' for financial evaluation. States of the world which are too similar in terms of the levels of advantage offered will be very hard indeed to evaluate financially.

DEFINING THE BUSINESS CASE – HOW TO SUPPORT THE 'BREAKTHROUGH'

When someone says the words 'business case' most managers think of a weighty, detailed document (or door stop?) with lots of hard facts and financial numbers. In larger companies managers typically see this as a necessary evil – required to get release of investment funds – within an adversarial environment. Some want to run for the hills (or even away to Alton Towers).

But the real point of a business case is to gain more clarity about the objectives of the project, its implications for the business, and particularly to expose and test the key assumptions which drive value. This can be achieved in a very succinct way, by for instance restricting the business case to a maximum of eight pages, as noted below (often less will suffice).

Format for a business case

- Executive summary (1 page).
- Project definition, objectives and scope (1 page).
- How the project adds value (new opportunity, tangible synergy, defensive or protective value) (1 page).
- Key external and internal assumptions (with an evaluation of importance and uncertainty) (3 pages).
- Implementation issues (1 page).
- Summary financials (1 page).

This brings the total length to eight pages plus detailed appendices containing technical details, detailed financial and non-financial measures and milestones, detailed financial sensitivities, detailed resource requirements – possibly another seven pages. This brings a typical case to just 15 pages.

Business cases will only add value therefore if:

- they are clear, succinct and written in a jargon-free style;
- they expose the most important and uncertain assumptions, and also address these both in the sensitivity analysis and via contingency planning;
- they do not fall into the trap of seeing the financial numbers as absolute measures of value, but use these creatively. For instance, in dealing with less tangibles it may be fruitful to put an illustrative value on 'what these might be worth', so that a more balanced, overall appraisal of the project can be achieved.

We have argued throughout the need to understand the key value drivers, and to expose and challenge the key assumptions before undertaking the sensitivity analysis. 'Better practice' means doing very rigorous testing of those key variables which are likely to be most uncertain and most important.

If needs be, for instance, one might reduce prices by, say, 5 per cent to reflect competitive rivalry and new entrants. (Coincidentally, this is the exact reduction in nominal prices between 1993–4 in the UK supermarket industry – something perhaps unthinkable before the event.)

It is only by working this way around that true sensitivity analysis is performed, otherwise all you end up with is 'insensitivity analysis' – playing with the assumption set to get the right answer – a positive NPV (which in this case means no more than 'numbers prevent vision').

Finally, an important issue is how to deal with the terminal value. This is the value which is put on the cash plans at the end of the time horizon of the projections. With slow payback decisions the terminal value can amount to between 40 per cent and 50 per cent of NPV. Yet terminal value may be subject to minimal, strategic and financial scrutiny. Invariably, terminal values can be proved more effectively using a quick competitive and financial scenario which, although broad-brush, checks that the assumptions make prima facie sense.

Key questions for compiling an effective business case are therefore as follows.

1. Does the business case specify clearly the scope and objectives of the strategic development project, its relationship to other areas of investment (capital or revenue) and to operational change?
2. Does it specify what the strategic routes to value creation are, e.g. competitive enhancement or protection versus synergistic value or creating future spin-off opportunities?
3. Are key strategic operational and financial assumptions clearly identified?
4. Are key uncertainties and interdependencies identified?
5. Does the 'sensitivity analysis' focus on key risks and also on exploring worst downsides (and also any 'upsides' which may strain capacity and push up unit cost levels)?
6. Has a break-even analysis been conducted to test the robustness of NPV, and does this take each of the high impact, external and internal assumptions in turn?
7. Have areas of 'softer' value, including intangibles, the protective value from slowing a declining base case, or the value of contingent and future opportunity been identified and, if necessary, isolated in the business case?

8. If the project is targeted at achieving a shorter payback, would this produce some useful reshaping of the 'project definition'?

9. Besides IRR, has NPV also been assessed in order to prioritize projects and has the NPV been compared across projects along with variations in payback? (All other things being equal, a project with faster payback may be preferable to another project with similar NPV.)

10. What is the basis for any 'terminal' or residual value which has been included?

11. How does this project affect the total financial balance of the portfolio of projects (or businesses) given its cash flow profile?

12. What is the likely impact on bottom-line earnings? Is this such that the proposal needs to be 'sold' back to the shareholders to highlight longer term benefits and to shift these perceived constraints?

13. What operational and organizational requirements are required to implement the project satisfactorily?

14. Have the 'critical success factors' for successful implementation been fully thought through?

TACKLING SPECIAL CASES

There are a number of special cases which require further discussion. These include:

- strategic development projects where the bulk of value is highly contingent;
- joint ventures;
- exit from a business.

Projects with contingent value

Strategic development projects with contingent value pose special problems of appraisal. Examples of these are new technology development, new brand launch and entry strategies into embryonic markets.

Managers find it difficult to value these projects simply because they are relatively unlikely to achieve a big payoff. Unless the probability of a positive outcome exceeds a particular threshold then it may be very hard for managers to feel confident enough to include this in the value of any investment case. There may also be difficulties for managers in including contingent value within an investment case where there is a major chance that it will not materialize.

Managers may well find it difficult to justify including a quantified value within a business case for a contingent project unless the balance of probabilities was at least in its favour. (One might speculate that this level of probability may be, say, over 50 per cent or even 75 per cent, depending upon how managers apply control measures.)

There may also be a further cut-off point, at which level of perceived probability a contingent event is deemed to be worth while, including within any qualitative assessment of value (that is as an upside to the business case).

A way of coping with this is to distinguish between:

- **demand which is conceivable:** it is relatively indeterminate as buyers may not have defined intent to buy something at all, nor what their specific needs might be;
- **demand which is contingent:** buyers are becoming clearer that they will have a need that will require satisfaction but they are unclear how best to meet that need;
- **demand which has crystallized:** buyers have made a clear commitment to a course of action, either through explicit decision or through establishing a predictable pattern of buying.

Estimating the value of opportunities which are based on conceivable demand appears to be best addressed by broad-brush thinking. This might involve exploring the overall shape and size of market demand and potential advantage of the product, given some view of competitor intent and insight into likely customer requirement. Where demand is contingent, a more firm estimate of demand might be assessable through more in-depth market analysis as the shape of demand firms up.

Where, however, demand is contingent or conceivable, there may be severe boundaries to the use of financial appraisal tools. This is, perhaps, the territory of the 'unknowable'. In this case, managers may find the use of techniques such as NPV to have a 'fraudulent feel' – unless of course they are aware that the measures, for example of NPV, are illustrative only. NPV would still be useful as a tool here, as it would be possible to work backwards to explore the kind of market conditions in which a positive NPV would appear viable (rather than using market and operational assumptions to generate the NPV).

To summarize, key questions to help value projects with contingent value are as follows.

- In what circumstances can value actually occur, and how remote are these circumstances?
- What steps can be taken to help crystallize value, or to avoid events which will prevent value from crystallizing?

- What makes the company think it will be well placed competitively to exploit the opportunity when it actually crystallizes?
- Is it appropriate to include an estimated value in the business case, an illustrative value (based on a 'what if'), or simply a qualitative statement about value as the use of formal NPV may be perceived as misleading?

Joint ventures

Joint ventures and other collaborative arrangements are often fruitful avenues for growth. Joint venture projects typically (but not always) involve lower investment outlays, but greater risks in terms of the sustainability of income. The literature on joint ventures (for instance, Lorange and Roos, 1992) suggests that joint ventures:

- are highly competitive arrangements where parties seek to maximize the leverage which they get out of the joint venture. This is done while revealing only to a minimum their own core competencies;
- are characterized in the early stages with 'things going well', followed by a period of increasing instability which precedes break down;
- rarely survive beyond around six years without one partner becoming dominant.

Joint ventures thus present special problems of appraisal. Frequently, they appear to generate very attractive NPVs and high IRRs. But this is perhaps due to projected cash flows being based on 'everything going right', instead of the high-risk scenarios painted earlier.

Joint ventures offer a rare possibility for using decision-tree analysis to explore different turns of events (with probability and payoff assessments). Here is an example.

Example

First five years NPV	£5m
After five years: 50% probability of becoming dominant partner	
Expected value (rest of life) 50% × £8m	£4m
20% probability of being bought out:	
Expected value (sale of shares) 20% × £5m	£1m

30% probability of the joint
   venture collapsing in acrimony
   30% × – £5m   (£1.5m)
                                                              ‾‾‾‾‾‾‾
Total expected NPV   £8.5m
                                                              ‾‾‾‾‾‾‾
(Which compares unfavourably against a simplistic
NPV of the first five years of £5m plus the rest of
life of £8m, of £13m)

Finally, exit from a business is frequently a strategic decision just as much as entry. Although accountants and managers appreciate the need to evaluate the incremental cash flows of new businesses, it is rarer to see them challenge existing businesses or projects.

Sometimes the 'exit option' occurs when managers have been considering a new investment project within an existing business. When evaluating the financial projections it becomes increasingly evident that the project is being pushed uphill, struggling to achieve justification. This can sometimes be because the business itself is in steep strategic and financial decline.

Another trigger to business reappraisal may occur because corporate-level management are uncomfortable with the strategic plans of a business. Despite its market place being fundamentally unattractive (very competitive, mature and low growth), and its competitive position being suspect, its financial plans still seem rosy. By appraising the business as a strategic project (using discounted cash flow), managers may be forced to:

- stretch their strategic thinking further out into the future than, say, just three years;
- understand and challenge where any positive net present value is coming from;
- surface and challenge the key competitive and other external assumptions on which NPV is based.

In some instances, reappraisal may reveal that the business is not currently contributing to shareholder value, and that it may be worth more to another parent. In other instances, regeneration options are flushed out and prevent the business from being starved of fresh investment.

CONCLUSION

This chapter has shown how financial analysis and strategic analysis need to be added together to perform any effective appraisal of strategies for growth. An opportunity may, based purely on strategic analysis tools, look like a breakthrough, but may ultimately result in financial breakdown. Finance should never be seen as being the enemy of strategy, but as its handmaiden. We have also seen how most of the analytical problems associated with appraisal are dissolved in part, or in whole, when applying the framework of strategic value management.

Managing for value is equally applicable at the level of the individual as well as the business. Often unintentionally, we fall into the trap in organizations of going along with the flow – often entailing lots of value-destroying or diluting routines. One way of heading this off is to have the 'red light implant'.

Imagine a light on your forehead which is on green when you are adding value, yellow when you are not sure and which flashes red when you are definitely not adding value. Having a red light implant gives you the confidence and air-cover to suggest other ways of doing things which do not destroy or add value.

Both strategic and financial appraisal therefore give merely two out of the three key dimensions of analysing potential areas of breakthrough strategies for growth. The third – organizational breakthrough – comes next.

ACTION CHECKLIST

- How do you define the scope and focus of the strategic development project?

- What unit and level of analysis have you opted for, and is this the unit which will best facilitate strategic and financial analysis?

- Is the timing of your business case appropriate – or are you building a business case for a strategic commitment already made some time ago (for example, market entry)?

- What key options exist for pursuing this opportunity which achieve growth while reaching for sustainable financial value?

- What key assumptions have you made (particularly concerning the external environment, and/or implementation)?

- What areas of less tangible value and interdependencies exist, and how have these been made more tangible or unravelled?

- Which assumptions are most important and most uncertain, and how does your strategy contain flexibility to deal with these 'danger zone' assumptions?

'Can we do it?'

5

ACHIEVING ORGANIZATIONAL BREAKTHROUGH

INTRODUCTION

We have now explored both the strategic and financial dimensions of breakthrough strategies for growth. But both strategic and financial analyses often fail to capture the implementation issues involved in making breakthrough strategies for growth a reality. Since around 1980 it has become once again permissible (if not fashionable) to discuss softer issues like leadership, culture change and, even more recently, organizational transformation in management.

Beneath the ideological surface of what one might call 'managerial sociology' lie some very important realities. So many strategies fade (or fail) because of strategic (implementation) droop. Although the analysis may have been sound, the choices made, so many strategies end up in effect in a state of corporate impotence.

Managers schooled in the art of tough business and financial analysis (especially those who love to focus on objectives, targets and controls) are extremely prone to overlook implementation realities. But it is precisely the soft issues which frustrate and bog down strategic development.

But are we destined to struggle forever to overcome implementation droop (of strategic proportions)? I think not. Implementation is an equal cornerstone of making growth which adds sustainable value a reality. This is important to support both strategic and financial analysis. The implementation link requires a little more than a single question: 'Can we do it?' It also calls for organizational analysis to help drive both the decision and the implementation process.

This chapter therefore focuses in on:

- the implementation process;
- tools for organizational analysis;
- developing an organizational strategy;
- conclusion.

The first two sections thus provide the framework for setting about organizational analysis. The third section helps to pull together the disparate issues in an overall programme for internal strategic development.

THE IMPLEMENTATION PROCESS

Figure 5.1 defines the five stages of implementation for strategic development. These stages are as follows.

- **Diagnosis:** what is the scope of the opportunity (or threat)? What are its objectives, and possible benefits, costs and risks? What is the overall implementation difficulty and who are the key stakeholders?
- **Planning:** what is the external and internal position, and how are these likely to change? What options are available for implementation and how attractive are they versus difficult to implement? Is the timing good and (specifically) what resources are needed, and when to deliver a result effectively? Which stakeholders now need to be mobilized to make it happen?
- **Implementation:** is implementation proving effective and, if not, why not? What new implementation forces and stakeholders have come into play, and how might these be handled? Do the original objectives need revisiting and are these more easily met by other strategies for growth? If so, what are the costs of refocusing efforts?
- **Controls:** is the strategic project on track in terms of its intended competitive, financial, operational and organizational effects?
- **Learning:** did you achieve what you set out to achieve? If not, what were the factors you might have controlled, or attempted to influence, but didn't. Or, do you need to revisit and change your recipes for strategies for growth (or for implementation)? Finally, were the implementation difficulties much greater than envisaged and, if so, why?

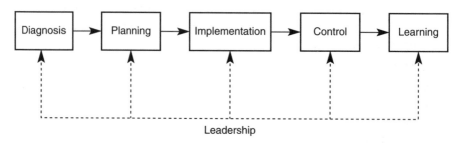

Fig. 5.1 Key elements in managing implementation successfully

Typically, managers focus 80 per cent of their efforts on those areas of the implementation process which carry only 20 per cent of overall importance. The following table graphically illustrates this tendency:

	Time actually spent	Time which should be spent
Diagnosis	2%	20%
Planning	10%	20%
Implementation	80%	40%
Control	6%	10%
Learning	2%	10%

Source: *Implementing Strategic Change*, A N Grundy, Kogan Page, 1993

Note the enormous difference in time between what, in an ideal world, it is felt that managers should spend on 'diagnosis' and what they actually spend. Also, note the need to spend considerably more time on learning.

Not only is it essential to manage all five stages effectively but this needs skilful leadership. This is particularly true when there is a need to revisit preceding stages (iteration).

Case study: Gold Bar Holdings (GBH) PLC

Several years ago, Gold Bar Holdings PLC (GBH) was a very rapidly expanding acquisitive company. GBH's business covered a range of high value materials. GBH's acquisition strategy was to buy small to medium-sized companies, and then to install better management systems and processes to make them significantly more effective organizationally and financially.

After a frenetic few years of acquisitive activity the board of GBH decided to hold an away-day to reassess its past acquisitions – its successes and failures. Most of these acquisitions had been successful, but there were a minority of cases where there had been some disappointments.

Four out of five cases of disappointments appeared to have been due principally to the underlying quality of management and key skills in the organization. These failures were not particularly affected by misjudgements about the company's products, its competitive position, or even the financials and the due diligence process (for uncovering strategic

The above case highlights the importance of revisiting strategic development projects so as to maximize learning, otherwise companies are liable – perhaps some would say fated – to repeat these errors.

Short exercise

For a past area of strategic development which you have been involved in, ask these questions.

- What were the strengths and weaknesses of each phase of the strategic development process, particularly:
  - diagnosis;
  - planning;
  - implementation;
  - control;
  - learning?
- What 'do's and don'ts' can you distil for the future?

Now that the need to have an explicit (fluid) process for managing the implementation of strategies for growth has been exposed, it is time to take a closer look at some very important tools for diagnosis, planning, implementation and control.

TOOLS FOR ANALYSING ORGANIZATIONAL BREAKTHROUGH

A number of key tools are available to analyse organizational breakthrough, as follows.

- Root cause analysis (fishbone analysis).
- How-how.
- Implementation forces ('IMF' analysis).
- Stakeholder analysis.
- From and to analysis (or 'FT' analysis).

The three core tools are IMF analysis, stakeholder analysis and 'FT' analysis. The other two tools have been added because many managers frequently need assistance both in problem or opportunity definition (root cause analysis) and also with brainstorming implementation routes ('how-how').

Figure 5.2 depicts the three core tools in triangle form. The tools in Figure 5.2 were successfully integrated at Hewlett Packard (UK) into a process for combining *hoshin* (breakthrough management) and applying the philosophy of total quality management to the change process. This management process is called 'accelerating business change'.

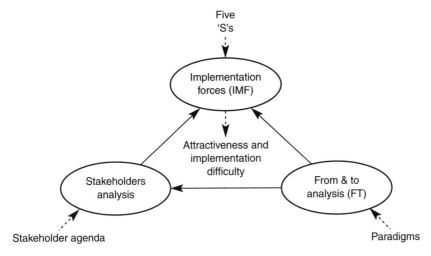

Fig. 5.2 The implementation triad

Root cause (fishbone) analysis

Root cause analysis is a very quick and easy way of going behind the more immediate definition of the problem or opportunity. For instance, Figure 5.3 indicates how root cause analysis can be used to identify why the quality management standard ISO9001 presented an opportunity. This figure enabled one leading company to identify that ISO9001 was not quite such an attractive opportunity (at least in the short and medium term) as was originally thought. In particular, the idea that the company might actually lose customers through not having ISO9001 was exposed as a doubtful assumption.

Many managers may have met root cause analysis in the quality management literature – but it seems much more rare to find it applied to

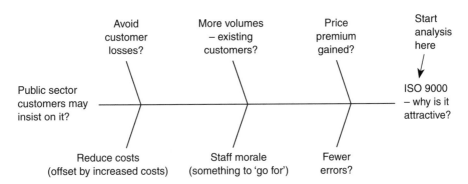

Fig. 5.3 Root cause/fishbone analysis

resolve strategic problems. As one manager put it: 'unless you pull a problem up by its roots, like a weed it always grows back'.

Where root cause analysis is used to depict an opportunity it is possible to show it vertically as a 'Christmas Tree'. Here the top of the tree is the perceived opportunity (where the fairy goes), and the branches break down the opportunity into parts. It is even possible to show the enabling influences as Christmas Tree roots.

How-how analysis

How-how analysis is useful in programming implementation (so that you have a fleshed out plan prior to testing it out with the core three implementation tools, which follow next). It is also useful in finding a way forward which might not have been thought about before.

Figure 5.4 gives an example of a how-how analysis, where until this picture was drawn up managers perceived that there was no way that the cost of bought in motors could be reduced.

While root cause analysis works backward from the current situation to find out how and why it exists, how-how works forward to see how it can be resolved in the future.

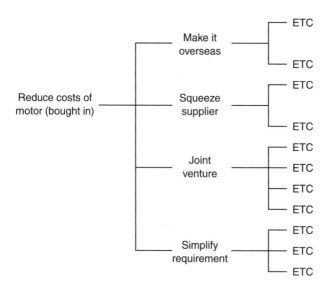

Fig. 5.4 How–how analysis – an example

Short exercise

For one area of external or internal breakthrough which impacts on strategic development ask the following questions.

- Why is it a problem or opportunity (look at the underlying causes or drivers using root cause analysis)?
- What (obvious and less than obvious) options are available for tackling this problem or opportunity (how-how analysis)?

Implementation forces

Implementation forces (IMF) analysis is derived from the original notion of 'force field analysis' from Lewin (1935).

Implementation forces analysis can be defined as follows:

Implementation forces analysis is the diagnosis and evaluation of enabling and constraining forces that have an impact on the change process.

IMF analysis is a tool which brings to the surface the underlying forces that may pull a particular change forward or may prevent progress, or even move the change backwards. These 'forces' can be separately identified as 'enablers' or 'constraints'. But neither set of forces can be adequately identified without first specifying the objective of the strategic development project or programme. The objective of strategic development is where you want to be or need to be, suggesting a gap with where you are now.

Turning back now to IMF analysis, the most effective way of evaluating the forces enabling or constraining achievement of the strategic development objective is to do so pictorially. This picture represents the relative strength of each individual change force by drawing an arrowed line whose length is in proportion to that relative strength.

A horizontal version of IMF analysis is depicted in Figure 5.5. Note in this case that, on balance, the enabling forces appear less strong than the constraining forces. This particular analysis is of the strategic plan of Dowty Communications for the early 1990s. It shows that although many of the plans, processes and programmes had been put in place, it was nevertheless difficult to envisage implementation being a complete success. (This picture is based on similar IMF pictures done internally by Dowty Communications managers in order to jolt top management to reshape implementation plans.) Subsequent events suggest that implementation difficulties at Dowty Communications were very severe.

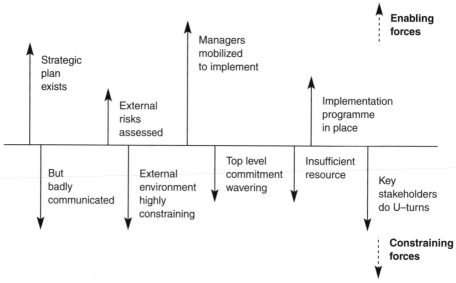

Fig. 5.5 IMF analysis of Dowty Communications strategic development plan for the early 1990s

As a rule of thumb, one would wish to see the enablers outweighing the constraints by a factor of at least 1.5 to 2 overall. Otherwise we should be concerned and potentially worried that implementation droop will set in.

Also, any stoppers really must be addressed, otherwise implementation really won't happen. During (and before) implementation the key implementation forces should be continually monitored to ensure that none threatens to 'go critical' and become a stopper.

The next issue that arises is how to evaluate the relative strength of the various forces. Two methods used successfully in the past include:

- scoring each force as having 'high', 'medium' or 'low' impact;
- scoring each force numerically on a scale of 1–5.

Most groups of managers work comfortably by using the high, medium or low scoring method. In exceptional cases (for example where managers have scientific backgrounds or have an inherent love of quantification) the numerical 1–5 scale appears to fit more comfortably.

One of the common objections to IMF analysis is that the whole scoring exercise is 'highly subjective'. This feeling normally occurs within the first ten minutes or so of any analysis exercise. It arises usually because all managers have done is to identify that a force is an enabler or a constraint without exploring questions including the following.

- Why is it an enabler or a constraint?
- How important an influence is it on the change process (and when)?
- What underlying factors does it depend upon in turn?

This highlights that any IMF analysis is dependent on many assumptions, many of which are implicit. A more successful and less 'subjective' analysis will have brought to the surface, shared and agreed these implicit assumptions.

A number of pitfalls need to be avoided in the use of force field analysis, which include:

- focusing primarily on tangible (as opposed to less tangible) implementation forces;
- missing major constraints because the team wishes to paint an 'ideal' rather than a realistic picture of the change (these issues will be dealt with below)
- failing to identify a 'stopper' – that is, a change which has such a powerful impact that it is likely to stop the change in its tracks. 'Stoppers' should be drawn either as a thick black arrow or, alternatively, as an arrow which goes right to the bottom of the implementation forces analysis and 'off the page'. (This assumes that you are using the vertical format for IMF analysis.)

A stopper can be defined as an influence or change which will effectively put an end to the initiative either through direct confrontation or passive resistance. (Initiatives may fail because of 'limpet management' – just as one constraint is loosened another reasserts itself.) Also, there may be cases where a specific enabling force can be made strong and prove decisive in moving the change forward. This kind of force may be described as an 'unblocker' and can be drawn as a very long (or thick) positive line on the IMF picture.

There may also be instances where a negative and constraining force can be flipped over to make a positive force, and in so doing transform the picture. For instance, if an influential stakeholder (who is currently negative) can be turned around in favour of the change, this can provide a major driver in the strategic development process.

It may be helpful to use the following checklist to brainstorm the enabling or constraining force. This is structured as five categories (which are a distillation of Peters and Waterman's original seven 'S's which in their original form also included staff and shared values – see Figure 5.6):

- strategy;
- structure;
- style;
- skills;
- systems.

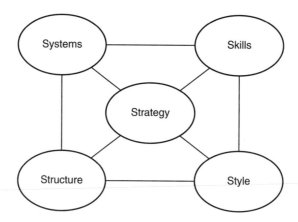

Fig. 5.6 Implementation systems

Strategy

- Do we have a simple and clear objective?
- Is this supported by a coherent plan?
- Does this plan fully address the key implementation issues?

Structure

- Are the roles of the key implementors sufficiently clear and well communicated?
- Have they got sufficient power and influence to achieve results?
- Does the project impact on a number of business and/or functional areas, and, if so, will it be effectively co-ordinated?

Style

- Does the project require new behaviours in the organization or changing old behaviours – if so, will these behaviour shifts materialize?
- Is there sufficient commitment to the project, and will this commitment be sustained?
- Does the project team itself have an appropriate leadership and team (with suitable interpersonal and political skills – not just technical)?

Skills

- Does the project require new skills within the organization and is this being effectively addressed?

- Does the project develop skills which may in turn generate or enable future strategic development opportunities to be detected and exploited?
- Does the project create skills bottlenecks which might either throw other projects off their critical paths, or create internal conflict, or both?

Systems and resources

- Does the project require new systems or processes to achieve success, and will this infrastructure be in place?
- Does the project require significant changes to existing systems or processes and are key stakeholders (the 'guardians' of these systems) on board with all of these changes?
- Are there actually sufficient resources?

The lessons of using the five 'S' framework at Hewlett Packard were that:

- the five S's is very good for exposing the soft as well as the hard issues in managing strategic development;
- but managers tend to get too absorbed in detailed and less relevant analysis until there was strong and direct facilitation.

Although some of the tools work better in some environments than others it could be dangerous to short-circuit the thinking process by just using one tool. The five S's gives managers much greater assurance that they have uncovered the hidden minefields of implementation.

Quick example: strategic development for an MBA programme

Recently a very successful MBA programme, which focused on part-time study, began to explore new ways of reaching its students, and to achieve substantial growth. The MBA board seized on the idea of launching a distance learning MBA. Using the above checklist, a number of enabling and constraining forces were identified.

Enablers

Strategy:

- Pressure from top business school management to expand
- Failure of other strategic growth initiatives

(and, I am afraid, that is the end of the enablers)

Constraints

Strategy:
- No overall implementation plan

Structure:
- No one really suitable to champion it

Style:
- Project will require considerable behaviour change (in lots of subtle ways)
- Commitment to the idea appears relatively tentative

Skills:
- Skills in preparing distance learning materials are underdeveloped

Systems and resources:
- Systems and processes currently don't exist
- The budget is woefully inadequate to achieve success

The IMF picture for a project to launch a distance learning MBA is shown in Figure 5.7. This project was abandoned (but this was only after market research had been conducted. Often it pays to do the implementation analysis before doing expensive, external analysis.) A better option was found which survived the IMF test much more effectively.

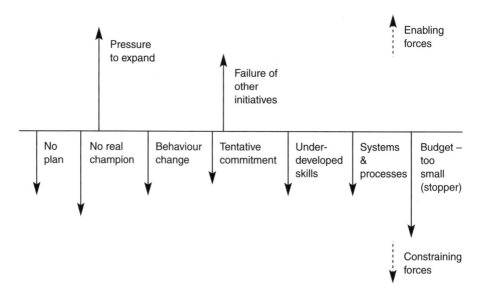

Fig. 5.7 IMF analysis of the distance learning MBA

The team involved in the decision were individuals with a collection of three MBAs, two PhDs and six other degrees! (Maybe that was part of the problem.) But overlooking the implementation issues isn't just something that management academics do – this is endemic in corporate management.

IMF analysis should not be used simply to reflect, but also to reshape, change strategy and plans. At the diagnosis stage, not only should it be used to map the existing pattern of implementation forces, but also to identify what pattern of forces is required in order to move the change forward at an acceptable pace. Frequently, managers relax exhausted or satiated by their analysis effort. The obvious application of IMF analysis – to redesign the project or programme to make it easier to implement – is all too often missed.

Some do's and don'ts of IMF analysis

Do:

- Brainstorm all the key tangible and less tangible forces impacting on the strategic development process.
- Include key forces drawn from your 'FT' analysis (see section later), and the stakeholder analysis.
- Test your judgements by questioning 'Why?' a force is strong or weak by reference to the strategic implementation objective and by thinking about its constraints within the overall process.
- Do the initial IMF analysis on an 'as is' basis – show the warts and be prepared to be provocative.
- Where a major constraint exists, draw this in as a stopper (that is as a very long downward arrow) to draw attention to its role in braking the change process.
- Use the tool throughout the strategic development process as the forces will change over time.
- Involve others to test and provide input to the analysis.
- Use 'How-How' and root cause analysis to reshape the forces.

Don't:

- Confuse IMF analysis with simple cost-benefit analysis. Benefits should only be included as a force if they are perceived by and owned by key stakeholders. Often, these benefits are in the eye of the programme initiator and are neutral in driving the change process forward.

- Use IMF analysis as a tool just to describe the current position. IMF analysis should be used to reshape actively your implementation plan to optimize the effect of enabling forces and to neutralize or flip-over the constraining forces to become enablers.
- Get bogged down in attempts to evaluate the forces precisely – IMF analysis is a soft science.

IMF analysis can be used in a number of ways. First, it can be used very formally, either within a team or individually. Or, it can be used intuitively – in effect as a form of 'organizational radar'. In fact, having used IMF analysis formally a number of time enables it to become unconscious. However, there are situations when you really do need to revert to a formal picture, if only to get a clearer mirror of your own intuitions.

Short example

I was involved in a number of major internal strategic development initiatives within an organization. My gut feel began to tell me that the prevalent organizational forces influencing those initiatives were extremely constraining. When I sketched up the actual IMF picture this not only reaffirmed my gut feel, but also suggested that the situation was *Mission Impossible*. The best option turned out to be to helicopter out of the situation and then to seek to influence it from the periphery.

At the earliest opportunity this is exactly what I did – to the surprise of some parties. This incident not only appeared to jolt the organization into taking these issues more seriously, but also enabled me to reassert (a hopefully benevolent influence) from a different position.

Managers find their own ways of innovating with IMF (implementation forces analysis). A brilliant and creative way of displaying the analysis came from two Volvo managers, who drew the enabling forces as tulips (to emphasize the need to grow these forces). The constraining forces were drawn in more conventionally as arrows (but as real arrows). See Figure 5.8.

Short exercise

For one area of past (or current) strategic development which proved (or is proving) hard to implement ask these questions.

- What were the key enabling and constraining forces which affected implementation (IMF analysis)?

- What was the overall pattern of these forces and were there any 'stoppers'?
- How could these have been reshaped to facilitate the implementation process?

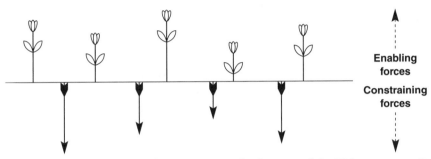

Enabling forces

Constraining forces

Fig. 5.8 Implementation forces analysis – a fresh approach by Volvo managers*

* Per Senninge and Erik Thormann, Volvo Cars Europe

Stakeholder analysis

Stakeholder analysis is the second change tool for analysing implementation issues. Stakeholder analysis has entirely reshaped the way in which strategic development has been implemented. Although Piercey (1989) and I (1993a) have drawn attention to the importance of stakeholder analysis as a practical tool, with some exceptions (for example, Goold *et al*, 1994a, p 315), it is seen in more theoretical terms.

Stakeholder analysis is the systematic identification of key stakeholders and appraisal of their influence on and posture towards implementation. It may also involve creating a strategy to reshape the influence of these or new stakeholders.

Stakeholder analysis is the second method of creating organizational radar. Like IMF analysis, it can be used not just on 'big picture' strategic development issues but also on much more micro-level issues, like getting something specific done in your job.

The tool is used as follows:

- first, identify who you believe the key stakeholders are at any phase of the process (the 'stakeholder brainstorm');
- second, evaluate whether these stakeholders have high, medium or low influence on the issue in question (you need to abstract this from their influence generally in the organization – Piercey, 1989);

- third, evaluate whether at the current time they are for the project, against it or idling in 'neutral'.

The above gives a good 'first cut' of the pattern of stakeholders. The cluster of stakeholders depicted on a stakeholder grid (see Figure 5.9) should then be assessed to see what the overall picture looks like, particularly:

- Is the project an easy bet?
- Or is it highlighting a long slog?
- Or, finally, does this seem like *Mission Impossible*?

Following the first-cut analysis you should then move on to the next phase.

- First, can new stakeholders be brought into play to shift the balance or can existing players be withdrawn in some way (or be subtly distracted)?
- Second, is it possible to boost the influence of stakeholders who are currently in favour of the change?
- Third, is it possible to reduce the influence of antagonistic stakeholders?
- Fourth, can coalitions of stakeholders in favour be achieved so as to strengthen their combined influence?
- Fifth, can coalitions of stakeholders antagonistic to the project be prevented?
- Sixth, can the change itself, in appearance or in substance, be reformulated to diffuse hostility to the project?

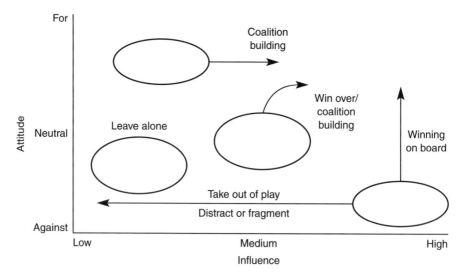

Note: This tool is based on earlier versions by Piercey (1989)

Fig. 5.9 Stakeholder analysis

- Seventh, are there possibilities of 'bringing on board' negative stake-holders by allowing them a role or in incorporating one or more of their prized ideas?
- Eighth, is the pattern of influence of stakeholders sufficiently hostile for the project to warrant re-definition of the project?

An example of stakeholder analysis in use is contained in Figure 5.10. This is again based on the position as assessed by internal managers of key stakeholders at Dowty Communications.

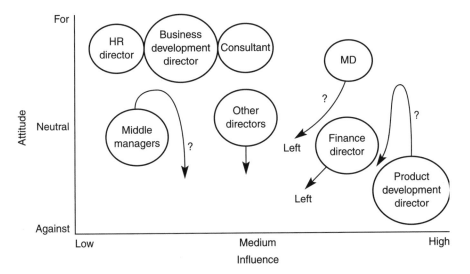

Note: This stakeholder picture is based on middle manager perspectives at the time.

Fig. 5.10 Stakeholders analysis – implementing strateges for growth at Dowty Communications (early 1991)

Short exercise

For any major management issue which you are currently facing ask these questions.

- What does the stakeholder analysis (per Figure 5.9) highlight in the pattern of influences?
- What (creative) strategies can you think of for enhancing support for what you (and presumably the business) are trying to achieve?
- What could go wrong in implementing these influencing strategies and why?
- How would you deal with these influences either before or during the event?

Once you have done the stakeholder analysis it may well be worth while revisiting the IMF analysis to either introduce one, or more, new forces, or to revise earlier views.

Although it might be more logical to do the stakeholder analysis first, strictly speaking, this might then fail to capture some of the agendas of stakeholders, as the wider issues involved in the project would have yet to be fully explored. Also, I suspect that many managers would become so involved in the stakeholder positioning they would not have time for IMF analysis.

Stakeholder analysis invites many questions as well as answers. These questions can be used to track potential positions of stakeholders (and their agendas) in specific meetings and chance conversations. Stakeholders change positions – suggesting the notion of 'snakeholder analysis' – tracking the wriggly players.

Often a particular stakeholder may be difficult to position. This may be because that stakeholders agendas might be complex. It is quite common to find that it is only one specific blocker that has made a stakeholder into an influential antagonist.

Where there are very large numbers of stakeholders at play on a particular issue, this may invite simplification of the project. The project may need to be refined, perhaps even stopped and then restarted, in order to dissolve an organizational mess.

In order to use stakeholder analysis effectively you may need to set some process arrangements in place where a team project is involved. First, the analysis may be usefully done in a 'workshop' environment so as to give the analysis a 'reflective' or 'learning' feel. This helps to integrate managers' thinking on a key change issue. Also, it may be useful to devise code words for key stakeholders in order to make the outputs from this change tool feel 'safe'. On several occasions managers have decided to adopt nicknames for the key players. The element of humour helps to diffuse the seriousness of stakeholder analysis.

As an aside note, obviously the stakeholder tool should not be used for covert personal and political purposes. It is there to get things done in organizations, not to obtain personal leverage for its own sake.

Stakeholder analysis is one of those techniques which does not really need much selling to managers. It has a natural appeal. I have seen senior managers suddenly bolt upright when I have put the stakeholder tool (Figure 5.9) on the projector in the 'dead slot' in a workshop after lunch at 2p.m.

I sometimes leave the overhead on deliberately at workshop coffee breaks. During a recent seminar at Management Centre Europe (owned by The American Management Association), Brussels, I left the overhead on and the door open – coincidentally a business process reengineering (BPR) conference was finishing next door. As the delegates came out a whole group of them stopped in their tracks, looked through the door, gazing at the stakeholder tool – wanting to know more, and causing a traffic jam. (In another case, one manager hadn't quite finished his analysis, and was found completing it in the men's room!)

So, once you have done your stakeholder analysis it may then be necessary to revisit your IMF analysis. You may need to introduce new forces or revise old forces. Although it might seem to be more logical to do stakeholder analysis first, and IMF analysis second, there are two big reasons for using the tools in my preferred order:

1. The stakeholder analysis is so inherently interesting that managers can tend to invest all their energies in refining it;
2. By doing the implementation forces analysis, the key issues and implications of implementation are more fully explored. This means that a more informed view of stakeholder agendas can be achieved.

Stakeholder analysis can prove to be an absolutely critical tool for achieving breakthrough. For it is often because of interpersonal and political reasons that perfectly robust strategic development projects are blocked.

Short exercise

For a particular strategic development project (or other issue) which you currently need to deal with ask these questions.

- Who are the current and likely stakeholders* in this issue?
- What are the key things on their agendas?
- Where (approximately) are they positioned on the stakeholder picture, and what picture emerges overall?
- What specific strategies for influencing stakeholders now appear appropriate?
- Should the project be refocused to make it more acceptable?

*Please think not only about the stakeholders making a particular decision (or influencing it) but also those who have either a direct or indirect influence over its implementation.

To conclude, to remember 'stakeholder analysis' think about what might happen to you if you don't do it. Are stakeholders whom you haven't thought about those who will hold you to the stake?

From and to ('FT') analysis

From and to (FT) analysis is another very powerful organizational analysis tool. Where a strategic development project has a significant impact on 'How we do things around here' (the 'paradigm') then it is essential that at least a rudimentary FT analysis is conducted.

The FT analysis can be done in one of two ways.

1. Brainstorm the key organizational shifts entailed for effective implementation of the project. Once this is done, these shifts are targeted to ensure that the project is sufficiently supported.
2. A fuller analysis of the impact on the paradigm is conducted.

The 'paradigm' represents 'How we do things around here'. The origins of the 'paradigm' are to be found in the theory of science (Kuhn, 1962), but the idea has been popularized in the US by Barker and in the UK more recently at Cranfield (Johnson, 1992; Grundy, 1993a). This 'paradigm' embraces a raft of organizational processes, some of which are 'hard' and tangible (the right-hand side of Figure 5.11) and some of which are 'soft' and intangible (the left-hand side of Figure 5.11), for example, signals from key stakeholders.

However, the idea of 'How we do things around here' as the paradigm extends into more tangible structures and processes, and beyond mere 'culture' – that is, if we understand culture as being the underlying values, attitudes, beliefs and behaviour within the organization.

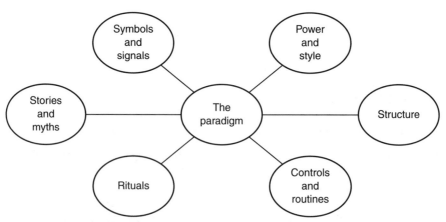

Note: This figure is a simplified version of Professor Johnson's 'culture web' at Cranfield School of Management.

Fig. 5.11 Paradigm analysis

The 'paradigm' works almost like the equivalent of the 'unconscious mind' of the organization, shaping how external change is interpreted, how strategic and tactical decisions are taken, and how internal change and development is managed. Newcomers to an organization – including recruits or, for that matter, consultants – will be a good deal more conscious of the peculiarity of 'the paradigm' than managers who have been with the organization for many years.

The 'paradigm' influences strategies for growth in a variety of ways including:

- it filters events in the external environment and therefore channels how managers understand external change;
- it shapes the organization's views on which newcomers it will 'bring aboard' – companies tend to recruit according to a view of fit with being 'one of us';
- it thus helps to reinforce existing recipes for strategic development;
- it also shapes in a profound way how strategic development decisions are implemented and also how day-to-day operations are conducted.

Paradigm analysis is thus a powerful technique in bringing to the surface forces which impede or constrain strategies for growth.

The paradigm can also be used to analyse progress of the project mid-way through. This can be done by comparing the current position against that at the very beginning of your current strategic development project. For each key element of the paradigm you wish to focus in on, ask: Where are we now (compared with where we were), as opposed to where we need to be?'

Managers within Prudential Life Administration in the UK successfully experimented with this approach. About 18 months into a major process of internal strategic development, they scored each dimension of the paradigm on a scale of 1–5 (1 being their starting point, 5 being the 'paradigm ideal'). This produced some revealing insights into the scale of the gap which still remained.

Paradigm	From	To
Power	Restricted	Resides at the lowest appropriate level
Structure	Hierarchical	Flatter
Controls	Instinctive and seat of pants	Measured objectives
Routines	Retrospective looking	Live and forward looking

Rituals	Loose plans	Structured plans
Myths	The 'Mighty Pru' 'Life Administration is OK'	Real world
Stories	Our job well done	Delighted customers
Symbols	Status hierarchy	Rewards for performance
Management style	Aloof	Open

Where FT analysis is done (either informally or via a full paradigm approach), this can highlight either new enabling forces which need to be brought in or further constraints (not previously identified) to be removed. The use of 'FT' as an acronym is no acronym – remember the famous advertising message –'No FT, no comment'?

Short exercise

For a particular strategic development issue which you are currently managing, have managed, are about to manage or 'How we do things around here', ask these questions.

- What is (or has been) the impact of the paradigm – in terms of forces enabling or constraining the success of the project?
- What particular actions or interventions could be mounted in order to achieve the necessary 'FT' shifts to support implementation?

Attractiveness and implementation difficulty

Now that we have led you through the three key tools of implementation analysis, it only remains to look at the trade-offs between attractiveness and difficulty.

The three implementation tools tell us little, if anything, about whether a particular strategic development project is beneficial. The tools are concerned purely with the implementation process. Benefits are only relevant in terms of shaping implementation forces insofar as they are perceived and shared by key stakeholders in the organization. Only if that is the case can they legitimately be introduced as enabling or constraining forces.

It is perfectly possible, for instance, to find a strategic development project which is attractive, with clear benefits, and yet where the implementation difficulty is extremely great. Alternatively, a project may be relatively easily implemented, but not particularly attractive or beneficial.

The attractiveness/implementation tool ('AID' grid) enables these trade-offs to be achieved. Pioneered in conjunction with Hewlett Packard, this tool enables a portfolio of possible projects to be prioritized. Figure 5.12 illustrates a hypothetical case.

Project A is seen as being both very attractive and relatively easy to implement. This project is non-contentious and will probably be given the go ahead. Project B is somewhat more difficult. It is only medium-attractive and is difficult. Project B requires a good deal of testing of the net benefits (Is it really that attractive?) (Would it be much harder than we currently think?).

Project C will probably end up being zapped unless it can be reformulated to make it both a lot more attractive and easier.

Project D presents the biggest dilemma of all. Although it appears to be very attractive it is also very difficult to implement. Yet managers will tend to focus on the attractiveness of the project rather than its actual difficulty. And that can occur even though they have gone through the IMF and stakeholder analysis thoroughly.

When piloting the AID tool at Hewlett Packard this happened twice. Quite separately, two 'D' type projects were identified and, as managers spent more time analysing them, commitment to action levels built up.

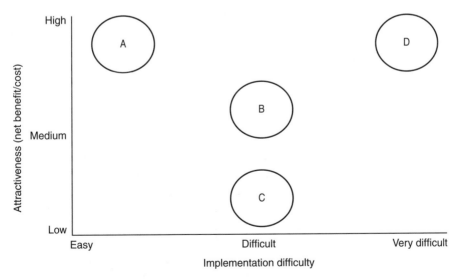

Fig. 5.12 An illustrative portfolio of projects – the attractiveness and implementation grid

Although neither of the projects went ahead – in their existing form – both myself and the internal facilitator Stuart Reed, had to be relatively strong to convince the teams that some further refinement was necessary.

Stuart Reed said to me at the time:

> 'I had gone through with them [the managers] both the implementation forces and the stakeholders. Although it did seem to be an attractive project our two organizational tools were telling us 'It is not going to happen'. I think because the managers were going through the analysis tools for the first time (and hadn't actually tried to implement the project) they hadn't quite realized that it really wasn't going to happen.'

Short exercise

For an area of organizational breakthrough that you are currently involved in ask these questions.

- How does its overall attractiveness (net benefits-costs) appear?
- To what extent are these benefits tangible versus less tangible, and can the less tangible be made more targeted and specific?
- Have you really thought through all of the costs, especially the indirect costs, and the costs of change?
- Using the implementation forces (IMF) and stakeholder analysis, how difficult does implementation appear overall?
- To what extent are your current perceptions liable to be disappointed during actual implementation, and why?
- What can you do to secure either higher attractiveness or easier implementation, or both?

So, to summarize, the organizational analysis tools help to see through a strategic development project to determine whether it is feasible or simply 'not going to happen'. These tools give us the means to do a kind of X-ray of implementation for projects – to see inside the outer surface of attractiveness into the inner implementation core.

Finally, to help oil the strategic development process you would do well to use a process tool (developed jointly by myself and by Dave King at Dowty Communications). This deals with the undesirable 'P' behaviour.

When beginning a strategic development workshop or contentious meeting one should ask all participants to brainstorm the 'P' behaviours that we want to avoid. To add some humour and reality, anyone caught behaving in a 'P'-behaviour fashion is asked to contribute £1 to the facilitator's or chairperson's favourite charity. A list of possible 'P'-behaviours is as follows:

- political;
- parochial;
- procrastinating;
- posturing;
- protectionism;
- pretending;
- pessimism;
- pettiness;
- preservation.

The real value of the 'P' process tool is that you rarely have to use it. But if you are facing a P-behaviour event or meeting and you don't get the P-behaviours out up front, then invariably the event becomes a quagmire.

Short exercise

Identify *one* meeting or other management event which might be greatly facilitated by using the P tool.

- How could you seek to influence behaviour by laying out the ground rules in advance (for example, this will be a politics-free meeting, or 'This is a politics (and other P-behaviour)-free zone'?

To summarize: IMF analysis, stakeholder analysis, systems of change and FT analysis gives you the four television screens (Channels 1 to 4) with which to manage implementation. In addition, the 'P'-behaviour tool gives you something akin to the volume control.

DEVELOPING AN ORGANIZATIONAL STRATEGY

This final section shows how internally oriented strategic development programmes can be integrated to form a coherent whole. It is not sufficient to address each strategic development project separately as there are likely to be common themes and issues across projects that also need to be addressed.

Traditionally this has been dealt with (if at all, and then frequently badly) by the route of functional or cross-functional strategy. Functional strategies include things like:

- human resource (or HR) strategy;
- IT strategy;
- operations (manufacturing, logistics or sourcing) strategy;
- financial strategy.

Cross-functional strategies include:

- total quality management;
- customer care programmes;
- BPR ('Business Process Reengineering') (see Chapter 10);
- strategic value/cost management (see Chapters 4 and 9).

The overall mix of programmes and interventions (such as GE's work-out programme led by Jack Welch) can be called organizational strategy. This can be defined as: 'The mobilization of people, processes and practices in support of strategic development and change.'

Organizational strategy goes far beyond individual functional strategies, particularly HR strategy. Arguably, separatist functional strategies should now be dissolved for the following reaons.

1. They do not add value in their own right but only by securing overall alignment within the organization.
2. If separate, then they are readily hived off to their traditional functional home (for instance, HR strategy becomes shunted into a cul-de-sac within the personnel department).
3. They become peripheral in the business planning process.
4. They relegate some of the key implementation issues (which are often soft and people-related) outside the strategic development process. They are frequently given cursory attention or even omitted from the business case.
5. Some of the key, soft areas of competitive advantage are then loosely managed.

In a recent UK study I conducted in the financial services industry on the links between human resources strategy and strategic development, I found that HR strategy was at best partly effective for a number of key reasons:

- The people issues were so interdependent with operational issues that they tended to get lost in the planning process.
- Top management's primary attention was on market moves, and meeting external competition and change even though in these particular markets one of the key sources of differentiation (or cost leadership) was the people element.

- Personnel departments felt nervous about putting HR strategy on to top managers' agendas, and top management felt nervous because (a) they sensed these issues were important, (b) they wanted to deal with them but didn't really know what the best way was; (c) they half expected personnel departments to come up with the answers.

The following implications for action emerged from this study.

1. It may not be a good idea at all to have a separately identified human resource strategy. It would be better to call it an organization (or 'organization and people') strategy.
2. The organizational strategy needs to bring together all the key themes which are involved in:
   - sustaining strategic development projects externally;
   - implementing internal change;
   - maintaining the existing set of competitive advantages;
   - co-ordinating cross-functional programmes and interventions like TQM, BPR etc.
3. Line management, assisted by other specialists (and not the HR department or anybody else!) should own organizational strategy.
4. In terms of the role HR can and should play, it is helpful to focus their efforts on the 'people value chain' (or 'PVC') – how do people add value in the organization (or inadvertently destroy value)?
5. In order to get a clear agenda for organizational strategy, it is essential that the competitive strategy is clear. For example, a company pursuing a twin differentiation and cost reduction route with equal vigour may well end up with a very confused organizational strategy. (For instance, it may be hiring lots and lots of graduates who are then over-qualified and over-paid – in the case of a cost leadership strategy.)
6. One of the key links between organizational strategy and strategies for growth is in brand strategy. This not only dictates organizational strategy but is also a limiting factor for the kind of brand strategy which is viable. (Remember British Rail's advertising campaign in the mid 1980s – 'We are getting there'? This was very laudable but unfortunately British Rail appeared to tell their customers before they told their staff 'we are getting there'.)
7. In some instances, strategic development issues which appear to make apparent product/market and operational sense fall down when subjected to organizational analysis. In both cases of the research study the companies had experienced some not altogether insignificant problems.

8. A key area of leverage in organizational strategy was the making of key senior appointments. These decisions play a parallel role to that of strategic decisions *vis-à-vis* strategic planning. It is often the making of a particular decision which is the driver of long-term organizational performance. It is that much harder to influence the stream of daily events through a planning process.

9. As the organization moves through different phases of development it may need quite different people at the helm. All too often the leader is fortuitously appointed and may be in sync or at odds with the emerging needs of their role. To assume that 'A Leader is Forever' is very dangerous and potentially damaging to longer term strategic development.

10. In order to develop an organizational strategy it is very useful to develop a future 'organizational scenario' to map out:

- the future 'way of doing things around here';
- the shape, size and structure of the organization;
- the interdependencies of this organization with its environment;
- the possible route (and transitional events) which might bring about that strategy.

In order to exploit this last idea, spend some time working on the next exercise.

Short exercise

- What organizational scenario can you envisage for your company in three to five years' time?
- What factors or triggers might bring this organization about?
- What will it feel like being in that organization (and do I wish to be there)?
- What would it feel like to actually travel there? (What programmes, changes in management and style are likely to occur to get us there?)

CONCLUSION

We have now shown how important it is to do a thorough analysis of the organizational issues impacting on strategies for growth. You are well advised to experiment in a real-life situation with:

- implementation forces (IMF) analysis;
- stakeholder analysis;
- from-to ('FT') analysis;

- the attractiveness and implementation grid (or 'AID');
- the 'P' behaviours.

These tools are there to provide 'softer' and certainly less frustrating strategic development. Managing implementation (and the organizational issues which go with that) is so frequently the graveyard of strategy. Indeed, what we are expecting managers to do is to manage in three dimensions:

- the external (and strategic);
- delivering the results (and the financial ones);
- making it happen (politically).

Figure 5.13 thus represents the three dimensions of managing strategic development. Success requires all three dimensions to be managed, not just one or two. One way of probing the support which a project might receive is to apply Porter's five competitive forces internally (as in Figure 5.14).

Figure 5.14 highlights the need to understand the agendas and influence of internal customers. It also draws attention to competition with existing and new projects, and with other means of achieving the same objectives (for example, a culture change programme might be seen as a substitute to TQM).

We leave organizational strategy by reflecting once again on the paradigm. Although increasingly managers are becoming more comfortable with this concept (for instance, by using FT analysis), it still feels to some as unreal and mere jargon. It is not. The paradigm enables and impedes breakthrough strategies for growth in a most tangible and everyday way.

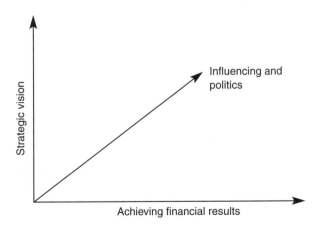

Fig. 5.13 Implementing strategic development – the three dimensions

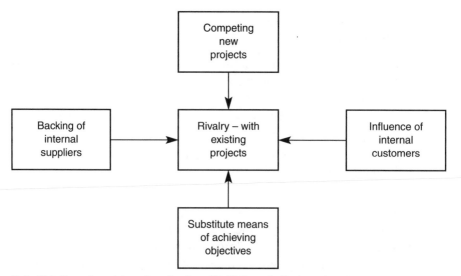

Note: This figure is an internal application of E. M. Porter's five forced model, 1985

Fig. 5.14 Applying competitive forces to internal projects

The very part of the word 'para' is shared with other words with similar meanings, which we can use to further underline its importance, as follows.

- **Paradox:** is a confused paradigm, with people 'doing many different things around here' (as in the 'emergency strategy').
- **Parasites:** those who 'do their own thing around here' (playing in the political dimension much more than the financial, or strategic).
- **Paralysis:** or 'how we stop things getting done around here'
- **Paracetamols:** the headache pills needed by the organization the night after the 'strategy for growth party' which became too wild and uncontrolled.

BREAKTHROUGH STRATEGIES FOR GROWTH –DETAILED CHECKLISTS

Finally, now that you have completed Parts 1 and 2 of this book, you may also find it fruitful to attempt the structured questions on your own breakthrough strategies for growth in Appendix I.

ACTION CHECKLIST

- What is the underlying nature of the problem or opportunity underlying a particular area of external or internal breakthrough (root cause analysis)?

- What are the key forces (enablers and constraints) impacting on the implementation of any key strategic development project (of your choice)?

- How can these be reshaped to make implementation easier?

- Who are the key stakeholders with influence over either the decision-making process or over its implementation? What is on their agenda, and what is their degree of influence and attitude towards this particular project?

- How can these stakeholders be repositioned?

- What shifts in how we do things (from and to analysis) does this whole target imply?

- Overall, how attractive is the project (net benefits less costs) relative to its degree of implementation difficulty?

It will be useful to read Appendix III on 'Strategic Development Workshops' for further practical help with the process.

Part III

MOBILIZING FOR BREAKTHROUGH

Organic growth happens in a predictable way. But its sources often happen accidentally. ...or, they have a very short half-life.

6

BREAKTHROUGH
ORGANIC GROWTH

INTRODUCTION

The bulk of this chapter applies previous breakthrough frameworks to the case study of Tesco PLC. This case study is particularly interesting as Tesco in the mid 1990s is at a crossroads following a very successful phase of growth. But before taking a look at Tesco, it will be useful to reflect on the wider role of organic corporate growth.

Organic growth happens in a predictable way. But its sources often happen accidentally, sometimes mushrooming very rapidly with a momentum of their own. Or, they have a very short half-life (like esoteric nuclear particles), expiring almost as quickly as they were born.

It was perhaps Mintzberg *et al* who were the first to uncover the messiness of strategic decisions. In their pioneering work they found that these strategic decisions often went through a relatively long gestation or pregnancy. During this time they went through phases of review or deliberation.

For Mintzberg *et al*, it was as if strategic decisions started off as a mountain spring, flowing down a stream, sometimes getting stuck in a stagnant pool before commencing the long journey down the mountain. As the stream became a river, suddenly the decision might be accelerated, going fast over the decision rapids and finally ejecting into implementation and value generation (where the estuary enters the sea).

Of course, many strategic decisions never make the sea, evaporating long before they ever get a big push or pull. During this sometimes long and fairly unpredictable journey, the decision might be buffeted by a number of factors. Figure 6.1 shows just nine.

First, power and personalities are very important drivers of organic growth strategies. Very commonly the driving force behind strategic development is one or more key individuals with considerable access to power. The late 1980s were replete with such personalities – Robert Maxwell at Maxwell Corporation, Ralph Halpern at the Burton Group, and many

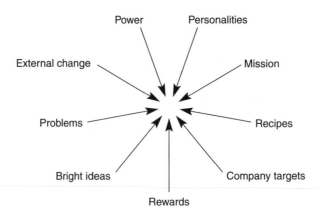

Fig. 6.1 Strategies for growth – key inputs

others. But even where the personalities are softer and the influence more subtle, personalities do have a tremendous sway over the execution of strategic development.

Second, corporate missions can exercise some sway over the direction of strategic developments. This sway can be helpful or indeed harmful. It can be helpful insofar as it can provide an overall umbrella (in effect, Mintzberg's 'umbrella strategy') for keeping emergent strategies within a reasonably coherent pattern. Or it can be very dangerous, suggesting inappropriate avenues for strategic development.

The role of recipes has already been mentioned elsewhere. These can play a profound role in amplifying commitment to a particular strategy, accelerating it, or deflecting and discouraging ones which do not appear to fit.

Corporate targets have a very direct and tangible influence over organic strategic development. Whereas acquisitive development is frequently given a kind of 'strategic handicap', organic development is more likely to have to stand on its own two feet, and early on. The influence of targets is also very much influenced by rewards systems, which have commonly much shorter time horizons and narrower focus than the time horizons of strategies for growth.

Turning now to innovation, in mature and maturing organizations it is common to find that strategic decisions are often typically driven by problems rather than by more positive, 'bright' ideas. Or, in more youthful organizations, there is a glut of bright ideas which then result in organizational overload. Organizations which grow mature yet remain sufficiently fluid and open to new ideas are hard to find – one exception that springs to mind is Hewlett Packard, where product innovation thrives alongside a hard-nosed, commercial culture.

Last, but certainly not least, is the impact of external change (especially driven by the PEST factors and competitive forces). This is only one out of the entire nine factors. It is now evident perhaps why organic growth strategies are often primarily driven by internal, rather than by external, factors.

Figure 6.2 now plots a more 'ideal' situation, where the strength of the influence is depicted by the relative length of the arrows. Note that the predominant drivers are those of bright ideas, external change and recipes.

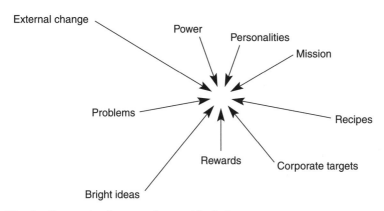

Fig. 6.2 Strategies for growth – an ideal picture

Figure 6.3 also plots a more 'realistic' situation. Note that this picture is almost a complete reversal of the 'ideal' situation (Figure 6.2).

Short exercise – organic growth in your organization

Taking one or more examples of recent organic growth ask these questions.

- What would your overall picture of the internal drivers look like?*
- What are the positive and negative consequences of this pattern?
- What particular things could be done to enable the organic growth process to be handled in a more balanced or appropriate way?

* Consider each one of the drivers in Figure 6.2 in turn.

From the above exercise you will probably have discovered that you may need to retune your process of strategic development considerably, especially by:

Fig. 6.3 Organic development – the realistic picture

- restraining key personalities, encouraging others and, where neces-sary, intervening to shift the balance of power;
- overhauling, dismantling or reinventing your mission (whether this is formally or informally spelt out);
- challenging, testing and refocusing your strategic and growth recipes;
- refining your corporate targets;
- resetting your rewards system (perhaps the hardest of all);
- creating safe zones of time and space for generating and amplifying bright ideas (some companies, for example Hewlett Packard, call this 'creating white space');
- putting in place processes to diagnose and resolve major problems;
- setting up processes (formal and less formal) for detecting and ampli-fying 'weak signals' (Ansoff) in the organization, and establishing task forces for dealing with the 'strong signals'. For example, at Hewlett Packard in 1994 a task force was created to help achieve breakthrough in the company's order fulfilment processes.

Now that some of the particular problems of managing organic, strategic development have been outlined, it is time to look at a particularly interest-ing case study. This is another major retailer, Tesco PLC, which, during the 1980s and early 1990s, achieved considerable success on the back of a growth strategy which was organically driven.

But before investigating Tesco it is worth while focusing briefly on the role of competitor analysis in strategic development.

ANALYSING COMPETITORS

Competitor analysis can add a lot of value to strategic development. But it should not become an industry – it is merely a tool for sharpening up thinking about strategies for growth. Competitor analysis involves a mix of 'hard' and 'soft' analysis. The 'hard' ingredients can include the analysis of:

- current operations and facilities;
- products and services – performance, quality and price;
- current financial resource;
- existing investment plans;
- management structure.

The 'soft' ingredients can include the analysis of:

- likely and possible strategic intent;
- the impact of past or potential organizational changes;
- leadership;
- style of operating;
- underlying competencies and processes.

Note the importance of people – particularly the behaviour and mindsets of competitors. In the long run these are often more important than the 'hard' factors. These softer aspects are particularly important when thinking about likely competitor reaction to a particular strategy for growth.

But the most powerful thinking comes through putting together both 'soft' and 'hard' factors. For instance, a company might be financially in trouble and a new chief executive is hired who is drilled in turnaround and cost cutting. A likely scenario is a series of redundancies, cost-cutting measures, and (potentially) a freeze on innovation and reduction in the level of servicing quality. Although the company's managers will be more alert (to achieving short-term results) in this scenario, any overemphasis on cost reduction may make the company's market share vulnerable to direct attack.

The fruits of competitor analysis can be distilled into probably no more than two pages each (or 'competitor profiles'). These could include, for example:

- current market and competitive strengths and weaknesses;
- financial strengths and weaknesses – derived from results, cash flows and balance sheet strength;
- current management – its likely strategic intent, style and mindset;
- strategic options, constraints which it faces and your view of what it is likely to do – again the broader scenario specific areas for external or internal breakthrough.

This broader competitive scenario acts as a backcloth to the analysis of a specific competitor. One way of creating a meaningful scenario is to begin first with the PEST factors, competitive forces and forces driving (or braking) growth within the industry. (This can be done in, at maximum, a couple of hours with sufficient preparation and good facilitation.)

Next, one (or more) manager(s) takes the role of a particular competitor and is asked to come up with their preferred set of strategies for growth. Then, as in a game of cards, the players are asked to show their hands to each other. Out of this last step of the role-playing some interesting and novel competitor scenarios are likely to emerge. Some new storylines invariably crystallize (see also Appendix II – Everyday Scenario Planning).

If carefully orchestrated, the whole process can be run in around five to seven hours – for a particular area of business. This process forces managers to think outside their own organization, looking at their own company and the market through the eyes of a competitor. (Obviously, some manager(s) have to play their own company.)

Short exercise

For one key strategy for growth think about the following.

- Identify one key competitor who poses a significant threat to you (either now or in the future).
- Draw up a quick competitor profile, on no more than two pages, based both on 'hard' and 'soft' characteristics.
- What key insights have you gained both into the competitor's and your own strategy?
- What might you now do differently or do even more vigorously than before?
- What key gaps in the data do you now need to plug?
- What value overall was this exercise, and should you roll this out to other competitors and other strategies for growth?
- Would it be useful to involve others in the management team and outside?

The reason why competitor analysis has been brought in at this juncture is that it is particularly pertinent to the Tesco case. When a company like Tesco faces an abrupt transition in its market place it becomes of paramount importance to think not only (mainly) about your own moves, but also those available to your competitors. And this should be done for the whole series of moves, not just the next tactical steps.

The Tesco case study

Tesco plc is a very successful retailer with its home base in the UK. Tesco is essentially a major operator of supermarkets (and hypermarkets) in the UK and, from the early 1990s, in niche areas of continental Europe.

Brief background to Tesco's History

Tesco was originally founded as a chain of grocery stores in the southern half of England. In the 1970s it expanded through offering customers exceptional value. It was a major combatant in the earlier bout of UK supermarket price wars, which preceded the development of superstores in the UK.

So Tesco's earlier strategic development was thus based on its popular appeal and a focus on the lower price end of the market. But in the early to mid 1980s things changed in two key ways. First, Tesco embarked on a strategy of repositioning itself to have an appeal to the middle income. This repositioning sought to shed Tesco's image of being a 'pile it high and sell it cheap' retailer.

These were very exciting times for Tesco. An early step was for Tesco to get a name for itself as a quality in-store butcher. This was followed by a huge success in Tesco wines, accomplished through considerable merchandising flair. Suddenly Tesco was being talked about as the place to buy economical, good quality wine. Other major ingredients of this repositioning were the introduction of in-store bakeries and also the upgrading of vegetables – the in-store greengrocery.

Second, Tesco played a leading role in the development of superstores in the UK, which revolutionized British grocery retailing.

The great superstore expansion

By the early and particularly the mid 1980s, Tesco (in common with other supermarket chains like Sainsbury, Safeway etc.) realized that the superstore market could be greatly expanded. This period was characterized by a most favourable industry environment, especially through the following.

The political and economic factors

- Thatcher's laissez-faire government which encouraged rapid expansion of sites and planning permission being relatively easy to obtain.
- The decline of the public transport network.
- Rapid increase in personal disposable income.

The social and technological factors

- Increases in personal mobility through car ownership.
- A big rise in women going out to work after having a family (putting pressure on time available to do shopping).
- Advances in information systems, making it easier and cheaper to run a large but responsive network of superstores.

Besides the PEST factors, a number of competitive forces facilitated Tesco's expansion strategy.

The buyers:

- lacked significant bargaining power and were in effect locked into their local superstore by virtue of convenience.

The suppliers:

- lacked bargaining power and were increasingly put under pressure by the superstore majors to cut prices, both of branded goods and by the expansion of 'own' or 'private label'.

The substitutes:

- were weakened (these were principally the small, local shops who were put in a vicious cycle of lower volumes, then higher prices, then resulting in lower volumes still).

The entrants:

- were dissuaded by the sheer cost of developing major superstores.

The competitive rivalry:

- was reduced by the availability of a fast-expanding market with room enough for all players;
- and through the erosion of the small corner shop sector of the market, which couldn't compete on price with the might of the superstore giants.

The industry mindset:

- was one of sustainable and profitable growth with the most critical success factor being grab maximum market share.

The industry (as at 1985–92) would therefore appear to have considerable inherent market attractiveness. Also, Tesco was greatly strengthening its own competitive position, thus moving north-west in the 'grow-earnings' (GE) grid towards a 'Big-Bang' positioning.

Tesco's competitive advantage as at 1990 can now be summarized as follows.

- Its prices were relatively competitive, now supported with an image of generally high quality and thus value for money.
- It had a number of niches of successful differentiation (especially in relation to the lower cost supermarket discounters) – particularly in wines.
- It had friendly customer service with appeal as 'the family supermarket'.
- Its market share was relatively high (particularly in southern and middle England), supported by a strong infrastructure.
- Its managers had a very strong determination to squeeze maximum business from the growing network.

In the above analysis no single source of competitive advantage appears to dominate over the others. There seems to be no special, single and outstanding technical strength underpinning Tesco's competitive position. On the other hand, it is hard to find any specific and major tangible source of competitive disadvantage to begin to build a 'black' or 'bad' onion model of competitive disadvantage.

But has Tesco anticipated and reacted to recent change in the external competitive environment sufficiently effectively? Read on to find out.

The transition – supermarket wars

Before taking a look at the forces reshaping the industry, here is an analysis of the market structure in the early 1990s.

According to Verdict (1993 analysis, *Sunday Times*, 17 July 1994) the relative market shares in the UK of the supermarket chains were as follows:

- Sainsbury (Savacentre) 12.3 per cent;
- Tesco 11.4 per cent;
- Argyle (Safeway, Presto and Lo Cost) 7.6 per cent;
- Asda 6.5 per cent.

These combined market shares amount to a total of 37.8 per cent. (Compared to the combined might of the majors, Marks & Spencer have only 3.1 per cent market share and Waitrose a lowly 1.5 per cent.) But interestingly this leaves a very large part of the market still being left to other players, suggesting the industry is split between (a) a heavily concentrated sector – the majors, and (b) other, more fragmented competition. (In early 1995, Tesco actually overtook Sainsbury – just in market share terms, helped by the William Low acquisition and its Clubcard (discount) promotion.)

We do, as always, have to be careful about interpreting market share data. For instance, Tesco's own figures (Tesco, Annual Report and

Accounts, 1994, p 56) suggest its 1994 market share is only 10.1 per cent (and not 11.4 per cent as per Verdict).

What is perhaps more interesting than the current figures is the trend, with Tesco's own figures for market share (in 'food and drinks shops') increasing from 8.4 per cent to 10.1 per cent over the five years of 1990–4. This suggests very strongly that Tesco has had a very clear strategic intent to achieve a high relative market share (in the UK), perhaps with aspirations to match or even beat Sainsbury, the market leader (in size terms).

Interestingly, Tesco achieved these gains with only a 13 per cent increase in the number of food stores in the UK (from 379 to 430). This reflects the development of stores of increasing size and also increased productivity within stores.

In profit terms, the four biggest players (as at 1993–4) stacked up as follows (*Sunday Times*, 17 July 1994) in terms of pre-tax profits (before exceptional items):

Sainsbury	£777m (6.9% of sales)
Tesco	£528m (5.7% of sales)
Argyll	£402m (6.8% of sales)
Asda	£201m (4.1% of sales)

With the exception of Asda, the top players were thus still able to report relatively healthy profits despite an increasingly fierce competitive industry.

The following analysis now takes apart Tesco's annual report and accounts both strategically and financially. This is an example of 'strategic financial accounting' where an annual report and accounts are analysed both from a financial and strategic perspective. These two viewpoints combined simultaneously often lead to either new insights or heighten awareness of existing trends. In the following analysis I was actually taken aback at the impact of the competitive environment on Tesco's financial numbers.

Strategic financial accounting (SFA) is another weapon in the armoury of the analyst for strategies for growth. SFA can be used to:

- contribute to the analysis of your own company's competitive and financial position;
- analyse a competitor's position and its potential strategic intent;
- analyse an acquisition opportunity;
- understand the strategic and financial health of a key customer or supplier.

Figure 6.4 summarizes Tesco's financial record over the period 1990–4.

Turnover	1994 £m	1993 £m	1992 £m	1991 £m	1990 £m
'Continuing operations'	8,347	7,581	7,097	6,346	5,402
Acquisitions	253	–	–	–	–
	8,600	7,581	7,097	6,346	5,402
Operating profit	521	529	463	388	311
Net interest receivable	7	32	66	19	10
Operating margin	528	561	529	407	321
Property charges	(93)	(2)	–	19	35
	435	559	529	426	356
Return on capital employed	15.7%	17.8%	18.8%	20.8%	22.2%

Figure 6.4 Tesco's financial record

(These figures were extracted from Tesco's annual report and accounts, 1994. 1990–3 figures have been restated to reflect more recent accounting policies so that the results are comparable. Reported profits for 1994/5 show an increase to £551 million, helped by lower property charges and by volume increases.)

Tesco's figures (in Figure 6.4) show the efforts of considerable expansion in scale of activities and in profit. They also show a quite marked decline in return on capital employed. This decline is only partly due to changes in operating margin. The operating margin actually increased from 5.8 per cent to 6.1 per cent between 1990 and 1994 (although it peaked at 7.0 per cent in 1993). Part of the decline in return on capital employed appears due, in fact, to the disproportionate increase in capital employed, as over the whole period profits before property charges and interest have actually risen by 64 per cent over the five-year period. (Note 10 to the five-year record – on p 55 – defines return on capital as 'profit *before* net (loss)/surplus of properties and interest divided by average capital employed'.)

In addition, there is a swing in property charges from a positive income of £35m in 1990 to a negative charge of £93m in 1994, a total adverse swing of £128m. Although not included in retail trading results, this swing nevertheless provides a second barometer of financial health. Tesco appears to be making a loss on its property-related activities and transactions.

Taking a step back to examine the wider business environment will make better sense of Tesco's corporate financial performance. Again, begin with the PEST factors as follows.

The political and economic factors

- The UK recession of 1990–2 did not have a very big immediate effect on the supermarket industry. This was principally because Tesco was narrowly focused on products which consumers were inclined to continue buying, even when their incomes were either reduced or threatened. The lack of impact of the recession probably gave the major supermarkets (including Tesco) the dangerous feeling that they were almost invulnerable to a recession-based mindset.
- However, the prolonged length and depth of the recession led to a profound change in consumer buying attitudes – inducing them to become more increasingly price sensitive and (where appropriate and feasible) to shop around.
- Media comment on the pricing and margins of the supermarket industry also generated a suspicion among consumers that the superstores were actually giving them a bad deal. The *Sunday Times* played a major role in this, running several headlines criticizing the grocery majors.
- Personal disposable income suffered a severe squeeze not merely from the UK recession but also from the impact of higher tax rates (this was a knock-on effect of the high government borrowing requirement which almost peaked at £50 billion – the equivalent I calculate as being around eight hundred crates of champagne a minute – priced at £130 a crate).

Social factors

- Increased pressure built up to halt the ongoing expansion of superstores. This rapid expansion was having a number of major, adverse effects including (a) increased traffic congestion, and (b) putting smaller stores out of business.

The above social factors culminated in the second half of 1994 with a major reduction in the success rate of new superstore planning applications. This change in regulatory sentiment had been building up for quite some time as local pressure groups began to bring to the attention of the government the disbenefits of superstore development. These stores had begun to erode the 'visability and viability' of town centres (according to a 1993 planning guidance note, called enigmatically 'PPG6'). According to Paul Smiddy, food retailing analyst at Nomura, the effect of PPG6 was to halve the number of successful planning appeals from 60 per cent to 30 per cent in 1994.

The assumption that the early 1990s rate of new superstore development was sustainable thus moved inexorably from the 'certain/not so important' to the 'very uncertain/very important' sector of the uncertainty/importance grid.

These PEST factors therefore highlight how easily a favourable industry environment can become at best of neutral attractiveness or, at worse, adverse. Besides this, we must mention too that, in any event, sooner or later the UK expansion of superstores would have run into constraints through effective saturation of the market. If the rate of expansion of the late 1980s and early 1990s had continued, one might speculate that by the year 2030 superstores in the UK would occupy areas of land comparable to the whole of the UK housing stock. This analysis underscores the need to conduct scenario analysis on the industry environment as a backdrop to making key strategic development decisions.

Turning now to the industry's competitive forces, the effect on total market attractiveness appears even bleaker.

The buyers:

- were now becoming far more aware (especially through media campaigns) of the favourable profit margins being enjoyed by the top grocery retailers;
- and were thus more able and willing to shop around.

The entrants:

- were attracted in by the potential of making good profits. The Aldi chain in particular has made inroads into the market by offering a low-cost but very focused competitive strategy.

The competitive rivalry:

- has multiplied, resulting in Tesco's launch of 'Value Lines' (a focused range of products at low price) and Sainsbury's campaign of 'Essential for the Essentials'.

The industry mindset:

- has shifted from being one of ongoing profitable growth (by expansion) and a race to open superstores, to one where frugality is the virtue and lower price is the key watchword.

The impact of these industry changes cannot be overstated. For instance, David Sainsbury, chairperson of Sainsbury, went on the record (*Financial Times*, 4 November 1993) as saying that:

> *'We won't be able to get the sales increases in percentage terms that we have had in the past. ... We're clearly now back in a period where people are again talking about discounting and price wars.'*[1]

Sir Ian MacLaurin, chairman of Tesco amplifies these thoughts (*Financial Times*, 22 September 1993):

> *'Quite clearly the aspirations of customers in the 1990s are very different from the 1980s. ... Whoever you are, you now have the Aldi's, Netto's and Ed's sitting in your car park. We have got to be as cheap as anybody on the basics, but offer additional lines and services.'*

And on 19 January 1994, Tesco announced that it was cutting its store opening programme, building smaller and cheaper stores, and beginning to write down its properties for the first time.

In the *Financial Times* (20 January 1994) Mr David Reid, Tesco's finance director admitted:

> *'Saturation of the market has been with us for some time, but what you are seeing now is just a continuation of that. ... Margins were going up between half and one (percentage) points a year, but now they've fallen. This is a numbers game and the numbers have changed.'*

This decline in margins was caused first by Tesco's Value range of low-priced goods and second by responses to price cutting by Kwik Save and by Sainsbury (the latter with its 'Essential for the Essentials' campaign). Sir Ian MacLaurin spells out the logic for Tesco's Value strategy as:

> *'There is [now] no point in customers going to an Aldi or Netto when they can buy the basics as cheaply at Tesco, as well as all the other things Tesco sells'.* (*Financial Times*, 20 January 1994)

Faced with an adverse shift in the external, competitive environment, the major players have therefore begun now to adjust both their strategies and their underlying mindset. David Sainsbury even ventured to admit at a major food retailing conference in late 1994 that the big food retailers had allowed the prices of basic commodities to drift upwards in the late 80s and early 90s. This had been rewarded by high margins which had also been increased by internal productivity improvements. But this upward price drift is credited with opening the gap in the market to allow Germany's Aldi and Denmark's Netto to creep into the UK. (This then resulted in a 'Duke of York' strategic retreat.)

At the same specialist retail conference, David Sainsbury, David Reid (finance director of Tesco) and Colin Smith (chief executive of Argyll) managed to conclude that in spite of short-term pressures the future in the UK was still bright. This 'brightness' entailed a mix of improving product ranges and reducing costs – thus emulating Marks & Spencer's recent UK strategy. But other views exist. According to Archie Norman, chief executive of Asda, the notion that the fall in industry margins is a one-off 'step change' did not hold water:

> *'I don't know how they can say that with a straight face. ... This [step change] was supposed to have happened a year ago, but gross margins have continued to decline in the past four months'. (Financial Times,* 16 December 1994)

He also went on to add, 'The tightening of planning is the best thing that has happened to the industry' presumably hinting that this would reduce the level of competitive rivalry considerably, relative to what it might have been.

The strategic facts suggest that Archie Norman of Asda may be right. Asda is pursuing the strategy which Sainsbury, Tesco and Argyll espouse – product and productivity improvement (with a 17 per cent increase in core trading profits in the half year to November 1994).

From organic growth to acquisition

In the mean time Sainsbury spent $US325 million in a stake in Giant Food, the Washington DC-based supermarket chain. According to David Sainsbury:

> *'This is very much a first step. We will see how things develop. We regard the North American market as one of the major areas of growth for the group in the future'. (Financial Times,* 4 October 1994)

The LEX column (*Financial Times*, 4 October 1994) commented on J Sainsbury's move by suggesting that this was consistent with Sainsbury's successful strategy diversification, identifying that this now gave Sainsbury a most significant foothold in the US market.

Tesco, for its part, has made a major move into Scotland with its contested acquisition of the William Low grocery group. William Low had 45 outlets in Scotland and 12 in the North of England but many of these stores were relatively small (below 20,000 ft^2). William Low's market share in Scotland was estimated at 6.6 per cent, and Tesco's (pre-deal) at 7.1 per cent. Post-deal its share of the Scottish market becomes 13.7 per cent, just behind the market leader Argyll at 16.5 per cent (source AGB).

Tesco's strategy is thus quite different in this respect from Sainsbury. While Sainsbury begins to play for big stakes in the US, Tesco has opted to strengthen its UK position, and to embark on a more incremental development strategy in Europe. It will be very interesting to see how both strategies work out in the late 1990s.

Returning to the William Low bid by Tesco, the *Sunday Times* (17 July 1994) described this turn of events:

> '*It was a phone call James Millar [chairman of William Low] had dreaded for years. His secretary told him that Sir Ian MacLaurin, the chairman of Tesco, was on the line. A good friend for many years, Millar hoped MacLaurin was phoning for a chat or to suggest meeting for lunch. But the call was not a social one.*
>
> *MacLaurin had a proposal to put: "James, I want to make an offer for your company" he said. After months of secretly researching the Scottish chain, MacLaurin's team had concluded that the best way for Tesco to expand into Scotland was to buy up one of the existing players. MacLaurin needed to know just one thing. "Could it be an agreed deal?"*
>
> *Millar was stunned ... he had dedicated much of his life to preserving the 126 year-old company's independence. ... But this year's decline in profitability had forced him to confront reality. Analysts were forecasting that 1994 profits would be just £14.5m, down from £21.1m last year.*'[2]

Tesco had offered 225p a share for William Low, valuing the company at £154m, a 33 per cent premium to market price. It would also take on £50m of debt. Apparently Millar felt he could recommend that deal to his board and shareholders. 'The crunch came for me when I realized it would be difficult for us to reach 225p by our own efforts' said Millar. Everything seemed to be settled and Tesco's finance director had apparently jetted off for holiday when Sainsbury entered the fray.

Sainsbury also had designs on William Low and had apparently talked to the company earlier on. Sainsbury only had four stores in Scotland. Sainsbury's response was to offer an uprated bid of 305p a share. Predictably, Tesco then bid 360p a share to secure the deal. Sir Ian MacLaurin denied that Tesco had been pushed into paying too much.

The acquisition by Tesco of William Low gave the company an immediate (if not cheap) contribution to its strategies for growth in 1995. During post-acquisition trading William Low's results have considerably improved. However, the question still remains as to what options for the future Tesco might and ought to pursue. These are very much backed up with the changing nature of the industry. Arguably in the early to mid 1990s was witnessed a major and predictable adjustment to the retail grocery industry as it moved from emergence and growth phases of superstore development to a rapid maturity.

Future options – from acquisitions back to organic development

Besides Tesco's UK stores it had also begun to expand into Europe through a relatively small acquisition of a French supermarket chain, Catteau. Catteau had 8 hypermarkets and 51 smaller supermarkets (as at the end of 1994) and has concentrated on the very north of France, adjacent to the Channel.

Presumably this close geographic proximity gave Tesco possible advantages through shared sourcing and logistics. But, like Sainsbury (in its venture to the US), this invites the question as to what opportunities for major development Tesco's should now exploit. Should these be, like Catteau in near – or middle – France, or in other nearby countries like Holland and Belgium? Or, should Tesco make a bolder move into one or more Eastern European countries and try to establish a strong position, reshaping the market as it goes? (On 12 April 1995 the *Financial Times* reported plans for up to 70 stores in Hungary.)

Acquisitive moves might be both expensive and cost a lot of management resource, so might Tesco's be advised to rely more on organic development in the future? Presumably its Catteau investment has helped considerably with the learning of how to operate a tailored Tesco formula outside the UK.

So, further international development is clearly one avenue for strategic development. Or, hypothetically Tesco might focus on repositioning and strengthening its current business mix, for instance by:

- introducing radically new products and service lines
- exploring new formats, like its experimental, back-to-the-town-centre 'Metro' stores (bringing it into indirect/direct competition with M&S foods)

- developing new ways of distributing goods, or perhaps via home shopping.

But still the focus is on managing strategic development within the existing industry paradigm ('How we do things in the industry'), rather than managing strategic development for the industry's future (Hamel and Prahalad). A first step to exploring new futures in strategic development is home shopping.

It may be that the time of home shopping (as at 1995) is just about to come. I remember vividly in 1989 I was involved in conducting some research for a then virtually unknown organization, CEST (Centre for the Exploitation of Science) on the application of information technology to reconfigure the retail industry. A Burton's IT manager at their Logistics Centre in Milton Keynes held up a bar code to me and said, 'If you can do anything for us to get rid of this, then you are really on to a big prize.' One of our key findings (as at 1989) was that once home shopping became cheaper and easier (both to customers *and* to companies) then it would reconfigure a number of adjacent industries.

It was on 1 January 1995 when I noticed (*Sunday Times* – 'Style' p 8) that CEST was actually doing a project to develop electronic bar code technology to replace laser scanners at check-out tills. According to the *Sunday Times*:

'A hand-held device will allow a shopper remotely to scan products. The device will not only give the price, but relay other details such as fat, sugar content in foods ... warning you if you are spending too much, or even if food purchases are threatening to break a calorie-controlled diet.'

Apparently this system enables the shopper to point at what they want to buy, pay for it remotely and collects it together for pick-up. (Never again will I have to take along the latest case study I am writing on Tesco to work on during the check-out queues!)

Unfortunately for Tesco, it is Sainsbury which is currently one of the partners in this project. It is certainly by no means easy for existing players to challenge their recipes of doing business by considering radically different ways of doing business along this kind of line. I recall in 1989 interviewing a very senior IT manager in the retail industry (in a pub on the A1):

'They [the board] don't want to think about home shopping as a possibility. Expand, expand, expand, is all they think about. I guess it is pretty impossible for them to even think about not needing all these stores any more.'

But besides the home shopping channel you may wish to think about more diverse market opportunities for Tesco. When Marks & Spencer diversified into food and later on into financial services, both of these moves must have appeared to be quite novel internally. Yet in each case there was a clear, strategic logic. Can we find similar areas which fit Tesco's competitive profile and capability?

One (perhaps unlikely) possibility for Tesco might be that of the holiday market. It hardly needs saying that this market is very competitive. However, if Tesco were able to offer a small number of higher value-for-money choices of family holidays this might enable it to achieve considerable scale economies. It might also be relatively cheap to sell, with a simple brochure handed to customers as they leave Tesco's store. Tesco's fit with this opportunity would be:

- Through its brand strength, as a reliable supplier;
- Its capability to tap into its vast stream of customers – and at low cost.

In order to add a differentiation angle to this venture, it might be possible to design holidays so that they all had something quite different to more common or garden packages. Perhaps one could have, for example, 'theme holidays' like visits to Tesco's sources of wine and cheese in France, or to entertainment centres like Disneyworld.

A number of other strategic tests need to be applied. For example, can Tesco's competitive position become 'very strong'? (It would have to be very strong given that the travel industry's total market attractiveness generally is not good.) Nevertheless, Tesco might well be able to add a useful niche product line here without distracting and diluting its core purpose and business activities.

Short exercise

Given the data on Tesco and the retail grocery industry in this case study answer these questions.

1. What avenues for strategic development would you see as worth while investigating?
2. Using the 'grow-earnings' or GE grid, how do you see these as being positioned (now and in the future) in terms of total market attractiveness and competitive strength?
3. How easy or difficult would it be for Tesco to implement these opportunities given their existing capability and mindset (which is primarily geared to running grocery stores)?

4. Can we make it sufficiently attractive financially? This would not be a massive opportunity but might be just about sufficiently substantial to be worth doing. Also, margins might be reasonable, given the (assumed) relatively low costs.

Lessons from the Tesco case study

The Tesco case study highlights a number of key lessons on strategies for growth primarily of an organic nature.

- When a company becomes very successful pursuing a particular set of strategies for growth, it becomes hard to adjust its recipes in the light of external change.
- A powerful way of making more coherent sense of this external change is to combine the strategic development tools within one or more scenarios of evolving industry development. This helps senior managers to 'think the unthinkable' and 'bring it' (strategic data, insights and conjectures) all together.
- Some more radical transitions in industry structure are relatively predictable (as was the shift in the grocery retail industry during 1992–4). But others are harder to predict, for example the impact of the coincidence of information technology and communications industries. This may play a profound role in shaping life styles and values towards the end of the 1990s. It is also possible to conjecture that radical changes in how people shop regularly are around the corner.
- Financial results (if read sensitively) can reinforce views that an industry has actually changed, and provide a kind of 'financial X-ray' to illuminate existing strategic intent and the more tangible aspects of competitive position.
- When an industry does go through a significant transition, companies often revert to old mindsets, rediscovering past strategic and growth recipes, rather than forward into the future. (For example, Tesco is moving back into smaller city centre stores with its 'Metro' concept.) Although these moves may make some strategic sense, they may also distract the company from exploring new, future-based opportunities.
- Where attractive organic opportunities for strategic development dry up, managers frequently also default to acquisition-based strategies. Again, some of these moves may be sensible but acquisition may then absorb the lion's share of financial and people resource, and also of top managers' attention.

- Acquisitive development inevitably involves a degree of organic development post acquisition (see Chapter 7). Also organic development may often embrace acquisitive elements, such as Tesco using an acquisition to expand geographically in the UK.

- Although Tesco's marketing over 1994/5 clearly gave it a tactical advantage (for example, through its Clubcard) over its rivals, this does not seem to have had a proportionate effect on its shareholder value. Tesco's (as at April 1995) stock market capitalization was still significantly lower than Sainsbury's. Ironically, Tesco's excellent 1994/5 figures caused a fall in capitalization in grocery shares as the financial markets awaited counter-attack. So the question – Do Tesco's achievements give it sustainable value? – is very much an open one.

- After years of largely parallel moves, the big players in the grocery supermarket industry are now at a crossroads. Sainsbury's attention is directed to the US while Tesco's is principally on Europe. Asda is focusing on continuous improvement. Of the big companies, Sainsbury has broken out of food retailing into DIY (and has strengthened its position in early 1995 with its acquisition of the Texas DIY chain). But it remains to be seen if (or when) a player will move into new (but related) products and services through new distribution channels and/or technology. Home shopping and recent information technologies suggest Sainsbury may be the first to achieve breakthrough – or will it?

Short exercise

Does the Tesco case hold very close parallels with your own company's strategies for growth, for instance in the following.

- The tendency to pursue a particular growth route, possibly beyond the point that it will yield the same value which it has in the past?

- Relying on growth drivers which can easily go into neutral or into reverse, and not really wanting perhaps to think through the vulnerabilities of the growth strategy, and possible turning points?

- The main focus being on (quantitative) revenue and profit growth, at the expense of competitive position, and ultimately longer term, economic value?

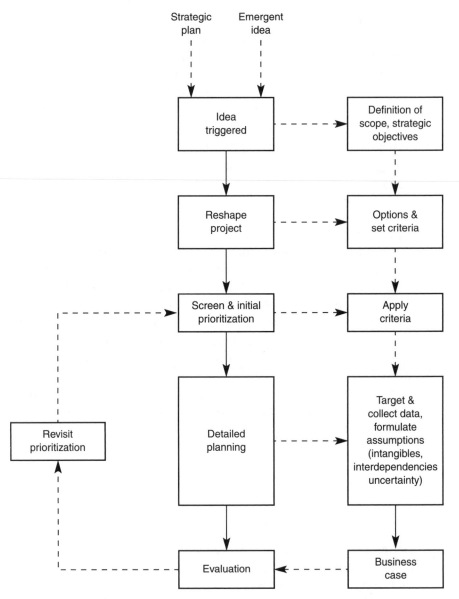

Fig. 6.5 The organic development process

CONCLUSION

Organic strategies for growth are frequently managed in an incremental way, rather than in a holistic way. The sheer momentum of one-track strategic development in an industry results in a hardening of strategic and growth recipes. These recipes enable opportunities within the same industry paradigm and mindset to be managed. But they are not so helpful with achieving novel breakthroughs.

To achieve effective breakthrough a process for managing organic development needs to be established.

Figure 6.5 sets down the key ingredients of this process, highlighting the importance of screening and prioritizing organic development projects. Note the importance of reconfiguring each strategic development project, rather than accepting this as a given. This process follows closely the financially-based analysis outlined in Chapter 4 (the right-hand side of Figure 6.5).

Now that organic strategies for growth in depth have been covered, the next step is to turn to acquisitive and then international corporate breakthroughs.

ACTION CHECKLIST

- **Who are the likely competitors (existing and new) that you will come up against, what are their competitive strengths and weaknesses, financial resources and strategic intents?**

- **How can you combat these competitors (especially new sorts of players)?**

- **What are the trade-offs between allocating resources towards organic growth versus acquisitive growth in your company?**

- **Where your industry is growing rapidly, when might growth stall and how quickly will the industry as a whole realize this and take action to reduce and refocus investment?**

- **What radically new directions for strategic development may exist which might be available by combining technology innovation, new channels to market and by reconfiguring the industry's value chain?**

---

[1] Reprinted with kind permission of the Financial Times © Times Newspapers, 1994.
[2] Reprinted with kind permission of Times Newspapers.

'A corporate advantage ...
equals Parenting advantage
plus Family advantage.'

7

BREAKTHROUGH
ACQUISITIVE GROWTH

INTRODUCTION

This chapter considers a very important avenue of strategic development – the acquisition route. Although in the early 1990s the level of
acquisitive activity tapered off after the excesses of the 1980s, by 1995
it was once again on the rise. Most companies are now likely to be much
more cautious in how they pursue acquisitive opportunities. However, the
often painful lessons of ill-advised acquisitions made around and before
1990 may be rapidly forgotten.

This chapter now helps establish a 'better practice' for the acquisition
process. This is achieved through a framework for managing acquisitions
strategically developed for programmes at Cranfield School of Management (a leading UK business school) and elsewhere. In Chapter 8 there is
also a major case study – the acquisition of Rover by BMW which illustrates this framework.

This chapter also examines the case of Hanson PLC – not to hold this
up as an 'ideal model' but to distil some key lessons for managing the deal-
making process. This naturally leads on to the short case of ICI which
became the target of a hostile bid by Hanson, and subsequently began the
demerger of ICI (now) and Zeneca. The final example in this chapter is
Sketchley PLC.

Acquisitions are by no means a new topic within this book (see discussions
of Marks & Spencer's international strategy (Brooks Brothers especially the
retail clothing acquisition in the US), and in Tesco's acquisition of William
Low in Scotland (and London International)). Certainly acquisition activity
increases the strategic and financial stakes involved – although the rewards
can be high (and also the penalties), the risks are substantial.

That is not to say that the advice is 'don't do it', or 'don't consider it' –
merely that you need to be especially careful when considering the acquisition route.

Introductory exercise

Assuming that you have had some experience of acquisitions in the past, think about these questions.

- What were the original objectives of a particular acquisition?
- Would you say that the acquisition has been a success in
  - strategic terms;
  - organizational terms;
  - financial terms?
- Why was it a success (or, if appropriate, a failure)? In particular, was it:
  - the right company to acquire?
  - bought for a reasonable price?
  - managed appropriately post-acquisition?
- What overall lessons come out of this analysis (whether the acquisition was successful or a failure) for your future acquisition process?

This exercise will probably have revealed some key strengths and weaknesses in your acquisition process. This chapter will sensitize you more to the pitfalls and take you step-by-step through a 'best practice' acquisition process.

This chapter does not pretend to be an exhaustive guide to all the specialist technical issues surrounding acquisitions (for example, legal and taxation). Although very important, these specifics are often less important than achieving an integrated process so that a single, complete overview of the acquisition is maintained by the acquisition project manager at all times.

ACQUISITION TYPES

There are a number of ways of categorizing acquisitions. For example, Haspeslagh and Jemison (1991) distinguish between:

- domain strengthening;
- domain extension;
- domain exploration;

depending upon whether they are aimed at acquiring a capability, a new platform or an entirely new business position.

For example, Tesco's acquisition of Catteau (in Chapter 6) looks very much like a 'domain exploration' acquisition. Sainsbury's acquisition might be viewed more as a domain extension (likewise Tesco's acquisition of

William Low). It is of obvious importance to distinguish between 'domain strengthening' and 'domain exploring' (as the latter focus adds value just as much via corporate learning as via more direct, financial benefit).

Another approach is simply to distinguish between acquisitions which:

- increase scope;
- are step-out;
- are infill in nature

An example of an acquisition which increases scope is that of Lloyds Bank's acquisition of Cheltenham and Gloucester Building Society in the UK (the deal was signed in 1994 to be consummated in later years). This acquisition gave Lloyds, at a stroke, a major increase in share of the mortgage market. Arguably, it is also in part a step-out acquisition as a UK building society is quite a different animal to a clearing bank. Building societies typically have a much simpler, cleaner product range, a different cultural feel and have traditionally been subject to rather different regulatory rules.

A classic step-out acquisition would be that of Dowty's (the defence and aerospace group) acquisition of a £100m turnover telecommunications business – Case Communications – in the 1980s. Following this acquisition, Case was only loosely integrated within the Dowty Group and was subsequently divested in the early 1990s, following takeover of Dowty itself by TI Group. Dowty's move into telecommunications was one of the key factors which made it vulnerable to takeover. Dowty failed to manage Case Communications, and the other information and communication business it acquired for shareholder value.

Examples of 'infill' acquisitions abound and will not be enumerated here. Infill acquisitions are in general terms lower risk than either acquisitions involving increase of scope, or step-out. The biggest cautions on acquisitions thus apply to major increases in scope and to step-outs.

The different kinds of acquisition may generate value in characteristically different ways, as will be seen below.

MANAGING ACQUISITIONS FOR VALUE

Introducing the three V's rule

Acquisitions are frequently mismanaged because of the build-up of untested commitment, over-enthusiasm and the 'thrill of the chase' (Jemison and Sitkin, 1986). Anyone who has ever been involved in an acquisition should quickly recognize what I mean. It is very hard (even with the best of intentions) to maintain objectivity and complete clarity about the rationale and value of an acquisition once the process gets under way.

Value does not come easily through acquisition. Very frequently value is actually destroyed by the acquiring company which suffers from imperfect information about the target. Frequently it is the divesting company that actually generates more value. In the earlier case study on Tesco, it is evident that the shareholders of William Low did very well out of the deal. The initial bid of 225p per share was 30 per cent higher than market value, and Tesco's eventually topped this with 360p, or double the pre-bid market value.

On three separate occasions I have been involved in helping put a value on a particular business strategy (because the conventional business plans did not seem to reveal the underlying picture). On all three of these occasions the business was subsequently divested and at very favourable prices. Partly this might have been due to the business being objectively worth more to another company, because of market or operational advantages, but at least some of the extra value (to the purchaser) was probably illusory.

So, valuing an acquisition is very much not simply a matter of playing around with the financial numbers. These numbers require concrete, strategic support. So how is this analysed? A useful framework is that of the 'three V's':

- $V1$ is the value inherent in the business strategy itself;
- $V2$ is the value added through the particular deal;
- $V3$ is the value created or destroyed through post-acquisition management.

The key test should therefore be 'Why and how do you claim to be adding value through acquisition? Is it $V1$, $V2$, or $V3$ or some combination of these?' (See also Appendix IV which explores value further.)

As McTaggart *et al* put it (1994):

'With millions of dollars and so much internal effort expended on this activity each year, one can't help but wonder why the odds of success are so low. On the basis of our experience in this area, the answer seems relatively clear: the odds are low because, for most companies, a series of secondary objectives interferes with realising the primary objective of creating shareholder value when they target and make acquisitions. All too often, managers pursue acquisitions in an attempt to utilise their company's excess resources, replace a major declining business, enter new geographic markets, exploit potential competitive advantages, or simply achieve an earnings-per-share growth target. While some of these secondary objectives may be desirable, the historical record suggests that they are frequently achieved only by transferring a portion of the shareholders' wealth to the acquired firms' owners in the form of an excessive price.

There are three prerequisites for beating the odds. First, a creative strategy must be conceived to direct the search for candidates and identify those targets with the greatest potential to create value. Second, to avoid overpaying, management must adopt a disciplined approach to analysing acquisition economics. And finally, each acquisition must be integrated successfully so that, at a minimum, the premium paid for control can be recaptured quickly.' (p 177) [1]

Examining our three V's (which are implicit in McTaggart *et al*) closer, V1 can be assessed by evaluating a variety of parameters.

- Is the acquisition's total market attractiveness 'high', 'medium' or 'low' (using the six, expanded competitive forces – including industry mindset, PEST analysis and the analysis of market growth-drivers)?
- Is the acquisition's competitive position 'strong', 'average' or 'weak', not merely currently but against changing customer and competitive needs?
- Does the acquisition fit the existing competitive strategy of your own core business (differentiation, cost leader, focus)?
- Is its competitive position supported by underlying sources of competitive advantage? Are these sources of competitive advantage hard or easy to imitate?

The above four tests are tough and may help to weed out businesses whose financial health seems to be reasonable but whose strategic health is ailing.

The next 'V test' is V2: what is the value added through the particular deal? To arrive at V2 you need to assess the financial consequences of the strategy (in terms of anticipated cash flows), and also the underlying value of business assets and liabilities. To what extent are you paying more than, or less than, a reasonable value for these cash streams or assets?

McTaggart *et al* (1994) describes the V2 as 'the bargain value' of the acquisition. Some companies (notably Hanson PLC and Hanson-lookalikes) have built corporate fortunes through exploiting V2 (and also, as will be shown later, V3). One very clear sign of V2 at work is where an acquirer buys a group for £X million, makes disposals which yield at least £X million, and is still left with one or more very profitable businesses.

In assessing the bargain value you also need to take into account the underlying investment requirements and cost of changes necessary to sustain assumed cash flows (see especially Appendix IV).

Exercise

For an acquisition you have had an involvement in or knowledge of, ask these questions.

- Was there significant value added by acquiring a business with a particularly solid strategy and competitive position? (V1)
- Was the deal done at a total cost (deal price, plus investment and change costs) which was particularly favourable (relative to cash flows and the underlying value of net assets), or not? (V2)
- Was post-acquisition management conducted in a way which created or destroyed value? (V3)
- Overall, did the acquisition appear to add to or destroy value? (V1 + V2 + V3)

The Hanson approach

For example, Hanson PLC acquired Imperial Group for £2.5 bn, and then subsequently realized £2.3 bn by disposing of the Courage drinks business, the hotels business, Golden Wonder, and Ross Young's frozen foods and several other food companies. Even after it had sold these businesses Hanson still had left a very profitable cigarettes business earning £200m in its first year post-acquisition.

This example is reminiscent of Chapter 4 the role of financial measures of return in appraising strategic development was discussed. Not only did the acquisition of Imperial Group generate a very good net present value (NPV), but it also had a very fast payback. With access to a stream of high value relative to the investment like this one, and ones where the value can be recouped quickly and ploughed back into similar opportunities, then you would have the recipe for very, very profitable strategic development. Hanson did – at least in the mid 1980s.

Although many may find the Hanson approach not necessarily to our liking, one cannot fail to be impressed with Hanson PLC's hard-nosed approach to value. In *Hanson – an Autobiography* (Brummer and Cowe, 1994) we hear about not the brains behind Hanson's acquisition success but another part of the human anatomy – the Lord White nose (which is deployed in the US).

As Brummer and Cowe explain, quoting interview material with Lord Hanson himself:

'Lord Hanson and Lord White represent a swashbuckling, entrepreneurial strain in the business world in which many of the most

significant decisions are based upon instinct rather than complex Harvard Business School models. "Gordon was the buyer", James Hanson has reflected. 'Gordon was the one who sniffed out the possibilities and then went on to conduct the takeovers. He's certainly the brightest person I've ever met in that way. He can sense a business. He can feel absolutely and he can sell you on an idea of it because he knows he is going to be right. But he's also the quickest one to throw his own ideas out of the window.'[2]

Lord White is credited with having a nose for recognizing an undervalued company, and also a nose for recognizing the hidden downsides of particular acquisition deals. This latter is very helpful when enforcing the discipline often required when claiming one's share of V2. Indeed, a strength of the Hanson approach is the discipline of setting and sticking by a walk-away-from price (as practised by Hanson Industries in the US).

Lastly, what about V3? In some cases V3 can represent the biggest ingredient of value – and also the hardest to ensure that value is created, as opposed to being destroyed. V3 can turn negative through ill-thought-through integration; this can occur especially when there is a clash of cultures and where the acquisition is one of 'absorption' (Haspeslagh and Jemison, 1992). Also, it can be quite neutral because no real post-acquisition management has occurred. A key lesson is the need to anticipate and manage the V3 stage at both V1 and V2 – to understand the possible ways in which value might be destroyed through integration in formulating strategy and in deal shaping.

The ICI story – from acquisition to demerger

Imperial Chemical Industries (ICI) was formed in 1926 by four chemical companies as a defensive move against the increasingly large European and US chemical companies. ICI grew along with the chemical industry during the 1960s (especially in Europe), and in the 1970s, becoming a giant, complex, vertically integrated and somewhat conservative organization. By the 1970s the chemical industry was becoming much more mature. As Owen and Harrison (1995) describe the chemicals industry was faced with new entrants – particularly oil companies – at the same time that growth slowed down.

In the early 1980s (and the deep industrial recession which ensued), ICI began to change itself internally. Sir Maurice Hodgson began this change process in the late 1970s. The now famous Sir John Harvey-Jones, ICI's then chairman, sought to shake up ICI's old ways. Between 1978 and 1982 ICI lost 50,000 jobs. The ensuing changes were reflected in very large redundancies and also a deliberate strategy moving away from the bulk chemicals/commodity end of the market towards higher value-added speciality chemicals and products. This was called the 'light brigade', symbolizing the move towards speciality products (*Financial Times*, 26 February 1993).

This shift in the corporate portfolio was brought about both by organic development and also some major acquisition moves. In particular, ICI acquired Beatrice (speciality chemicals) in the US in 1985, Glidden paints (in the US) in 1986 and Stauffer (agrochemicals) in 1987. Alongside these extensions in corporate scope, ICI pharmaceuticals became the jewel in the corporate portfolio as its most profitable division. According to Trevor Harrison – ex ICI – (LSE Management Accounting Research Conference, March 1995) ICI had become 'a prisoner of its own success'.

But even before these acquisitions, ICI had become an increasingly complex set of businesses. Not only was ICI seeking to move upwards towards speciality effects chemicals, but also westward to the US, and eastward in Europe and the Far East. It was also spreading its wings into new business areas like seeds.

This made it hard to track the strategies of the diversified group and for the corporate centre to really add value. Every year the corporate centre reviewed the three-year business plans of all of its business portfolio. This review became so intensive and time-consuming that it was named internally as 'hell fortnight', an experience which I went through in 1987, while on secondment to ICI.

Although Sir John Harvey-Jones had made some inroads to the traditional ICI culture, as David Barnes (now chairman of the demerged Zeneca) reflects (1995), the ICI corporate umbrella was a protective shield under which managers could shelter from some of the higher competitive and commercial realities and pressures.

The next chairman of ICI, Sir Denys Henderson, then picked up Sir John Harvey-Jones's baton of strategic development. In 1990, Sir Denys set in motion a number of strategy task forces to take a fresh look at ICI's corporate portfolio. This was triggered by a variety of factors:

- first, a number of businesses in the portfolio were hard to characterize as 'winners' – some needed considerable attention, some to be sold off;
- second, ICI had become vertically integrated to such an extent that head office felt that some of this was both unnecessary, and actually diluted shareholder value;
- third, ICI faced a capital shortage and difficulty in sustaining its dividend at the high levels that had been set in the late 1980s.

These task forces led to a new round of restructuring of the various businesses. In October 1990 another factor intervened. ICI's third quarter results were considerably worse than expected. In fact, profits were £100m down relative to what had been hoped. Although ICI may have appeared slow to react, ICI was actually three to six months' ahead of many other companies in sensing the onset and scale of the early 1990s recession. For instance, at a presentation in late summer 1990 by one of ICI's financial directors to an off-site gathering, the bad news about pending recession was delivered. (This was not just a gloomy occasion but one for passing around handkerchiefs.)

According to Owen and Harrison, these combined strategic and financial signals caused Sir Denys to initiate a fundamental rethink of ICI's corporate strategy. Although the word is not used in other commentaries, 'shock' may seem appropriate to describe the effect which the £100m profits shortfall had had on Sir Denys. The ICI board concluded from its review that the ICI portfolio had become not only too diverse and in parts competitively weakened. It also concluded that it also needed to do something (and quite urgently) about its shareholder value. An analysis of its stock market value indicated a 'value gap' between its actual and potential worth (Chrysler is a recent classic case of this value trap). In 1990 if one applied a pharmaceutical price-earnings ratio to ICI's pharmaceuticals business, this alone gave ICI's market capitalization. This may appear bizarre as the rest of ICI was technically worth nothing, unless one reflects that the group paid a chemicals-style dividend, reinvested pharmaceutical profits in chemicals and effectively behaved as a chemicals group. ICI appeared to be condemned to being perceived as in essence 'A chemicals group', and thus underrated in terms of its price to earnings ratio. This undervaluation of ICI had not gone unnoticed by one very major predator. Hanson PLC appears to have realized that ICI would be a large but interesting corporate morsel. By taking a 2.8 per cent stake in ICI in May 1991, Hanson made its opening shot in a potentially hostile takeover of ICI.

Although Hanson did not (in public) make any clear statement that it did wish to acquire ICI, its likely intent was manifest from the very start. Unfortunately (for Hanson), Hanson allowed ICI to marshal its defences, and Hanson appeared not always totally prepared for what was about to come. ICI then made a vigorous counter-attack on Hanson's own track record and its management style generally, and contractual arrangements with one of the two top players – Lord White. Sir Denys proved not to be the pushover which Hanson appears to have assumed – indeed there may have been some permanent damage to Hanson's image as a result.

For once, Hanson's timing may have been slightly out, particularly as in the UK a general election began to loom. The Labour party could undoubtedly have made considerable capital out of attacking Hanson as the destroyer of British industry (rightly or wrongly). One senses behind the scene political pressures on Hanson to back off from this sensitive move.

ICI then also accelerated its plans to restructure the group. No doubt the Hanson débâcle had focused the minds of its top team wonderfully. Prior to, and during, the demerger of Zeneca, ICI:

- lost 40,000 jobs between 1991 to 1993;
- closed 40 factories;
- sold 40 businesses;
- moved decisively to becoming a 'no frills' operation.

ICI also wrote off £949m to cover this vast restructuring (Source: *The Sunday Times*, 28 February 1993).

This is possibly one of the biggest examples of 'corporate strategy re-engineering' in recent times.

Another strand to the restructuring was the realization of demerger as not so much a threat but as an opportunity. When Sir Denys Henderson invited John Mayo, corporate finance specialist at Warburgs, to give him an objective assessment of ICI he got a very direct and incisive response. John Mayo spent several months analysing the various synergies (or lack of them) within the ICI group. His conclusion was that there was a noticeable fault line between ICI traditional chemicals businesses, and the two newer areas of pharmaceuticals and agrochemicals. This fault line led to the separation of ICI (now) from Zeneca.

John Mayo found very little synergy in marketing technology, people terms, and in the value added by head office *vis-à-vis* old versus new Zeneca businesses. There were also some profound negative synergies, including the investment constraints on organic and acquisitive growth, particularly for pharmaceuticals.

Owen and Harrison (1995) relate this explicitly to ICI's corporate parenting style. It would seem that the fit between ICI's parenting advantage (Goold, Campbell and Alexander, 1995) was no longer positive. On a number of fronts, pharmaceuticals (and to a lesser extent, agrochemicals) would add more shareholder value by being separate from ICI.

It is obviously an open question whether ICI might have demerged along different lines, for instance by retaining agrochemicals in the old ICI, or selling this business off. The demerger is notable not just for what did happen but also for what did not happen – a major divestment. Perhaps the influence of key stakeholders within the company might have played a role here.

The actual demerger of Zeneca appears to have added considerably to shareholder value. According to Owen and Harrison, the combined shareholder value of both ICI and Zeneca was £13.2bn in December 1994. This compares with a mere £7.6bn in June 1993. Allowing for a significant injection of cash (to reduce Zeneca's gearing from what it would otherwise have been), this represented an increase in shareholder value of 57 per cent over that period. This was substantially in excess of the 23 per cent increase in the *Financial Times* general stock index.

The ICI and Zeneca case study thus highlights a number of main lessons for strategies for growth.

- Corporate complexity can easily increase incrementally beyond the point at which shareholder value is added and beyond the ability of the corporate centre to add value to the businesses.
- Creating a spread of businesses can generate good financial results in good times but this may cover up competitive weaknesses. In recessionary times these weaknesses are rapidly exposed. The underlying strategic health of a group is therefore easier to interpret in a recession than during economic boom.
- The bigger you become, the more difficult it can be to take shareholder value seriously.
- Size is rarely, if ever, sufficient protection against break-up and predatory attack.
- Timing plays a bigger role in shaping strategic development than it is usually given credit for.
- Signals may converge from a number of sources and may precipitate a sudden change in corporate mindset. But these might have to build up over a period before they are listened and responded to.
- Even in a group as vast and as complex as ICI, it pays to have a sharp and incisive mind from the outside to cut through the often artificial claims of 'corporate synergy'.
- Corporate restructuring is rarely the end of the story. (A 'detergent strategy' – see Chapter 1 – often moves through several cycles in a very large and complex organization.) Will Zeneca be big enough to survive independently in a world of ever larger pharmaceutical companies? (Zeneca was tipped to bid for Wellcome in 1995, but did not, leaving it a potential prey for other pharmaceutical companies.) The *Sunday Times* (28 February 1993) even hinted at SmithKline Beecham as a possible new corporate parent for Zeneca and in July 1995 it was rumoured Zeneca was in play as a bid target.)

Short exercise

Does the ICI/Zeneca tale suggest to you anything about your own business portfolio, particularly the following.

- Are there any areas where you may be diluting or even destroying value, albeit inadvertently?
- Is your set of business activities becoming unduly complex, and cloudy, with supposed 'synergies' which are actually hard to cash in, in value terms?
- If you were to 'think the unthinkable' about what businesses you would like to be in (and not be in), what would your portfolio actually look like?
- Working backwards from your ideal set of businesses, how might you get from where you are to where you might wish to be (à la ICI/Zeneca)?

On a final note, Goold, Campbell and Alexander (1995(a) and (b)) rightly emphasize the importance of corporate parenting style, particularly in acquisitions. For instance, they highlight how BTR's parenting skills (and advantage) is built on margin enhancement, and that this works well with acquired industrial companies, but less well on acquired distribution companies. However, the words 'corporate parenting' arguably put undue focus on the headquarters role. It may be a more rounded way of looking at corporate strategy to focus on 'corporate advantage' or the way in which the different businesses collectively add more value than they would as separate units in addition to the value brought by these corporate headquarters. Expressed in its simplest terms:

Corporate advantage
therefore equals
Parenting advantage plus **Family advantage**

On a lighter note, in one company the lack of value added by head office was humorously captured in the expression of 'nose office' (implying a much-needed shift from 'nose office' to 'brain office').

The Sketchley experience

The next case example is that of Sketchley PLC, a UK-based service company, in the late 1980s. Sketchley embarked on an acquisition spree to diversify out of its core UK, dry-cleaning business. It began to see itself as an 'industrial services company' (in effect a Mintzberg-type, 'umbrella' strategy). It acquired a range of businesses including industrial cleaning and vending.

At the time Sketchley would have very definitely claimed to have had a 'strategy'. Yet it is unclear whether this strategy was sufficiently thought through and tested in detail in the way this book has so far set out.

For instance, it is doubtful whether the thought processes suggested by the GE grid were used to help screen new business opportunities at Sketchley in the late 1980s. At least one account of Sketchley suggests that what was needed was both the process and the personality to act as a check on the high level of enthusiasm for the expansionary strategy pursued.

What actually happened to Sketchley is perhaps best described directly by the analyst Walter Wright in his seminal article (1992) on Sketchley:

'The first real public indicator from Sketchley that all might not be well was the publication of poor half-yearly figures in November 1989. Profits were down by a quarter on a year earlier and with dry cleaning and vending hit by summer weather and the market for computer peripherals said to be becoming more competitive ...

After what must have seemed an uneasy three months, the whole situation came abruptly to a head. Two hostile takeover offers were received and summarily rejected, three of the four executive directors departed, the true financial state of the company was revealed, by stages, as being far worse than anyone imagined (with an overall loss of £8.1m being reported for the year to March 1990).'[3]

Walter Wright also explains that these trading losses were then followed by a number of disposals of acquisitions (at losses) resulting in extraordinary charges of £11.5m.

The situation was so dire that the initial hostile bid (by Godfrey Davis) was actually withdrawn because of the ongoing bad news from Sketchley's results. The second bid for Sketchley from Compass was actually lower than the first.

A number of problems obviously contributed to this strategic development disaster. Walter Wright lists 'window dressing' of the financial numbers and 'management-based policies' (that in an absence of managing-for-shareholder-value'). But the two most interesting to us at this junction are over-enthusiasm and high-risk strategies.

Of over-enthusiasm Wright says:

> 'The atmosphere at successive head offices must have been absolutely crackling with cerebral activity. They seemed to feel that they were engaged in an undertaking only a little less difficult than establishing a human colony on the moon.'

Indeed, on a short visit to Sketchley in 1989 I could not fail to pick up this electrostatic myself. This was by no means unique to Sketchley, as one might think Wright implies. I can think of at least several companies where strategic excitement has reached such a pitch as to drive out calm, strategic thought.

Second, Wright says of high-risk strategies:

> 'In the easy-going days of yore, companies used to diversify into unknown areas. Now they know better. The established core businesses are there. There was no suggestion [at Sketchley] of a cautious approach, learning as it went along. It was big money right from the start.'

In summary, Sketchley's 'strategy' for growth failed because:

- it was largely based on pre-acquisition rather than on sufficiently tested strategy – very frequently companies confuse an acquisition programme with a strategy;
- it appeared to have overpaid for certain of its acquisitions;
- it did not succeed in adding significant value post-acquisition. This was in part due to hoped-for 'synergies' being elusive and partly due to the additional expense of corporate overhead.

Short exercise

Are there any situations in your own business (or group's) strategic development where the Sketchley tale rings particularly close to home? For one of these situations ask these questions.

- How well was managers' commitment to the strategy for growth tested, monitored and steered?
- What might have made things different (for instance, intervention by some key – existing or new – stakeholder), a reality – shock, a change in the management team or a new analysis of the businesses?

Managing acquisitions strategically – the process

So, how might Sketchley have managed its acquisitions more strategically? Figure 7.1 charts the process in five stages.

Figure 7.1 highlights the importance of developing (at least as a first cut) an overall strategy before commencing a search process. There should also be clear objectives set for the acquisition, both in terms of its strategic and financial contribution, and also in its organizational contribution (for instance, in adding to corporate learning and capability).

Where there are softer objectives (like the organizational ones) these should be really very specific and tangible, not loose and vague. This will enable performance indicators to be set up so that achievement of objectives can be monitored.

Second, the search process needs to be focused on the acquisition criteria – the do's and don'ts of the strategy (see next section).

Third, the valuation and evaluation process involves integrating the strategic operational, organizational, financial, taxation and legal aspects of the acquisition.

Fourth, 'the deal' involves the execution of negotiations to achieve an acceptable and favourable agreement.

Fifth, and finally, 'integration' involves the execution of post-acquisition management. At this stage not only is the acquisition's performance against expectations monitored, but also important learning lessons should be captured.

Although Figure 7.1 shows five linear stages they are all very iterative. For instance, during the evaluation and valuation, the strategy itself should be re-examined, reshaped and fleshed out. Also, the integration plan needs to think through the key issues associated with implementing the strategy. This may entail considerable forward thinking about present and future investment requirements. It also involves thinking through, targeting and costing out any change programmes to be implemented post-acquisition.

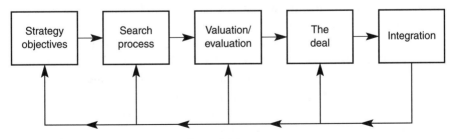

Fig. 7.1 Strategic management of acquisitions

Otherwise those areas of investment and change tend to be emergent, rather than deliberate and foreseen. And, when doing the deal it is important not to saddle the post-acquisition management phase with burdensome integration difficulties.

Short exercise

How does the acquisition process (Figure 7.1) compare to the actual process followed in your organization?

- Which of the five stages would you say your organization is strongest at or weakest at?
- What additional tools and processes could be deployed to strengthen the weaker stages, and what additional skills are needed?

The next section examines the pre-acquisition process (especially the search-and-screening process, the deal process and post-acquisition management).

The pre-acquisition process

Many models of acquisition management fall into the trap of being opportunity (if not opportunistically) driven. They emphasize the search of industrial sectors to establish favourable product/market or niches (for example, with growth potential) and then to identify specific companies which are 'available'.

But with this approach, although there may be pretensions to 'fit a strategy' it is more common to find rapid strategic amnesia setting in once the chase begins. Also, with an approach which is primarily concerned with exploring product/market opportunities it is extremely easy to target the fit of underlying capability and culture. Unless the acquisition is a Hanson type (with post-acquisition management being exerted through strong financial controls), then mismatch of capability and culture clash may prevent adding value in the integration phase.

Arguably, if you have to find out so much about an acquisition target from scratch, then you are unlikely to be able to extract value from it because of the steep, corporate learning curve. Few companies have made a success out of this kind of acquisition approach except where a financial control style, post-acquisition (Goold and Campbell, 1987), is in place.

Competitive analysis can often generate (indirectly) acquisition targets. These acquisition opportunities ought to be identified within the ongoing strategic planning and scanning process. In particular, industry analysis (using Porter's competitive forces) can identify:

- opportunities for forward integration (through distribution channels or to customers) or for backward integration (through acquiring suppliers);
- substitutes which might provide growth opportunities and improve competitive position;
- existing competitors who have close fit and are strategically and organizationally complementary.

A vital part of the search and screening process is to apply the strategic do's and don'ts which form the company's key acquisition criteria. These strategic do's and don'ts should supplement more conventional acquisition criteria (which are frequently bent or relaxed to suit the tastes of an over-enthusiastic management – or 'OEM' – team).

Strategic do's and don'ts can play a pivotal role in the acquisition process as the short case on EXOCET reveals.

An insurance broker – EXOCET

An international insurance broker decided to review its process for making acquisitions. Reviewing its past criteria it found that these criteria had been largely ineffective in thoroughly sorting out quality prospects. Instead of a listing of criteria which could all be relatively easily fulfilled, the company decided to list the do's *and* the don'ts.

The list of 'don'ts' turned out to be far more powerful in sorting out the company's (called EXOCET here) opportunity stream. It enabled some important grey areas to be clarified, particularly one which was whether EXOCET would be prepared to acquire a broker *and* allow it to retain the original name. As EXOCET's strategy was founded on developing its brand strength, for the very first time its management were able to establish that it would definitely *not* acquire a broker and allow it to retain its original name.

In the above case, EXOCET also defined a small number of 'might do's', but also specified the tight circumstances under which it might be prepared to do certain things. It was thus able to adopt a 'deliberate' strategy with sufficient flexibility to incorporate emergent opportunities. Indeed, I would argue that the more emergent the strategy is, the more tight and deliberate the screening process and criteria have to be.

EXOCET also went on to specify other 'do's and don'ts', such as in the difficult and messy legal area. This had been an area of some contention and discomfort as its in-company lawyers were finding themselves being drawn into making, in effect, executive decisions, just because they were dealing with legal issues. This can be a fraught area, and by establishing in advance some legal ground rules both managers and their corporate legal advisers felt more comfortable about dealing with exceptions.

Short exercise

For your own organization, compile a list of the strategic do's and don'ts for potential acquisition targets.
You may wish to think very specifically about:

- size (relative and absolute).
- market focus;
- competitive style;
- brand and image;
- ongoing cost and effort;
- risk;
- degree of relatedness to existing business;
- extent of integration needed;
- degree of control required (both formally and informally).

For the pre-acquisition process it is therefore important to go back time and time again to the strategy. The competitive strategy for the acquisition provides a much clearer lens through which to judge financial value. Through competitive analysis the sustainability, and upside and downside potential of cash streams can be more reliably judged.

The key areas which require evaluation are therefore as follows.

- **The overall industry and market attractiveness:** this includes market growth rates (projected). But it also includes the levels of competitive intensity, impact of regulation or deregulation, environmental issues, economic cyclicality and technology impact. It should also include an assessment of the vulnerability of the industry to restructuring, for example through a breakdown of industry boundaries or through merger of a smaller number of players.
- **The target's competitive position:** this is not merely as at present but also future. Also, barriers of competitive advantage in some areas may be undermined by competitive weakness elsewhere, especially, for example, where the product and service range has proliferated and the focus of its competitive strategy has become fuzzy. (Remember here that competitive dominance has, more often than not, many financial rewards.)
- **Analysis of underlying drivers of competitive position:** this includes quality of production, plant, technology know-how, organizational

rigidity or flexibility, management strengths and weaknesses, life cycle characteristics of key product lines, information systems, etc.

- **Specific key sources of uncertainty and risk:** managers often seem to excel in burying these from view if they fall victim to OEM disease (over-enthusiastic management) or they seek to exorcise these through the rituals of bland 'financial sensitivity analysis'. (Or perhaps one might rather call this 'insensitivity analysis' – by exploring the range of variables that can still be tolerated and still get to the 'right answer'.)
- **Further resource requirements which are needed:** often major capital and non-capital requirements to harvest the value of acquisitions are overlooked. Also, organizational change may take longer than anticipated and be more costly than envisaged, not merely financially but also in absorbing integration effort. Indeed, 'integration difficulty and effort' should be a key element in the evaluation (i.e. it is not just an issue for post-acquisition management).
- **The softer factors:** these are likely to include organizational culture and differences in management style. Remember that the more significant market and operational synergies are in the acquisition case (and the bigger therefore the inherent integration task), the more important these softer factors become. Conversely, if a 'leave-alone' approach is adopted to integrating the acquisition then the full potential value of the acquisition may not be realized.

You may well sign on to the above argument on acquisition appraisal. But the chances are that in the past your appraisal has been skewed in favour of:

- financial, rather than strategic appraisal;
- internal, rather than external assumptions;
- tangible, operational analysis, rather than analysis of culture and style

The deal process

The first thing to consider is the pricing of the deal. Pricing of an acquisition is again an art rather than a science. Managers typically yearn for a simple and mechanistic way of valuing and pricing an acquisition, but this proves elusive for a variety of reasons.

First, managers most separate in their minds what an acquisition might be worth to them, what they might offer tactically for the deal and also what a 'walk-away from' price might be.

Second, valuing an opportunity needs to be tackled from several angles. To begin with, an assessment of asset value may provide one perspective on the value of an acquisition. The book value of net assets may be very approximate, however, and some have recommended instead the use of written-down value of replacement assets. But in many cases the asset value may be considerably divergent from the fundamental value of the business. This is because of the acquired company's ability (present and future) to generate cash.

Therefore it is imperative to look also at the cash generating capability of the business. Discounted cash flow (DCF) techniques offer managers a theoretically robust way of evaluating these cash flows, but managers again need to beware how they arrive at the assumptions these projects are based on, for example how any assumed 'terminal value' for the end of the time horizon of detailed forecast is derived. This can frequently form the majority of a deal's net present value. Again, you need to revisit the lessons of Chapter 4 on managing financial value.

Further, a popular (and perhaps the most popular) method of evaluation is the use of market-based methods. For example, a company earning £10m (post tax) might be in a sector which characteristically has a price divided by ratio earning (p/e ratio) of eight. On a p/e basis a valuation of the company might thus be worth £10m × 8 or £80m. But this method is crude from a number of points of view, including:

- the base year may not be representative of longer term trends;
- historical accounting performance is backward, rather than future looking;
- financially measured profits may be misleading – lesser instances than Polly Peck, the Maxwell Group and others are more widespread than perhaps is believed – and these were after all public companies – private companies may be even more suspect generally;
- the current level of p/e's may be subject to hype in the acquisition market place.

For instance, in early 1995 Glaxo, the major pharmaceuticals group, made a hostile bid for Wellcome, another smaller pharmaceutical company. The p/e ratio of the Glaxo bid was over 25 times last reported earnings. Within the pharmaceutical sector a p/e ratio of this magnitude is not unusual. This is because the industry's earnings are growing and, it is believed, will continue to grow.

So initially the proposed deal looks generous (if not over-generous). But hold on a minute. First of all, if you were to look at the implicit price/earnings of the bid based on current year's reported earnings (which are expected to be substantially higher than last year), then the implicit p/e ratio is significantly less. Also, it is very likely that in the post-acquisition (V3) phase, Glaxo will seek to strip a substantial amount of cost out of its combined operations. This may add considerable value to the overall deal, making the Glaxo bid look not quite so generous as at first sight.

Returning now to the distinction between negotiating price, walk-away price and ultimate value to the business the following can be seen.

- All methods of appraisal can be used in negotiating to present a value for a business in accordance with your own negotiating interests (for example, if using DCF, use a deliberately high discount rate – few managers really understand the basis of how the cost of capital is arrived at).
- A walk-away price does not have to equate with the ultimate value to the acquirer. But when the acquisition chase reaches its crescendo, it is tempting to 'go all out' to 'win' the business. You may also get the reputation of being a 'soft touch' in the acquisition market – turning away from a deal may in itself be an investment for future deals. Certainly Hanson has profited from its tough reputation. Finally, 'going the whole way' leaves no margin for error in what is, after all, a subjective process where you can easily overpay for a deal.
- Price may well be determined by competition conditions – what is the 'target' likely to be worth to other potential acquirers? And what is their strategic intent and likely binding psychology?

Ultimately, an acquisition is worth 'whatever someone is prepared to pay for it'.

Short exercise

For a particular acquisition which your organization acquired in the past ask these questions.

- Do you think that you over or underpaid for it, and why?
- How could you have bought it on more advantageous terms or, alternatively, could you have decided to back away from it?

A fruitful way of helping manage the negotiation process more effectively is to ponder the following deal-making do's and don'ts: these do's and don'ts have been compiled with the help of the distilled experiences of over 150 managers with acquisition exposure in acquisition seminars throughout Europe. Additional explanatory comments are shown underneath each section in italics.

Deal making Do's

Clarify the deal rationale – Do's

1. Understand the reason for and underlying pressure driving the vendor.
2. Be clear what it is that you are getting.
3. The 'walk-away-from' price must allow a good margin of worth to you of the deal.

Although these are three simple points, they should be branded on the foreheads of the acquisition team.

Track the deal fundamentals – Do's

1. Know your 'tradables' in advance of the negotiation
2. Get early agreement on the essentials
3. Keep ongoing track of the benefits (value) of the deal and total costs of the deal as any changes occur

These three points need continual work and a great deal of stamina. In particular, you cannot assume that the accountant on the team can necessarily capture all the implications of fast-moving negotiations in real time.

Managing the deal process – Do's

1. Hold a pre-negotiation meeting(s) *before* deal-making with your advisers
2. Remember that the deal is a learning process: you may learn things which cast new light on (a) attractiveness of the target, (b) attractiveness of the deal and (c) potential post-acquisition management difficulties
3. Establish a series of check points at key stages to stand back and take an objective look at the proposition
4. Take time out from negotiations if a log-jam exists and go back to essentials/tradables.

Because of the momentum which the deal process acquires, you need to invest considerable effort to manage the process in a calm, structured way.

Managing the communication process – Do's

1. Work hard at communication – within 'the team' and with the vendor.
2. Focus all information through *one* key point.
3. Be absolutely clear on who has the final say.

These points are again easier said than done. Acquisition negotiations can become extremely complex and the opportunities for miscommunication abound. These opportunities are multiplied further with cross-border decisions where at least one side works in a second language.

Managing the relationships with the vendor – Do's

1. Keep on thinking 'I am not here to make friends'.
2. Have a 'negotiation game plan' in place in advance – especially to give advantage over an unsophisticated/inexperienced vendor .
3. Exploit disagreement or fragmentation of views in the opposition.
4. Where an unsophisticated vendor is involved, be prepared to provide support:
   – to talk them through the key stages in advance;
   – when it all begins to seem 'too much' at later stages.
5. Avoid alienating key managers you wish to retain.
6. Make provision for continuity of employment, systems etc., where you are buying part, not all, of a business.

It is not possible to offer rigid prescriptions in the area of managing relationships – essentially these should be managed on a situation-by-situation basis. However, the above six points flag up some important pointers.

Achieving tactical advantage – Do's

1. Look for skeletons (by continual probing).
2. Be prepared to 'go for the extra' at the last stage of negotiations (the vendor's emotions take over here).
3. Reflect on your negotiating skills and style, and its strengths and weaknesses before finalizing the team.
4. Encourage candour from managers of target.
5. Keep out of any areas clouded by lots of subjectivity on the part of vendors.
6. Be aware of who thinks they are driving the deal but without necessarily letting them influence the out-turn of negotiations (you can still be proactive!).
7. Be prepared to use financial tools as both valuation tools and as negotiating weapons.

Obviously point 2 needs to be weighed against the situation – late, deal-wrecking tactics are not being advocated here. Point 5 stresses the need to avoid getting into debates which involve lots of feeling about what the business might be worth – always go back to the strategic, financial and other facts.

Managing the acquisition team – Do's

1. Appoint an 'acquisition project leader' (and, if necessary, a manager – to co-ordinate detailed information flows).
2. Involve 'the integrator' at key stages – indeed, consider making the integrator the project leader.
3. Ensure that the maximum experience of acquisitions is within the team, e.g. where the leader lacks 'experience' this needs to be counterbalanced.
4. Adjust your normal duties – it is not a part-time job.
5. Control the players in the team and the commitment 'up to the top'.

The organizational issues surrounding acquisition teams cause endless debate, often of a heated variety. It is imperative that roles and responsibilities are very well defined, otherwise there is a very real threat of going down the slippery slope into political in-fighting (points 1, 2 and 5). Also, point 4 actually means what it says – you can't lead a complex acquisition effectively at the peaks of activity alongside a heavy operational role – something has to give.

Deal-making Don'ts

Managing the deal process – Don'ts

1. Assume that your professional advisers *individually* know 'the whole picture'.
2. Allow ambiguity to persist in key areas, particularly in leaving it until too late to raise key legal, tax, pension or related issues.
3. See the deal in any sense as 'final and agreed' until formal closure.

The final point is critical – as soon as you think you have 'won' you may well have lost – in value terms.

Managing relationships with the vendor – Don'ts

1. Get involved socially with vendor and representatives without a clear strategy (particularly for the inexperienced).
2. Give vague assurances of continuity of employment which you may not wish to be held to.

These speak for themselves. Sometimes experienced acquirers greet point 1 with incredulity. But it does happen. I have even known of situations where an acquisition manager and the vendor's representative swapped stories about their mistresses – maybe this was harmless, maybe it was not.

Achieving tactical advantage – Don'ts

1. Put all of your cards 'up front' on the table (be prepared to ask *them* what they are looking for – depending on the context).
2. Be stampeded by artificial deadlines.
3. Become impatient with apparent haggling over minutiae – this can be very important and have a big impact on value.
4. Give in to the temptation of 'giving in to' perfectly sound arguments without a fight.
5. Conceal skeletons where it will be evident you have been obviously manipulative as the concealment will be transparent.

Points 1–5 above again appear self-evident, but remember acquisitions can become very much an emotional experience where reason gets left behind unintentionally.

Managing the acquisition team – Don'ts

1. Let any of your team display excessive enthusiasm
2. Air your team disagreements in front of the opposition.

These issues are picked up very quickly by an experienced opposition, especially through unconscious, non-verbal behaviour.

Exercise – deal process

For a past acquisition deal which you were involved in, or aware of, what do these checklists of 'do's and don'ts' suggest were the key strengths and weaknesses of the deal process?

We turn now to the legal and tax issues. Acquisition management is made even more difficult because of legal and taxation complexities. This complicates not merely the evaluation of the deal (a fundamentally sound 'business deal' can be negated or made marginal by contingent, legal liabilities, or because of tax advantages).

Also, detailed legal and tax advice is often sought *too late* as the bid is made without clear attachment to exact conditions. This risk is heightened still further if the deal is led by a non-financially literate manager or where the finance manager has inadequate 'close support' from legal and tax experts – and at the right time.

These complex, technical issues also complicate the number of players on both sides who are involved in the process. This may already have included financial institutions, technical consultants, auditors and the watchful eye of head office.

As deals are often set against deadlines (whether false or real), the negotiation process may run around the clock. The over-eager, acquiring team may be tempted to cave in out of frustration and keenness to make headway.

The post-acquisition process

Post-acquisition or integration planning should begin at the point at which a target is identified. If a target is likely to be inherently difficult to integrate, this has an immediate bearing on its value.

Also, the more thorough integration planning is done, the more chance there is to harvest the full potential value of the acquisition, especially where synergies are assumed in the business case and it is essential that these relatively fragile areas of value are actually captured.

Post-acquisition management is often a complex and lengthy process. It calls for project management techniques and skills of a high order (see Chapter 11). Where this is not realized, what typically occurs is that the managers face severe strain or may make fatally damaging mistakes (or, worse still, suffer both of these problems). These mistakes (for example, in timely and sensitive dealings with customers, suppliers and staff) can often do irreversible damage to value. A key criteria of acquisition success in some successful groups is therefore 'the quality of integration'.

As a final point, the process of post-acquisition management may take much longer than managers believe. This is especially so when dealing with softer aspects of integration, such as the resolution of cultural differences.

Post-acquisition management is therefore an exhausting task demanding attention to many details in managing change at the same time as trying to keep the business performing well. Not surprisingly, there is often a dip in performance associated with an acquisition integration – this may lead to a vicious cycle of increased pressure to perform which is resisted by acquired staff (assuming that they stay).

Post-acquisition management cries out to be project managed. During post-acquisition management there are likely to be a number of project areas, some of them 'hard' and some of them 'soft', for instance:

- communication with customers;
- communication with staff;
- financial reporting systems;
- updating budgets and targets;
- areas identified for cost reduction;

- integrating joint activities (for instance, distribution);
- implementing a new organizational structure and roles;
- team-building (or rebuilding);
- ensuring that all the legal and fiscal requirements of the deal are complied with.

This daunting list could easily be added to. The range and difficulty of these activities highlights the sheer amount of work that needs to be consumed – in relatively short periods of time. Many of the key activities are also time-critical, for instance communication with customers and staff.

A really valuable exercise is to plot all the key activities (on a weekly basis) for the first three months post-acquisition and also for the next three months on a month-by-month basis. This should identify critical dependencies and any critical paths. (See also Chapter 11.) During the post-acquisition phase it is tempting to focus mainly on internal change and to overlook key changes in the external competitive environment. Also, lessons about the real competitive position of the company may be overlooked and it may be as long as two years or more into integration that the need for a full strategic review is realized. By then it might be too late – which leads on to post-acquisition learning.

Post-acquisition learning is a vital but often missed stage in an effective acquisition management process. This can be performed not merely in terms of financial performance but across a range of areas, as follows.

- **Strategic learning:** is your strategy the right one and do you have to change it in the light of evolving circumstances?
- **Operational learning:** are there processes and skills that you can transfer which were not appreciated prior to the acquisition?
- **Organizational learning:** what has the acquisition told you about the quality of management you have acquired (and also our initial judgements on them)?
- **Learning about the acquisition process:** what lessons are there for how you manage acquisitions generally that we can apply in the future.

Post-acquisition exercise

For an acquisition which you were involved in or are knowledgeable about, ask these questions.

- What were the key strengths and weaknesses of the post-acquisition management process?
- If you or the organization were to do it all again, what things do you think could be done differently to avoid the post-acquisition pitfalls?

A final warning is that while the 'financial numbers' may have been squeezed to look OK, the fundamental strategic health of the company may not be quite as thought and may even be deteriorating. The big problem during post-acquisition learning is to ensure that management first looks at all the key indicators of success (and not just the short-term, financial measures). Second, management needs to make sure that these indicators are examined in a genuinely open way. Again it is fruitful to hold a 'strategic amnesty' in order to maximize the learning (so that this doesn't become blame-time), otherwise your organization may be destined to repeat errors because of cover-ups.

CONCLUSION

This chapter has explored the role of acquisitions in strategies for growth and sounded a number of cautionary messages against over-enthusiastic management. The case of Hanson PLC helped draw some important lessons about maintaining objectivity, the need to have a 'nose' for the downsides and for being crystal clear about how an acquisition is likely to add value. (Sadly, Lord White died in August 1995.)

The ICI case highlighted the perils of incremental, strategic development beyond the point at which the group is manageable. The result was the painful process of repelling Hanson and the demerger of Zeneca. Zeneca has now to forge its own independent destiny as a two-business group, and against the increasing might and size of its pharmaceutical brethren.

Sketchley showed that although companies may think they are clear about how they will add value strategically (V1), and through post-acquisition management (V3), they have often just begun to think through the issues. Valuing a deal (for instance, Glaxo versus Wellcome) is very much an art rather than a science.

In the deal process itself managers often start with good intentions but their process and level of commitment can be swept off-course by events in negotiations or moves by the opposition. It is an absolute imperative to have a clear negotiating strategy – to know what you want (and what you don't want). You need to know what the tradables are and to seize the initiative (sometimes by stealth) when you can gain the advantage.

Post-acquisition management (sometimes called 'integration') is so often the graveyard of acquisition value. Besides project management (see Chapter 11), it is also useful playing through integration scenarios before and during integration (see 'everyday scenario planning' in Appendix II). This can also benefit from stakeholder analysis (Chapter 5).

It should be apparent that acquisitions are certainly not a task for everyday management. Now that you have been alerted to the potential and pitfalls of acquisition, it is opportune to move into BMW's acquisition of Rover as part of its international development.

ACTION CHECKLIST

- How does your acquisition opportunity add value (a) through its tangible contribution to existing competitive strategy (V1); (b) through getting a particularly favourable deal (V2); or (c) in terms of adding value via post-acquisition integration or development (V3)?
- What is the total deal cost (deal price, plus investment and change costs)?
- What businesses are you in which might be worth more to other companies and might thus be fruitful to divest or unbundle?
- Does the acquisition add to business or corporate complexity unduly and thus dilute longer term value?
- How risky is the acquisition (overall)?
- Does the acquisition really fit (or just get squeezed into) your acquisition criteria (do's and don'ts)?
- Are managers just a little over-enthusiastic about the opportunity, maybe the result of too much commitment, and thus being prone to over-play or underplay the risks?
- Do you have a very clear and deliberate negotiation strategy or one which is essentially emergent?
- Do you have a clear and detailed post-acquisition strategy?
- How do you plan to avoid 'everyday management' in your approach to the acquisition (for instance through appointing an acquisition project manager – full-time – and support team)?
- What scenarios for integration are likely to unfold and how is this likely to be affected by key stakeholders (stakeholder analysis)?

See also Appendix IV on Aquisition and value.

[1] *The value imperative*: Managing For Superior Shareholder Returns James M. McTaggart, Peter W. Kontes, Michael C. Mankins. Copyright © 1994 by The Free Press, a Division of Simon & Schuster, Inc. Reprinted with permission of the publisher.
[2] Reprinted by permission of Fourth Estate Ltd from *Hanson – A Biography* by Alex Brummer & Roger Cowe © 1994
[3] Wright W, *Sketchly was taken to the cleaners*, Long Range Planning, Vol 25 No 3, pp 108–116, 1992, reprinted with kind permission from Elsevier Science Ltd, The Boulevard, Langford Lane, Kidlington OX5 1GB, UK.

'International development requires a degree of strategic pickiness.'

8

INTERNATIONAL STRATEGIES FOR GROWTH – THE BMW AND ROVER CASE

INTRODUCTION

I have been using BMW as a case study for five years and Rover for eight years. So it perhaps was not a surprise that three years before BMW's bid for Rover my MBA students came up with the suggestion that this might occur. This idea crystallized out of Rover's migration towards a BMW-type of focused-differentiation strategy.

Also my students (rightly) identified Rover as being below critical mass to compete independently on the world car market. Although Rover has been supported for many years by its strategic alliance with Honda (which supplied engine technology) even with Honda's support its longer term future looked hard to sustain. Rover's parent, British Aerospace, lacked the resources to really position Rover as a significant car company even within its chosen niches.

This case study explores the BMW acquisition of Rover (again based on publicly available data), and also using the tools and processes from this and other chapters.

This chapter combines organic and acquisitive development and international alliances in a single case study. The acquisition of Rover by BMW is a response to competitive changes in the international environment and also in consumer sentiment. The case illustrates once again a number of techniques, including:

1. PEST analysis;
2. competitive forces;
3. Porter's generic strategies;
4. deliberate strategies;
5. the 'onion model' of competitive advantage;

6. the 'grow-earnings' or GE grid;
7. the acquisition process;
8. the three V's of acquisition value;
9. the value drivers;
10. the growth drivers;
11. the uncertainty/importance grid.

THE CHANGING CAR INDUSTRY STRUCTURE

When I use the car industry as a case study on a strategy programme in the New Forest, England (indoor, regrettably), managers plunge enthusiastically into analysing 'the industry'. Rapidly they discover that the UK doesn't really have a single industry, but several overlapping industries. For example, it is possible to examine:

- the UK versus the European industry;
- European versus North America versus the Far East;
- the executive car versus volume car market;
- initial sale of cars versus the second-hand market and also the parts market;
- the car industry as a self-contained industry or interfacing industries including motor insurance and financial services.

Clearly your choice of focus needs to depend upon which company(s) you are interested in analysing and for what purpose. Nevertheless, it is possible to do some generic analysis of trends, particularly using PEST and competitive forces analysis. But first, the scope should be narrowed a little to the European car industry.

Analysing the main PEST factors reveals the following.

- The political (and regulatory) factors:
  - increasing regulation of emissions;
  - European Union (EU) import tariffs encouraging Far Eastern car companies to invest in plants within the EU;
  - increasing taxation on company cars (specifically in the UK);
  - (in the UK) major curtailment of the road building programme.
- The economic factors:
  - gentle economic recovery stimulating demand a little;
  - but demand remaining very cyclical.
- The social factors:
  - increased car theft and higher motor insurance making some types of car effectively uneconomic;

  - a shift away from high performance for perfomance's sake cars;
  - downsizing of cars, both in the primary and second-car market;
  - increased traffic congestion eroding the notion of 'driving for pleasure'.
- The technology factors:
  - improved safety and security systems;
  - much more fuel-efficient cars using new designs, materials, engine technology;
  - pollution-reducing devices;
  - new, futuristic shapes in the form of 'concept cars'.

Besides these PEST factors, there are also a number of market growth-drivers, including the creation of more substantial niches, for example for 'people movers' (with Renault's Espace and lookalikes), and also four-wheel drive, 'fun' vehicles.

This general backdrop paints the picture of an industry which is subject to relatively intense pressure for change from the PEST factors. Yet it is still one which is ensconced in its original industry paradigm, albeit with shifting recipes. But one can easily imagine a future car industry, post the year 2000, which is quite different.

A whole new market in micro cars with very light fabrication and very high efficiency dual motors (petrol and electricity) for urban use. This market could supplement a much more environmentally friendly market for mid-range cars for larger family use. A third market might be the two-seater high performance but again fuel efficient commuter vehicle.

Turning next to the competitive forces, these reveal the following.

Buyer power:

- company (fleet) buyers have very strong bargaining power;
- private buyers have, traditionally, had relatively weak bargaining power, but have become more astute in shopping around for best deals.

Buyer power is thus strong, and getting stronger.

Entry barriers:

- are significant, but not insurmountable, especially by determined new players from the Far East. This has impacted on the executive car sector (Toyota's 'Lexus' marque) and also at the lower end (with Subharu and even Daewoo, a conglomerate who have reduced their costs of entry by being mainly car assemblers).

Entry barriers are thus becoming less difficult to surmount.

Supplier power:

- is not particularly strong and is thus a favourable industry force.

Substitutes:

- are less important directly (for example, public transport) with the exception of telecommunications where video conferencing is a part substitute to business travel.

Competitive rivalry:

- is intense, and likely to get even more intense with the establishment of new Far Eastern-owned plant within the EU. This could further weaken the balance between supply and demand, leading to substantial overcapacity (in the late 1990s). This overcapacity would be 'sticky' because of relatively high exit barriers.

Competitive rivalry is thus unfavourable and could get even worse, unless it is rescued by further industry concentration through takeover or strategic alliances.

The industry mindset:

- is still making the adjustment away from old recipes (high performance, prestige and cost company cars) towards a new set of recipes.

In all, the car industry is thus a really challenging environment in which to be operating. Successful companies will need to offer very high quality standards even where they try to be low cost. Differentiated companies will need to have truly outstanding products and service. It will probably be very difficult to achieve this across the board. There will be scope for differentiated players with a very clear and appropriate product/market focus, but such players will need to achieve a lowish cost base simultaneously. With these strategic imperatives in mind, this chapter now looks first at BMW and then at Rover.

BMW'S STRATEGIC POSITION

BMW is a very successful company which has exploited important niches in the car market with a very strong, differentiation strategy. Originally renowned for its quality motorcycles after the Second World War, it diversified into small cars. Although once regarded as the poor relation to Mercedes it has actually reached a position on a par with (and some would say ahead of) Mercedes. In late 1994 BMW displaced Mercedes as the supplier of engines to the next generation of Rolls-Royce cars.

In a manner reminiscent of Marks & Spencer, BMW has built an impressive brand. This was established by very clear market positioning, very high quality product and service from its dealer network to match. The very success of BMW does however mean that it has become a prime target for competitors to emulate, possibly by moving into direct attack.

Bernd Pischetsrieder, chairman of BMW, explains his company's positioning:

'We as a company, and our cars, want to appeal to people who want to be successful, active, successful because of their own strength. And this goes very well with the sporty character of our cars'. (The Money Programme, 1994) [1]

Figure 8.1 shows BMW's onion of competitive advantage, as at the early 1990s. This highlights a number of very powerful sources of measurable competitive advantage. Note that its market focus is displayed towards the edge as it can be imitated, and also customer loyalty is particularly fragile in the very competitive market which has already been painted. Also, although BMW has a very strong distributor network, this too can be copied.

Harder to emulate is the underlying quality of BMW cars. A useful competitive benchmark is that of motor magazines, which consistently rate BMW's 7 and 5 series as excellent. Other cars are measured up against the BMW range.

It could be argued that the motor press are so taken with the BMW range that they unfairly weight their ratings against other cars. For example, the Mazda Xedos (which is directly targeted at BMW's 3 and 5 series) is considered to be by some as relatively inferior (curiously the Xedos has been rated worse than the obsolete Vauxhall Astra GSI in terms of handling – which might be thought bizarre).

But, if the motoring press is biased towards BMW then this is in itself a source of competitive advantage. How much would a write-up on the Vauxhall Omega saying that it was 'much better quality than BMW 5 and 7 series' be worth to Vauxhall?

Maintenance of BMW's strong brand is therefore an absolutely critical success factor both operationally and for any strategies for growth which BMW embarks on.

But is BMW (as of the mid 1990s) capable of sustaining its competitive position against competitor attack from both Western and Far Eastern sources (such as from Toyota's Lexus marque)? There are some symptoms that a turning point was reached in BMW's strategic health around the early 1990s.

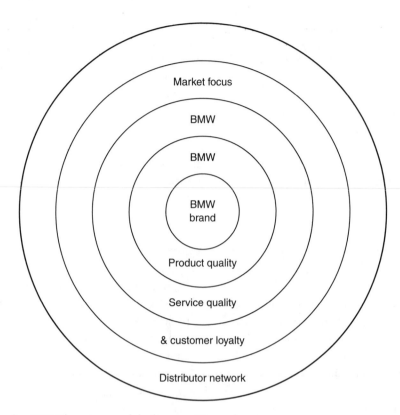

Fig. 8.1 BMW's onion model of competitive advantage

First, BMW's reputation for quality has not been unblemished. Certain of the early 3 series models in the early 1990s had significant quality problems. Bernd Pischetsrieder, chairman of BMW, accepted (*The Money Programme*, 1994) that there had been some quality problems but counters:

> *'There is a very subjective element in it, because we are obviously aiming for much more discerning customers, and therefore they will complain about items for which other cars' customers aren't complaining.'*

One might have some sympathy with BMW's predicament here. However, it does seem to be an inevitable consequence of BMW's positioning that its quality has to be absolutely unblemished. Indeed, Mr Pischetsrieder himself admits to some embarrassment:

> *'Nevertheless, it is being beaten on quality scores by certain other marques – that is an embarrassment, and it is one of our prime objectives to improve that.'*

But BMW is by no means inactive in meeting this challenge. Mr Pischetsreider says that:

'Zero defect is the objective and every single person in the organization plus 250,000 working in our network worldwide, have to have this approach.'

Achieving and sustaining top product quality is clearly a critical success factor for BMW. But this is not sufficient, given the impressive gains in quality of competing cars, particularly over the early 1990s. In the tighter economic climate of the early and indeed mid 1990s, some BMW customers are at least beginning to stray. One customer (interviewed by *The Money Programme*, 1994), Bob Cattle, who switched from a BMW to a Vauxhall Omega, puts it as follows:

'The BMW 5 series is a good car and I enjoy driving it, but with the number of vehicles that are now on the road, which are better value for money, you need to shop around.'

But besides the increasing threat of competition, BMW also faces some broader shifts in its competitive environment. According to John Lindquist of the Boston Consulting Group (*The Money Programme*, 1994):

'There is increased environmental consciousness amongst affluent groups who have been their targets. Consumer trends in luxury vehicles are undergoing a state of change. They are often looking for lower engine sizes which have less fuel consumption and less pollution. They are also increasing needs for smaller cars because of parking congestion in major urban areas, and in general conspicuous consumption through large size and large engine is not as fashionable.'

This naturally pushes BMW in the direction of medium and smaller sizes. Although BMW sells a lot more 3 series than 5 series, and also a lot more 5 series than 7 series, it is actually the top of the range cars which are rated as outstanding by motor magazines. So is the move to downsize a strategic temptation that will ultimately weaken BMW? Also, the competitive forces traditionally tend to be more acutely adverse when you consider the volume end of the car market.

But even before BMW actively considered buying Rover it had decided to experiment with the smaller end of medium-sized cars with its BMW Compact, launched in 1994. About the same size as a BMW 3 series, the Compact is a hatchback, taking BMW into new terrain.

According to consultant John Lawson of DRI Europe:

> *'The Compact is one effort to go a little bit more downmarket to tap some part of the market which they ... haven't been able to reach with mainstream product lines, and it is difficult to do that because one of the risks that you run is you undermine the image of your more top-scale cars and put them in a lower segment of the market. I think it remains to be seen whether in retrospect the Compact will be regarded as a success or not.'*

Summarizing BMW's strategic position as at 1994 (see Figure 8.1), BMW:

- had been (and still was) a very successful company which had achieved market leadership in executive, high performance cars in Europe;
- with a worldwide reputation for quality which is now being imitated by a variety of players;
- with a product line which was beginning to appear out of synchronism with the changing market environment, and which appeared somewhat limited and perhaps over-focused.

Bernd Pischetsrieder concludes (*The Money Programme*, 1994) that: 'Either you become a global player or you will be out of business in 20 years' time.'

But does this actually follow from the analysis in this book? It is now worthwhile for you (the reader) to spend some time pondering what other options were available to BMW.

Exercise – BMW strategic options

What options were available to BMW (as at 1994) (other than to acquire Rover as a central plank of its strategic development) and how attractive are these? You may wish to explore, for instance:

- other acquisition options;
- specific strategic alliances;
- organic development (of new products) to broaden its range;
- migrating its competitive strategy to have less emphasis (or even more emphasis) on differentiation;
- maintaining and protecting its current niche position;
- exploiting new technologies for engine and vehicle design.

ROVER'S STRATEGIC POSITION

Rover Group has a long and often tortuous history. In the 1960s the then Labour government nationalized a very large part of the UK-owned car industry because of perceived national strategic importance (and, no doubt, political reasons). British Leyland was formed to weld these disparate companies together. The plan was not perceived an economic success as British Leyland (BL) required not only massive investment but also ran up spectacular losses in the 1970s. BL was also at times an open sore of industrial relations, although Sir Michael Edwardes, who led BL, was credited at the time with sorting much of that malaise (known as 'the British disease') out.

BL's problems were not merely to do with poor organization, industrial relations and management. They were also to do with a reputation for poor quality and unreliable cars. Also, BL's businesses were for the most part not particularly large when set against world markets. Critical mass was then, as it is now, an issue for BL.

When Mrs Thatcher's government came to power in 1979 it was perhaps only a matter of time before a radical solution was found for BL (subsequently renamed Rover Group, to appeal to the original brand strength of the Rover name).

The Conservative government clearly wanted to privatize Rover but for obvious political reasons did not want it to fall into foreign ownership (for example, of Japanese disposition). Then a deal crystallized with British Aerospace (BAe), which on purely financial grounds was rather favourable. BAe acquired Rover for £150m in 1988. This price included other businesses which were subsequently sold at a substantial profit by BAe. (Indeed, it was later perceived to be so favourable that Lord Young, the Conservative minister responsible for the deal at the time, was obliged later to explain why Rover had been sold so cheaply.)

BAe seemed to be a perhaps unlikely partner as it was hard to imagine what BAe could bring as a corporate parent to Rover (other than finance for investment – assuming that BAe actually had that).

When Rover was sold to BAe, BAe was prohibited from disposing of its shareholding for a period of five years. This five-year period expired in 1993, leaving Rover once again 'up for grabs'.

But in that five years things had changed for BAe, which had been itself badly hit on three fronts. First, the ending of the Cold War put enormous pressure on its military business. Second, the recession and financial difficulties in the airline industry had badly affected its civil airline business. Third, its perhaps unwise diversification into property development (at around the time it acquired Rover) weakened its financial strength. In short, BAe was desperate for cash and so, if a willing buyer for Rover could be found, there was a very willing seller. Honda may not have thought just how desperate BAe was for cash.

Focusing now on Rover, the company had achieved its own transformation from the mess of the 1960s and 1970s to being a credible car company in the late 1980s and early 1990s.

This transformation has even been called 'Roverization' (*Financial Times*, 7 April 1993). In the five years to 1993 annual productivity per worker was up from 10 to 14 cars (although still short of the 20 typical of Japanese companies) (*Sunday Times*, 8 August 1993).

Part of this success is attributable to the involvement of Honda which supplied Rover's key engines. Honda had taken a 20 per cent stake in Rover Group, and this strategic alliance appeared to be working very well. Honda began to see Rover as a central plank of its European strategy.

The Honda connection enabled Rover to tap into Honda's technology economies of scale. It was thus able to reach economic sustainability at a smaller size than it would have had to have been were Rover to be completely independent. The Honda link came at a price, however, as Honda's bargaining power enabled Honda to extract value out of the relationship through its technology licensing arrangement.

But the second and third major planks of Rover's strategic turnaround were to reposition its product range to become much higher quality and also through productivity breakthrough. We will focus here mainly on the product repositioning but the internal organizational benefits have been substantial: 'We have acquired an insight into Japanese best management practices and processes', says George Simpson, chairman of Rover, *Financial Times*, 7 April 1993.[2]

Rover had previously had a product mish-mash with large executive cars alongside the Maestro, Allegro, Metro and Mini. In the earlier 1980s Rover appeared to be trying to be a broad-based provider (with some niches), and simultaneously pursuing a differentiation and lower cost strategies. In Porter's terms, Rover (then BL) had made the mistake of being 'stuck in the middle' on the Porter grid of generic strategies.

But from the mid 1980s Rover sought to:

(a) move up market; and
(b) have a much tighter focus of its car range.

As John Towers, Rover Group's chief executive said in 1994 (*The Money Programme*):

'If you think about the world as we see it in the future, full of very good, ordinary cars, Rover does not want to be a part of ordinary cars, Rover wants to be a part of extraordinary cars.'

The product range improvements made by Rover include the following.

- The launch of the 200 and 400 series to gradually supplant and replace the Allegro and Maestro.
- The acclaimed (in the UK) launch of the 600 series (which even pre-BMW bid looks a little bit like BMW cars). Although built on identical platform to the Honda Accord, the Rover 600 commands a premium of around £2,000, this price premium being a classic test of a realized differentiation strategy.
- The huge success of the Discovery range of four-wheel drive vehicles.
- The rebadging of the Metro as the Rover 100 in late 1994, backed up with an advertising campaign to give the car a feel of 'style' (moving it from the 'grey market' – the over-50s to the young market).
- The restored reputation for reliability.

Although it would be difficult to draw a particularly large onion model of competitive advantage (as at 1994), Rover's key competitive strengths were now (see Figure 8.3):

- the restored marque of Rover;
- its increasingly strong and competitive product range;
- its productivity.

But offsetting these relatively fragile sources of competitive advantage we can also identify (see Figure 8.2):

Rover's competitive advantages: **Rover's competitive disadvantages:**

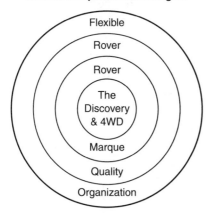
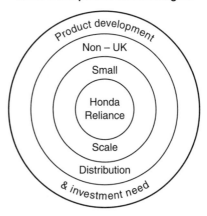

Fig. 8.2 Rover's onion models

- its relatively small size and dependence on Honda technology;
- the need for investment on a scale which was difficult to finance through internal cash generation.

The *Sunday Times*, 6 February 1994, analyses the Honda arrangement:

'Rover paid Honda substantial sums for the car floorpans and the engines for its larger models – plus a royalty on each jointly developed car Rover sold. Moreover the agreement barred Rover from selling Honda-based models in markets Honda wanted for itself. Rover was not allowed to sell the 600 in America.

Rover was caught in a Honda bear-hug: it gave the British company protection, but it prevented Rover's cars from breaking into real profit. All Rover could do and Simpson did it very well, was to squeeze every penny out of the pipeline that Rover itself controlled.'[3]

This account of the Rover–Honda strategic alliance underscores the risks which any medium or smaller-sized player exposes itself to when joining a strategic alliance with a larger and more powerful partner.

As a measure of the vulnerability of Rover, one car industry consultant (*The Money Programme*) explains:

'*The last car it developed from the wheels up was the Montego in 1984. Apart from four-wheel drive, Rover has lost key elements of its design capability.*'

Rover's sales were still (in the 1990s) predominantly concentrated in the UK. Also, outside the UK its models have very low market share (even in continental Europe) and are sometimes not known at all. For instance, when running a strategy programme for a major European country (with a British parent) I tried to run Rover as a case study on acquisitions. Almost all of the non-British managers had very little knowledge of the Rover range – beyond Rover's four-wheel drive Discovery.

So, overall, Rover emerges as having (as at 1994) a still fragile competitive position. Outside the UK its brand is weak, its market share is low and it lacks a strong distribution network. Its parent, British Aerospace, was no longer fed by an entrepreneurial visionary, eager to develop an industrial conglomerate but by an ex-BTR, financially hard-nosed chartered accountant. With the government's five-year brakes on BAe's exit off, the scene was set for the sale of Rover.

Given BAE's reluctance to continue as Rover's parent left Rover with a number of strategic options. Simpson concluded that there were three options. These were:

'A full takeover by Honda, a management buy-out, or acquisition by a German car company. The first looked unlikely; Honda had no interest in a bid, its existing relationship including a 20 per cent stake in Rover cars delivered all the cost benefits the Japanese needed.

But the management buyout option was interesting: a serious attempt was made to launch a buyout ... Simpson and Sir Graham Day, Rover's former chairman, were taking soundings in the City about its feasibility. They quickly ran into a roadblock: the problem of raising finance to support Rover's ongoing investment and working capital needs.

"Buyouts are not about getting people to invest in the equity, they are about getting people to organise finance to run the company. Rover needs about £1 billion in daily banking capital just to keep it going." Simpson said. "It was easy to find people to pay £400m or £300m for the equity but we couldn't find someone to stand by the £1 billion."' (*Sunday Times*, 6 February 1994)

Only Mercedes and BMW were likely candidates for the third option as Volkswagen was still struggling to digest its late 1980s growth. So now it is time to look at BMW for the strategic development rescue of Rover Group.

BMW'S ACQUISITION STRATEGY

This chapter has already decribed how BMW wanted to broaden its product range and to increase its relative market share. It sought to become of sufficient size to have a global reach in ten and more years' time.

According to *The Money Programme*:

'When it [BMW] realized that Rover might be for sale, the company realized that it had a once-in-a-lifetime opportunity for a dramatic leap forward.

The BMW–Rover [deal] appeared to solve two problems at once. It [Rover] is brand leader in the profitable four-wheel drive sector which BMW was keen to get into. Rover also had a much improved range of cars and low cost production, and an owner which was desperate to sell.'

	BMW	ROVER
Four-wheel drive	None	Range Rover and Discovery
Large executive	7 series and 850 coupe	None
Middle executive	5 series	Rover 800
Smaller executive	3 series	Rover 600
Medium sized volume car	3 series compact (but limited numbers)	Rover 400 and Rover 200
Small cars	None	Metro and Mini

Figure 8.3 The fit of BMW and Rover Group's product ranges

The complementary fit of BMW and Rover's different product ranges is depicted in Figure 8.3.

The Money Programme continued:

'Rover has made a remarkable recovery from the crisis days of British Leyland. Now its new strategy is taking shape: to charge the same price premium in cars as BMW does in big ones. Rover will be more exclusive and innovative than the mass market competition.'

The *Financial Times* described the deal process (1 February 1994):

'With £800m on the table from BMW, it took the British Aerospace board less than five hours last Thursday to decide that it would quit the car industry and put an end to its five-year relationship with Honda.

Mr George Simpson, Rover's chairman and the man who believed the relationship with Honda to be 'the natural path', was told to take the next flight to Tokyo to face a company which had thought its offer was a fait accompli. Six days earlier Honda had agreed to increase its stake from 20 to 47.5 per cent, pumping £165m into BAe and valuing Rover at £600m – 40 per cent less than the eventual winner.

Honda had started from a seemingly unassailable position, given its 20 per cent stake and its 14-year relationship with Rover. But ultimately, it was BAe's desire to find an exit from its five-year-old investment that proved the key.'

BMW had done a thorough job in stalking Rover:

'BMW's assault started last September, when it identified Rover as a target that would extend its car range and achieve economies of scale in distribution, component sourcing and R&D.

Its initial offer to BAe was repulsed because of Rover's relationship with Honda. Dr Hagen Luderitz, director of corporate planning at BMW, says BMW delivered a letter to Honda chief executive Mr Nobuhiko Kawamoto, stating its interest in Rover. No response was received.

Mr Kiyoshi Ikemi, councillor to Honda's president, denies any direct approach, claiming Honda received only indirect hints of BMW's intentions. "We weren't informed properly until Friday last week", he protested.'

BMW had done its strategic homework on Rover very well. According to the *Financial Times* (1 February 1994):

'Unperturbed by the original rebuff, BMW went ahead with its scrutiny of Rover. Mr Wolfgang Reitzle, BMW's research and development director, unobtrusively visited the UK plants. Back in Germany in test drove the entire fleet. After two months, he was convinced.'

After BMW entered the fray, Honda responded rapidly:

'Having been informed of outside interest in Rover, Honda was under pressure to act. 'If we took a larger percentage, BAe said it would be a clear signal that the rest of the company was not for sale,' said Mr Ikemi.

On January 21, Honda agreed to increase its stake to 47.5 per cent. This offer was also before the BAe board on the Thursday morning.'

But BMW accelerated along the finishing stretch:

'It was a fierce race to the finish. Mr Luderitz admits the speed of the deal limited BMW's ability to perform due diligence, although he was confident the synergies justified the £800m price tag – valuing Rover at £1bn. He delivered the formal offer personally on January 26.

At 9.15 on the following morning, the British Aerospace board of directors sat down to decide. Before them was the prospect of selling a business which was non-core and required substantial capital spending. The BMW offer had a deadline of midnight last night. The BAe board decided it wanted out – and Mr Simpson was sent to Tokyo to see if Honda would make a better offer.'

George Simpson, Rover's chairman was dispatched to Tokyo to see if Honda would make a better offer, but Honda decided that it didn't want control (at a price which beat the BMW offer).

The *Sunday Times* of 6 February 1994 gives an inside account of Simpson's meeting with Nobuhiko Kawamoto, Honda's president, who reacted to the BMW bid terms as follows:

> 'Kawamoto was visibly startled. He protested, insisting that BAe had already agreed to sell Honda an additional 27.5 per cent stake in the Rover operating company, lifting its total to 47.5 per cent. They had a deal.
>
> Simpson shrugged, 'I tried to explain that I was sorry, but Western business had to deal with issues such as shareholder value, that it was extremely difficult to evaluate things like a 15-year partnership and moral commitments, but that when the sums were done the bird in the hand – the £800m – was worth much more than what Honda had offered.'

Mr Kawamoto telephoned George Simpson at his hotel two hours later to say that there would be no deal.

When BMW initially began talks with Rover it offered around £550m (*Sunday Times*, 6 February 1994). But this figure was considerably less than Rover's book value of nearly £1.3m. Initially BMW made formal suggestions to Honda to co-operate in a Rover–BMW deal that would preserve the Honda-Rover link by direct association with BMW. According to the *Sunday Times* (6 February 1994), Mr Kawamoto didn't reply.

According to the *Financial Times*:

> 'They met on Saturday, but with an unequivocal 'no' from Honda, it was a relatively straightforward decision. Neither BAe nor Honda wanted control of the British carmaker. So BMW had won.'

Honda's offer of £167m to move its stake from 20 per cent to 47.5 per cent valued Rover group at about £650m. This was beaten on two counts by a BMW offer in January 1994 of £700m (in price and for total control).

Then, on 16 January 1994, two Rover senior managers flew to Munich to meet BMW to enable BMW to make a full bid for the whole of Rover – for Rover's holding company (and not just the subsidiary, in which Honda had a 20 per cent stake).

'When the offer finally arrived at BAe's London office ... at 5 pm on Wednesday, January 26, it had been raised to £800m – for the holding company. BMW would also take in Rover's average daily debt of £200m and its £700m in off-balance-sheet commitments. ... After February 1 the bid would be withdrawn'. (*Sunday Times*, 6 February 1994)

The core bid value of £800m looks, on the face of it, generous when stacked up against Rover's recent profits track record of pre-tax losses in 1991 and 1992 of around £50m, and a pre-tax profit of over £50m in 1993. But Rover's underlying recovery potential is significant even before BMW's involvement. In 1990, Rover made pre-tax profits of over £60m, from a weaker strategic base. But a price tag of £800m indicates that BMW sees considerable incremental strategic (and ultimately) financial benefits flowing through from Rover.

Even though BMW had out-manoeuvred Honda it still had another hurdle to jump. George Simpson and Bernt Pischetsrieder both saw Tim Sainsbury, the UK industry minister, to press their case. Tim Sainsbury was persuaded on the argument that Rover would be unattractive to private shareholders with the continuing involvement of a minority shareholder Honda, which had control of Rover's engine technology. (This is an interesting example of a strength in one argument being turned into a weakness in another, to positive advantage.)

That BAe got a good price for Rover Group is undeniable. The *Sunday Times* (8 August 1993) foresaw (based on informed industry comment) that Rover would be sold for between £400–500m plus debt, just over half the BMW price tag.

There were, however, always other options for BMW:

'It [BMW] could have continued to go it alone and develop the necessary products itself, but that would have taken time and would have been expensive.

Instead, it has chosen the riskier fast track of acquisition.'

The strategic benefits of the deal are summarized as follows

'● Control of Europe's only credible manufacturer of four-wheel-drive sports/utility vehicles in the shape of Land Rover. Long the jewel in the Rover crown, the Land Rover operates in one of the fastest-growing segments of the world market.
● A viable way of entering the small car market without diluting its own precious brand image.

- Access to a low-cost European production base and control of the European carmaker that has probably learned most in recent years about Japanese production and engineering methods.
- A novel way of developing a presence in some of the fastest-growing auto markets in the Far East and in Latin America, where BMW's traditional products largely price it out of the markets.'

(Financial Times, 1 February 1994)

Although BMW was exploring the possibilities of developing its own four-wheel drive vehicle, this would have taken several years to develop. Rover gave BMW a market leader in four-wheel drive in Land Rover. Land Rover's Discovery had considerable growth potential in the US. As Land Rover did not compete with any BMW products their access to BMW's US dealer network would have considerable synergistic benefits.

Although other car manufacturers would have been very happy to take Land Rover off Rover's (and BAe's) hands, BMW was prepared to take the whole of Rover on. This made it a much more attractive deal to BAe.

BMW was also prepared to invest sufficient funds to replace the 30-year-old Mini, which is a particularly ambitious plan considering the costs of investment against the volume potential of a niche vehicle. This kind of investment delighted Rover's management.

But now BMW and Rover/BAe had agreed a deal the new owners had a new strategic headache – what to do about Honda, its 20 per cent majority shareholder and partner in engine technology? As John Lawson, research director of the consultancy DRI Europe put it:

'All of the major selling models have been based on Honda platforms so Rover has indeed been living off Honda for development resources to a large extent. It would be extraordinarily difficult for them overnight to put those resources back in place'. (The Money Programme)

When asked by a journalist whether Honda's link with Rover would continue after present agreements had expired, Toshio Ishino, managing director of Honda UK, responded brusquely:

'No, I don't think so. After our present agreement continues which we support ... but after that nothing.

We have certain agreements for the supply of engines for some models, and as far as that agreement continues we co-operate, but once the period [is] finished, we won't continue any more.' (The Money Programme)

And when asked if the ultimate ending of the Honda relationship would be a great loss, John Towers, Rover Group's chief executive said: 'I think it would be a shame. I think it would be a shame for them and a shame for us as well.'

Rover is clearly disappointed at Honda's reluctance to look at the commercial and strategic upsides to an ongoing link with Honda. It must be a very difficult and emotive topic between the two companies, given their very close links. For instance, Roland Bertodo, Rover's director of strategic planning, told me in 1991: 'I am not sure whether I am living or working in Coventry or Japan or somewhere continually between the two.'

Honda had put its strategic commitment into Rover and clearly felt let down by this turn of events. But perhaps Honda might have thought harder about how BAe's corporate psychology and intent had changed since the departure of its former chairman and its weakened financial position.

According to *The Money Programme*:

'Rover shouldn't have a problem with its large cars like the 600 and 800. BMW can provide platforms for this in future. Honda is helping replace the medium-range 200 and 400 which will start to appear next year. Its most urgent problem is how to replace its smaller vehicles, the Metro and Mini.

Now the company has confirmed its plans for a radical replacement Mini, all Rover needs is the go-ahead from its parent.

The new Mini will be a luxurious fashion item. To develop such a car would be an enormous and costly gamble for BMW, with a very uncertain pay-off.'

But Rover still has considerable problems. Being acquired by BMW does not suddenly make Rover a quantum amount larger overnight. John Lawson of DRI says:

'I think in the volume area of the car market, the price of entry is high and is becoming higher. To produce a class-leading product a billion pounds is the sort of entry figure you have to pay. And it is extraordinarily difficult to justify that if you are only turning over 100,000–150,000 units a year.'

In addition, BMW has the problem of strengthening Rover's distribution channels, particularly in continental Europe. Rover's market share, for example, in three European countries is:

- Portugal   4.1 per cent
- France   2.4 per cent
- Germany   0.3 per cent

(Source: *The Money Programme*)

It would be tempting to let Rover into BMW's existing dealers. But as Mr Pischetsrieder says:

> 'We almost certainly could sell overnight in countries, even in Germany, many more Rover cars, many more Land Rover cars, by opening the BMW network and BMW showrooms to Rover cars. But I think that you have to resist the temptation to have a better business today **when you know for sure you will harm your longer term business**.' (Author's emphasis) (*The Money Programme*)

At least the top end of the Rover car range is now positioned in similar niches to BMW. It is therefore conceivable that some BMW buyers might switch to Rover if cars sit side by side in the same dealership. Clearly BMW would not wish to cannibalize its existing sales. Also BMW management might feel (rightly or wrongly) that the Rover range is just not up to BMW standards.

Nevertheless, a key dilemma still remains longer term. Even with a separate dealer network, should BMW seek explicitly to link Rover's brand to BMW's brand, some BMW buyers might defect to Rover. This assumes Rover cars have parity of quality and are positioned slightly cheaper than BMW. You don't have to physically see the two cars sitting side by side in a dealership to make the mental comparison.

Figure 8.4 shows the possible flows of value which are being discussed. This shows the value of the BMW brand cascading to further reposition Rover. There is also a possibility that associating the brands dilutes BMW's own premium. Given the stretched nature of Rover's products (from the 800 to the Mini) this is a significant threat. In particular, even the rebadged Metro (now the Rover 100) seems to hold little in common with the BMW 7- series.

It is also possible to see the threat of value destroyed by potential cannibalization of BMW sales by Rover. (However small, this would no doubt be regarded as serious.) According to *The Times* (8 April 1994), only 3 per cent of BMW customers would consider buying a Rover, and a wider percentage vice versa – but one might question such low figures, as does the *Sunday Times* (29 January 1995).

Also, the possible gains to BMW through acquiring the learning, indirectly, from Honda technology and approaches to quality now well-bedded in at Rover can be seen. Finally, there is the potential value added by

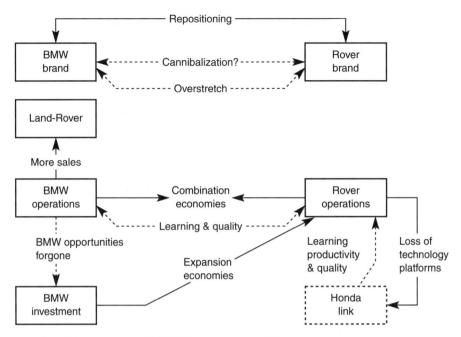

Fig. 8.4 Value streams of BMW's acquisition of Rover

greater economics of scale from rationalizing certain operations and sourcing in the enlarged group. There is also the value added in expanding
Rover's operations by BMW's investment. But this needs to be offset
against the value destroyed by perhaps neglecting other organic opportunities which BMW might otherwise have pursued. Not only do investment
funds need to be reckoned in here, but also the time spent by BMW managers in making sure that Rover 'comes up to scratch'. Figure 8.4 also
highlighted the synergies between selling Land Rover's Discovery through
BMW's US dealer network.

Finally, Figure 8.4 shows the loss of the Honda technology platform.
Although existing Honda supply agreements continue, giving BMW and
Rover some breathing space, the time will soon come around when Rover
has to recover its fuller independence, alongside support from BMW.

Honda's adverse reaction to BMW's involvement is also something of a
loss to BMW. Although BMW would no doubt not have wanted to have
fallen into the trap of an unequal alliance with Honda, Honda might nevertheless have served as a very suitable longer term partner (having a low
cost base). Instead of creating a friend BMW might have increased
Honda's hostility. Indeed, one of my sharper MBA students recently took
an extreme but nevertheless interesting view:

'I think Honda will never let BMW forget what they did with Rover. I think that Honda will have long memories and will take any opportunity (even if it costs them) to create disturbances for BMW in the very long term.'

Returning now to the issue of Rover's distribution network, BMW is apparently planning a separate distribution network for Rover.

'So Rover's German owners are contemplating some very expensive options, a new worldwide dealer network on top of the cost of developing cars in Britain. The stakes are high. Mr Pischetsrieder has effectively gambled the reputation of both companies on the outcome. True to BMW's style, he is playing for the long term'. (*The Money Programme*)

Not only has BMW played for the long term in its plans for Rover's dealer network, but it has also done the same for Rover's product range. For instance, Rover's 800 series is the more elderly in Rover's executive product line. The 800 series would therefore be the 'most obvious' to replace before the 600. But BMW has resisted this move and plans to replace the 600 series first. Mr Pischestrieder says:

'The father of 90 per cent of mistakes is the urgency to take decisions. And we will again resist the temptation to take an obvious decision just for the sake of being obvious – BMW, as a corporation, I think, was so successful in the past because we never decided the obvious ...

   BMW's success [in the past] always was that we resisted the temptation for short-term success for the sake of longer term success.' (*The Money Programme*)

And according to the *Sunday Times*:

'The logic of this move is that BMW feels that despite its UK success, the 600 is not yet a product which is fitting the BMW stable. BMW believes that it will need to further strengthen the 600 as a basis for launching a truly world-class executive car at the 800 series level. The relaunched 600 would then serve as a migration platform for aspiring executives who would then move on to the 800'. (*Sunday Times*, 16 October 1994)

There may be another reason why BMW might have opted to relaunch Rover's 600 series first. As was shown earlier, the agreement with Honda prevents Rover from selling the 600 in the US. Perhaps if BMW substitutes the Honda technology then this would open up the US market to the 600.

POST-ACQUISITION MANAGEMENT

This analysis of both companies' strategic positions and the deal already highlights a number of post-acquisition management issues including the following.

- **Brand management:** to what extent would the two brands become closely associated, and over what time scale?
- **Product development:** what existing models would be given priority for development and with what targeted positioning in the market? Also, what new models were to be developed to extend Rover's product range without resulting in proliferation?
- **Technology and design:** how to substitute the Honda technology and over what time scale? In the interim the Honda relationship still needed to be managed to avoid operational disruption and destruction, commercial or legal disputes. (Honda had, by February 1994, already sought to renegotiate its contracts with Rover.) These annual contracts are worth £400m per annum (*The Times*, 18 March 1994, which claims that if Honda put up the price ... then the cost to Rover could be enormous). In fact, in late 1994 Rover announced a £25m expansion of its design centre in Warwickshire. Rover was at pains to go on the record as having a 'complete capability to design both cars and four-wheel drive in the UK which was unaffected by the Group's being taken over by BMW'. (*Financial Times*, 1 December 1994)
- **Distribution:** BMW planned to integrated both companies' logistics networks. Accordingly it also planned to open parallel but separate showrooms for Rover cars, for example in Germany. (The question that obviously surfaces is 'Will this work' – in keeping the brands separate?) According to *The Times* (18 March 1994) BMW is hoping that Rover's sales in Germany will jump from around 12,000 in 1993 to around 100,000 annually.
- **Operations:** it can be assumed that BMW cars are unlikely to be made by Rover, at least in the foreseeable future. (But this is perhaps an option – could BMW market cars made by Rover if their quality was sufficiently assured?) What is undeniable is that potentially Rover has major potential for capacity expansion. According to the *Financial Times* (13 August 1993) both Longbridge and Cowley plants could produce a million units per annum (twice current capacity).
- **Organization:** it is unlikely that Rover will need to undergo major restructuring in its structure (other than in its logistics). The issue of Rover's design capability poses questions about "Who will do what?" in the big task of product redesign.

- **Culture:** this is inevitably a big issue. Rover has developed considerably as a flexible, lean organization over the past five to ten years. It is proud of its independence and recent achievements. BMW no doubt believes that it has the recipes for achieving and sustaining world-class quality. Could this result in a culture clash? And, if so, what would be the outcomes?

Post-acquisition management therefore poses major challenges for the combined BMW–Rover Group. It is also conceivable that some of the potential value created by the deal could be destroyed during the post-acquisition phase. This is even considering that given their strategic options available to Rover, certainly at top level, the BMW bid must be seen as 'sent from heaven'. But down at the level of the design teams, for instance, it could have been seen as an entirely different story.

According to the *Financial Times* (22 February 1994):

'BMW's Chairman has indicated that BMW will be more than willing to place some of BMW's own designers at Rover's disposal ... "600 BMW engineers? – I don't know what we'd do with them", said one Rover executive, "we are fully capable of seeing through our new car projects."'[4]

Besides the culture issues, extricating Rover from Honda could be very costly. *The Times* (18 March 1994) puts it neatly:

'As one analyst put it in Geneva [the Motor Show], "They [Honda and Rover] are like an old married couple trying to decide who gets custody of the Beatles albums and how much maintenance payments will be."'

OVERALL EVALUATION OF THE STRATEGY

Revisiting the overall strategy of BMW's acquisition of Rover, using the STAIR tool, reveals the following.

- **S for Simple, clear strategy.** Overall, although some of the fundamentals of the strategy are simple, there are several complexities. But overall BMW's strategy seems to have a coherence and logic to it.
- **T for Timing.** The timing of the strategy was extremely opportune. Not only was Rover 'available' but also, other than Honda and Mercedes, no other company was in a good position to enter the fray. BMW was therefore able to acquire Rover without substantial overpayment. Also,

Rover's UK sales had recovered from their recessionary low, and in the first half of 1994 reported a rise of sales of 16 per cent and production up 22 per cent.

- **A for Advantage (internal and external).** The advantages of the deal (internal and external) were on the whole tangible and positive. Internally there were a number of areas of competitive and operational leverage which generated value (see Figure 8.4 again). Externally, it is harder to see that BMW has bought into a market niche which is inherently attractive, given the increasing competitive rivalry in both executive and smaller car segments (this point is amplified below).

- **I for Implementation.** BMW's implementation plans seem to be well thought through – as far as the tangible aspects of post-acquisition management goes. However, whether BMW has given as much thought in approaching some of the softer, organizational and culture issues remains to be seen. So the jury is out as to whether BMW passes this element of the STAIR test. (Already Rover's European head of marketing has been 'poached' by Audi.)

- **R for Resources.** BMW currently appears to have enough resources to support Rover's considerable requirements. But by making this move BMW effectively opens up a second battle front precisely at the time when its own products are coming under increasingly fierce competitive attack. Should BMW's financial revenues in its core business be eroded, say around 1996–8, then what seemed once ample resources may evaporate.

In terms of external and internal attractiveness (see the third bullet point above), some further analysis of Rover's product portfolio is required.

Figure 8.5 uses the GE grid to analyse Rover's product/market niches. Both the 600 and 700 series are shown as being pushed to the right due to advancing competitive position. The 800 series is now (but only just) market leader in UK executive cars. Also, as the executive car market declines in attractiveness the 700 series moves downwards (as well as to the right).

By contrast, the Rover 400, 200 and Metro niches become very marginally more attractive (due to the assumed trend by customers to fewer smaller cars). The Metro and Mini are not seen as competitively strong, and the Mini in particular is deputed (without new investment) as being dangerously close to the brink.

The overall portfolio is not strong. Some readers and commentators might quibble with these assumptions but it would be hard to deny that Rover's model range needs considerable further strengthening.

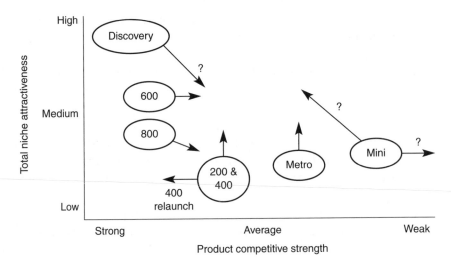

Note: these positionings and shifts are pre-BMW's development plans and also pre any major new organic investment by Rover.

Fig. 8.5 Rover group's product/market niches 'As is'

The obvious jewel in the crown is the four-wheel drive Discovery. It has a very strong competitive position and is focused on a fast-growing market segment. But two factors make one nervous about the niche attractiveness. First, competitive rivalry is increasing rapidly. Although currently this can be healthy – as the Discovery often captures customers who, having tried substitute four-wheel drive vehicles, now want to have a go at 'the real thing'. This, according to the *Financial Times*, 13 July 1994, can amount to 50 per cent of customers. However, as other vehicles improve this transfer factor is likely to diminish.

Offsetting these factors is clearly the success of the Discovery marque. In 1994 its price range was £19,000 to £28,000 allowing for trade-ups from the volume market while retaining its differentiation premium.

The success of four-wheel drive vehicles has been put down to their:

- high status image;
- flexibility as people carriers and for luggage;
- towing capacity;
- commanding driving position and road view.

Also, should the key growth drivers become neutral or reverse, this could easily compress market growth. Here are some possibilities.

- The interest in four-wheel drive may fall away (like the once popular, 'hot' and high-performance hatchbacks). There is clearly a strong element of fashion driving this niche. As the *Financial Times* (13 July 1994) puts it, 'measured by many conventional motoring criteria, the success of "lifestyle" four-wheel drive vehicles, defies logic'. The majority of four-wheel drive vehicles hardly ever see much duty off-the-road so a good deal of the need is psychological. As one commentator put it, 'what is the point of taking your 4WD up a mountain where no one will see it and when your friends are in the shopping mall?'

- Four-wheel drive vehicles like the Discovery have the image of safety (which is increasingly prominent in customers' minds). However, recent stories of four-wheel drive vehicles overturning at speed (with unpleasant effects for their occupants) cannot help but suggest that they do carry additional risks. These scare stories do not have to be true to have an effect, and even though recent official investigations suggest there is no real problem it is possible that perceptions of safety have been marred.

- These vehicles are typically significantly more thirsty than the average car on fuel. Should the price of fuel increase substantially in real terms (as it is predicted to do, for instance in the UK, due to green and fiscal reasons), then the enthusiasm of drivers might be eroded.

As a substantial part of Rover's current profits are reputed to be earned by the Discovery alone, then these issues are very important value drivers of the acquisition. Clearly BMW is banking on the growth-drivers winning out – as penetration of Europe is only 2.5 per cent (compared to 10 per cent in the US) there is still a belief that growth will win out.

Another useful way of analysing BMW's acquisition strategy of Rover is to examine some of the key assumptions which underpinned the strategy. Using the 'uncertainty/importance grid' BMW's likely perceptions (as can be best inferred from the story) can be contrasted with those which emerge from this analysis.

Figure 8.6 considers BMW's perceptions. This highlights the prospects for the Discovery being strong, being a very important but relatively important assumption. My own perceptions (Figure 8.7) are that this assumption is also relatively uncertain.

Figure 8.6 also suggests that BMW perceived Honda to be relatively acquiescent as a reasonably important assumption but one which is not acutely uncertain. By contrast, this assumption is seen as both very important and very uncertain.

The assumption that BMW and Rover cultures will fit similarly heads east – this assumption is viewed as considerably more important. Also, the assumption that Rover won't eat significantly into BMW's own sales heads

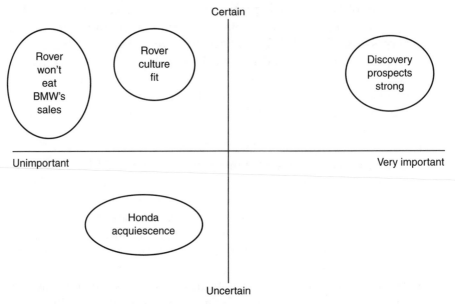

* As best inferred from publicly–available data.

Fig. 8.6 The Rover deal – analysing key assumptions BMW's perceptions*

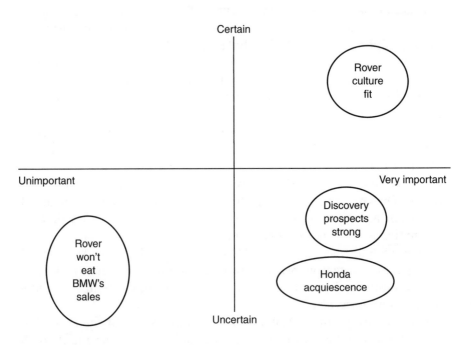

Fig. 8.7 Author's own perceptions – assumptions on the Rover deal

south (as being more uncertain). Arguably one could view this, too, as being even more important.

So, what does the uncertainty/importance grid reveal in this particular case? It shows that the strategy is significantly more risky than appears on the surface. Also, remember that four particularly interesting assumptions have just been picked. A fuller analysis might reveal even more rocks beneath the shoreline.

It is apt to conclude with *The Money Programme's* summary of BMW's strategy for international development:

> 'BMW is now embarked on an uncertain road into uncharted terri-
> tory. The standard is being set by its rivals in quality and design are
> getting higher all the time. The company will need all of its proven
> skills – and many new ones – to transform itself from European spe-
> cialist into world-wide success.'

The initial signs in mid 1995 are that BMW's post-acquisition strategy for Rover is wobbling. Although Rover's sales of four-wheeled drive vehicles are very strong, its other cars are experiencing lower sales. Although this is due in part to pending model launches a first half fall in sales of 12% over-all (the *Sunday Times*, 16 July 1995) is still worrying.

LESSONS FROM THE CASE

The BMW–Rover case is replete with lessons on managing strategic development internationally, as follows:

- organic development;
- managing alliances;
- acquisitive development;
- international development.

Organic development – key lessons

- Having a very clear and deliberate strategy can pay considerable div-
  idends. This was evidenced both by the impressive success of BMW's
  focused, differentiation strategy and also by the turnover of Rover
  through a similar strategy supported by the enabling competencies
  of Honda.

- The product range of any company needs to be managed as a 'strategic project set' (see again Chapter 4). In the car industry in particular it is critical to have a consistent and customer-relevant theme across the model range in order to define the brand. Although individual models can be appraised to some degree incrementally, nevertheless a lot of the value added is dependent upon interdependencies.
- There are invariably organic alternatives to acquisitive development (and vice versa) unless the acquisition is principally concerned with financial re-engineering. But managers tend to operate according to either an organic development mindset or an acquisitive development mindset.
- Unless a really deep and detailed strategic appraisal is performed, organic development programmes may fail to surface as the iceberg of all key longer term needs. And, unless this iceberg is surfaced in full, it will be the most observable, immediate and most 'politically hot' projects which are approved, at the expense of other needs.

Managing alliances

- Strategic alliances are invariably enticing as they often promise high strategic and financial pay-offs, with apparently low investment and risk (Lorange and Roos, 1992). But in reality they are more frequently 'lobster pot strategies' – easy to get into but hard and expensive to get out of. The benefits are easily eroded or destroyed by conflicts between the partners and/or competitive pressure.
- Strategic alliances can lead on into acquisition. Indeed, if they don't, then that is what leads to the destruction of value. In the BMW and Rover case, probably both Rover and Honda lost out through the failure to consummate an acquisition follow-through.

Acquisitive development

- The strategic appraisal of any acquisition target requires a clear and detailed appreciation of what will happen during post-acquisition management, how it will happen and with what likely results. This means not just analysing the acquisition target as is, but also in terms of how it will change and develop post-acquisition. This means thinking through what the difficulties will be and how these will be overcome.
- Once again, the financial appraisal of an acquisition requires a careful assessment of the value inherent in the target's existing competitive strategy (V1), the value obtained by a favourable deal

(V2) and the value added through effective integration. The BMW–Rover case showed that V1 was suspect (as Rover lacked significant competitive strength 'as is'), the deal price was a relatively full one given the considerably further investment required in Rover's product range (V2). Also, V3 – the value added or destroyed during post-acquisition management – could easily turn negative. All in all, this suggested that despite its attractions on the surface (witness the exuberant press comment), the deal could easily be overall of marginal longer term benefit financially.

- In the rush to snatch power from underneath Honda's nose, one wonders whether the 'thrill of the chase' (Jemison and Sitkin, 1986) didn't take over. Did the race to complete a deal obscure the apparently minor imperfections to the strategy which might later result in disappointment and contention?

International development

- When there is increased competitive pressure internationally, the urge to achieve a bigger mass intensifies. While this may be part-rational, it is often frequently intermingled with a defensive instinct. The BMW acquisition of Rover thus seems to be at least partially motivated by the instinct to protect. However, this may not be effective. If your castle is under attack, it may not be sensible to build an extension.
- Production and design economies of scale clearly push an industry in the direction of globalization. However, differences in regional consumer tastes inhibit standardization across markets. Does BMW really need to be a 'globally spread player' or is it sufficient to have very strong penetration of selected markets (especially Europe and the US)?
- If BMW is right and does need to become truly 'more global', then probably Rover is the wrong vehicle to achieve that goal. Apart from the Discovery, Rover's models and distribution are not strong outside the UK.

The lessons of the case study all highlight the need for international development to steer clear of bold, too broad strategic moves. International development requires a degree of strategic pickiness which is more commonly sought in the more mundane, domestic front.

To conclude, think about the following key questions for your own organization.

Exercise

- What key similarities does the case study have with your own business, for instance in terms of:
  - product/market development;
  - capability development;
  - strategic focus;
  - type of strategy (deliberate, emergent, etc.);
  - acquisition targeting and evaluation;
  - acquisition deal-making;
  - post-acquisition management;
  - strategic allowances;
  - managing the strategic development process.
- What specific lessons can you draw about areas of strategies for growth which:
  - if you were to go back in time you would now do differently;
  - you may need to rethink present plans;
  - may have an impact in the future?

ACTION CHECKLIST

- Where you have entered into an alliance, what not so obvious competitive disadvantages may result, especially in the long run?

- Using the GE grid, where are your individual (major) products or product groupings positioned?

- What investment is required simply to sustain this position?

- Where you have products in the far north-west of the GE grid, how can you keep them there and what is the long-term basis of their Total Market Attractiveness?

- Where you have an 'international strategy' what does this actually mean (and not mean), and does this strategy always deliver sustainable financial value?

- Given your total organic, acquisitive (and possibly international) growth ambitions, does the whole strategy simply require too much effort – and all at once – to be achievable?

[1] Reprinted with kind permission of the Money Programme.

[2] Reprinted with kind permission of the *Financial Times*.

[3] Reprinted with kind permission of Times Newspapers © Times Newspapers/Supplements Limited.

[4] Reprinted with kind permission of Times Newspapers Limited from 'BMW turns the ignition on a new era for Rover' by Kevin Eason © Times Newspapers/Supplements Limited 18.03.94.

*'Cost – the land that strategy
forgot'*

9

REACHING FOR VALUE – STRATEGIC COST MANAGEMENT

INTRODUCTION

In Chapter 4 I argued that strategic and financial analysis should be very closely integrated. This chapter focuses on cost management which offers opportunities for achieving both internally and externally led breakthrough.

Although cost management is very much a traditional concern of finance, it does seem to be 'the Land that Strategy Forgot' (Grundy, 1992a). Perhaps strategists have found more interesting and larger things to concentrate on. Yet much of what counts as 'strategy' materializes in practice through the allocation of budgetary resources. Most practising managers would recognize this simply as cost management, but in reality many areas of cost have major longer term and external competitive benefit.

The idea of 'strategic cost management' was born simultaneously on both sides of the Atlantic, In the US, Shank and Govindarajan (1993) presented a framework which integrates:

- value chain analysis;
- strategic positioning analysis;
- cost driver analysis.

This framework is content-led, consisting of a variety of tools from strategic, financial and operational disciplines.

Strategic cost management (SCM) has also been developed as a tool in parallel in the UK at Cranfield School of Management. It has been applied (in varying forms) in a number of major companies including the Prudential (Grundy, 1993a) and at Mercury Communications (Grundy, 1994a). Not surprisingly, many of the tools in the US version appear in the UK. However, much more emphasis is placed at Cranfield on implementing strategic cost management as an organizational change and learning process. It is feared that full-blown SCM, US-style, would be difficult for managers virgin to SCM concepts to assimilate. What is therefore presented in this chapter is a perhaps simplified framework for SCM which is closely married to a feasible process of implementation.

In this chapter I argue that cost management needs to be managed strategically for both financial and competitive advantage (or 'FCA'). Much of the chapter therefore gives practical guidance on how to apply strategic cost management but it is useful to begin by exploring different theoretical perspectives to the issue of cost management.

WHAT IS STRATEGIC COST MANAGEMENT?

Strategic cost management is about managing costs for both financial and competitive advantage, longer term as well as short term. To achieve these objectives a number of things need to be done simultaneously:

- Manage costs for improved financial performance – balancing longer term against shorter term priorities;
- achieve this by adding to, rather than subtracting from, the business strategy;
- make explicit and continuing trade-offs between costs against value added – both externally and internally;
- prioritize expenditure against agreed, complementary, strategic and financial criteria;
- identify, understand and manage key cost drivers.

Some of the elements of strategic cost management are old and some are much newer. For instance, the problem of balancing longer term against shorter term priorities is a very old one. But explicitly linking to the business strategy and the competitive context in which value is created is newer still. The fundamental difference is that strategic cost management provides a disciplined and coherent framework for managing the cost process in a strategic rather than in a purely tactical manner. This process is inseparable from that of managing organizational change. It involves managing the cost base in a way which is competitively targeted and benchmarked. It also involves appraising and minimizing the costs associated with strategic change.

In order to manage costs in the round it is necessary to explore a number of quite different but often complementary perspectives on cost.

WHAT DIFFERENT PERSPECTIVES ON COST EXIST?

This section gives an overview of perspectives on cost which they are then related to the strategic cost management process. They will be dealt with as follows:

- strategic management;
- financial management;
- operations management;
- organizational behaviour.

Strategic management

Cost is rarely mentioned by strategic thinkers as being a key issue (with a small number of exceptions). These exceptions are however, important, as taken together they help build a framework for strategic cost management. A number of key strategic notions are helpful, namely:

- the experience curve;
- cost leadership strategies;
- competitor analysis;
- differentiation strategies;
- the value chain;
- capability building;
- environmental shifts and scenarios.

The experience curve

First, cost plays a role in the experience curve – which extrapolates the effect of learning experiences and physical economies of scale. The experience curve works as follows: as an organization produces a particular product or service in greater and greater volumes, its unit costs tend to fall. In some industries, particularly where the end product or service is complex, and/or the process of production and delivery, this decline in costs can be dramatic.

In some industries the fall in costs can be so steep as to present a straight line over time against a log scale (see Figure 9.1). For non-mathematicians this means that the costs fall over time. This rate of decline of costs occurs disproportionately over time in proportion to cumulative volume. The caveat here is that volume is not achieved at the expense of adding complexity – invariably dramatic cost reduction is achieved at least in part by simplification – of product, of process or of both.

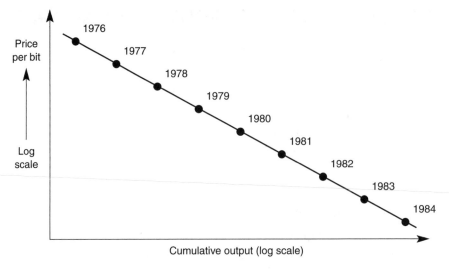

Source: Building on the Experience Curve, Pankaj Ghemawat, *HBR*, March/April 1985.

Fig. 9.1 Experience curve – example dynamic rams

The reduction in costs relative to cumulative volume can be dramatic, for instance when dealing with IT or telecommunications hardware. For instance, recently the price of a modem virtually halved in the UK in just over one year mainly due to experience curve effects.

Experience curve effects can be of vital strategic significance. If a company is able to achieve a high relative market share early on in the development of a product or market then it can drive down its costs using the experience curve effect. This can be achieved by attaining a cumulative volume far in excess of its nearest competitor. Should an early lead therefore be established, then the benefits in terms of both competitive and financial advantage are also cumulative over time.

Despite early airings of the experience curve phenomenon in strategy theory, this effect is often underplayed largely because most industries lack such dramatic gains to scale as were seen in the IT or telecommunications industry (Ghemawat, 1985). However, it is still possible to achieve a creeping reduction in cost through a much more gradual but nevertheless real experience curve.

The gains in less technology-intensive industries are not so easily and precisely measurable. However, even in service industries, like professional services, there can still be pronounced experience curve effects. The experience curve effect can therefore still play a major role in facilitating breakthrough strategies for growth both by enabling price to become lower (stimulating demand) and also by reducing costs.

For example, in the UK the accounting profession is currently dominated by a small number of very large players. Each of these players has a relatively 'full range' of products and services, from audit and tax and corporate finance (traditionally their core businesses), through to information and management consultancy, and also a range of more exotic, specialist services.

During the late 1980s and very early 1990s the mid-sized players and bottom three of 'the top ten' UK accounting firms sought to expand their management consulting practices. The 1990–2 recession virtually wiped out these mid-range players who struggled to sustain small volumes of consulting work across a fairly wide range of consulting services (see again Chapter 3).

Meanwhile, the more successful of the bigger firms were able to achieve profit through dominating specific product/service niches. This enabled these bigger players to:

- reduce initial marketing and sales costs;
- achieve much greater operational efficiencies ;
- secure more referred or follow-on work, again reducing both marketing/sales costs and time spent by consultants in between projects;
- add more value in the same time, or the same value with less time, and cost – relative to the mid-range players.

These bigger firms thus achieved a virtuous cycle compared to their weaker competitors.

Although perhaps few of these firms explicitly saw cost base as a competitive weapon, by 1993–4 (and after a shake-out of around 25 per cent of staff in some of these firms, according to some sources), cost levels were very much seen as a crucial, competitive weapon.

The lessons from this example are that:

- cost levels tend to increase when there is a proliferation of business activities relative to business size;
- during periods of major industry and competitive change, cost levels which were supportable at one time may now threaten to sink the company – this situation can crystallize very rapidly;
- larger firms may carry more substantial overheads, but they may be better placed to drive down unit costs through product/service specialization, or by achieving high relative market shares, and thus reaping the benefits of the learning curve and sheer economies of scale.

The impact of the experience curve needs to be evaluated on a case-by-case basis. Shank and Govindarajan (1993) rightly point out that managers often make decisions to expand product line or volume which assume easy-to-reap economies of scale. Often the incremental profits (and cash flow) are elusive because this incremental business is not truly profitable.

This may be because of inappropriate cost allocations through fixed or semi-fixed costs rising to sustain additional activity, or because of distraction effects. So there are some major riders to the experience curve in pursuing SCM – managers should not delude themselves that higher volume and relative market share necessarily yields lower cost relative to competitors.

Shank and Govindarajan's critique underscores the need to dissect the impact of marginal business. This needs to be achieved by unravelling the complex internal and external interdependencies which are not always self-evident when evaluating a project on a strictly incremental basis.

Cost leadership and cost management

A discussion of the experience curve leads on naturally to the topic of cost leadership. According to Michael Porter (1985), cost leadership is achieved only when a company has the lowest cost position in a particular industry. This does not necessarily mean that the cost leader has the lowest price (although low price and low cost are often closely associated in practice). This test of being the lowest cost player is a strenuous one. In practice, where an industry is made up of a number of fragmented groups of players (for instance in retailing) it is often better to define cost leadership relative to a group of competitors (or 'strategic group').

Being able to achieve the lowest cost position in an entire industry is contingent upon customers being relatively uniform in terms of their buying expectations and needs. For example, in the UK motor insurance market most customers are indifferent as to whom they buy insurance from – what matters most to them is price. This means that the 'blue-chip', traditional players were not well protected against a new, low-cost player. Indeed a cost leader – Direct Line – has now become market leader in the UK. Direct Line achieved this position in a very short period of time. In effect, Direct Line has reconfigured the industry value chain, achieving breakthrough growth while simultaneously delivering financial value.

In this case it is much easier to define the cost leader than it is in a much more fragmented industry – like management consulting – where there may be a number of 'cost leaders' operating in different strategic groups.

Differentiation and cost management

The next kind of generic strategy of relevance to cost management is differentiation. Differentiation involves adding more real or perceived value to target customers relative to competitors – with costs slightly higher or on a par with key competitors.

Where competitive rivalry has increased substantially (for instance in a maturing industry), companies are saddled with the challenge, however, of both improving service and value, and reducing costs. Strategies to sustain advantage through differentiation need to be underpinned by strong cost management.

Frequently the process of ongoing reduction in the cost base is managed in part by publishing targeted reductions in the cost base for several years, rolling into the future. While possibly unsettling to many managers, this at least creates a climate and awareness of challenging cost. But rolling cost reductions do need competitive justification. Also they need to be made without subtracting from the business (and competitive strategy).

This example also highlights that cost programmes should be managed as a central part of any strategic change process – otherwise they will damage organizational capability.

As has already been said, with a differentiation strategy the core value of the superior product or service should be delivered at a cost not substantially out of line with competitors – this is a message worth enforcing. Additional costs over and above those of competitors are then tolerated and, indeed, are selectively encouraged if and only if they add disproportionate value to customers. This incremental value must then be harvested through premium price or additional volume, or both.

This suggests that the successful differentiator needs to achieve a high value/cost leverage for the more discretionary areas of cost, particularly those associated with service and product performance. Where brand is an important means of achieving competitive advantage, a successful differentiator may also require a high relative market share to gain sufficient value/cost leverage for its advertising and promotional spend (A&P).

Few companies are in the happy situation of managing cost to achieve both differentiated and low cost at the same time. Practice appears to follow theory (Porter, 1985) by and large – but with some exceptions. Revisiting the Marks & Spencer case (where SCM is applied intuitively as can be inferred purely from publicly available data), a twin strategy is at work.

Because of a tighter product line focus than many of its competitors, and because of its absolute market share, Marks & Spencer also achieves low cost through its restricted range of high volume products. It has also controlled its costs (as shown in earlier chapters) by very close links with its suppliers.

But another major point is that the style of cost management adopted by M&S is of crucial importance to its (successful) business strategies within M&S. Costs are challenged continually through each and every aspect of the series of linked activities through which M&S adds value.

In conclusion, Marks & Spencer highlights that costs do need to be strategically targeted and controlled, particularly in a very competitive and challenging environment, like the UK retail industry.

Competitor analysis

Another key input from strategic management is that of competitor analysis. This can yield very powerful insights about relative cost levels. For example, at Dowty Case Communications (for full case, see Grundy, 1993a) competitor analysis revealed that rivals were deploying much heavier sales teams on key accounts. Although at first sight this seemed to be more expensive, in fact sales costs relative to sales revenues at Dowty were higher because their hit rate was actually lower.

The value chain

Strategic cost management can also help identify 'What business are we in?', but to do this the notion of the 'value chain' must first be explored.

The value chain helps companies define where and how they add value, for instance in:

- procurement;
- logistics;
- manufacture;
- marketing;
- personnel, finance and administration support.

The value chain is one way of exploring 'What business(es) are we in?' and also what business(es) we should be in – from the inside out. It should be distinguished quite clearly from the more simplistic notion of 'added value'. The value chain involves analysing the company's value chain, and its existing and potential fit with the value chains of both customers and suppliers. As Shank and Govindarajan (1993) highlight, the notion of the value chain is superior because, unlike 'value added', it doesn't just stop on delivery to the customer. Equally, it doesn't just begin on delivery from the supplier. SCM must consider not merely the impact of some cost option internally, but also externally, within the customer's value chain.

A linked point is that the balance of competitive power in the industry value chain is also important. A firm may invest very heavily in the quality of its service, adding value to the customer, but may fail because of limited bargaining power to harvest this value through any price premium.

Porter's value chain is thus a first, albeit crude, step along the journey of identifying key business processes. Bundles of these processes can be

viewed as mini-business units in their own right. For instance, a data processing centre might sell its services externally, becoming an external profit
centre for a distribution or retail company.

The value chain can be used to analyse each key business process or
function to try to gain greater leverage of value over cost. For instance, at
ICL the company's overall competitive strategy was aimed at differentiation. Yet an increasing competitive market forced ICL to look at ways of
managing certain areas of cost more effectively. In a more detailed case
elsewhere (Grundy, 1993a), I describe how ICL logistics in the UK
redesigned its distribution activities using a zero-based approach. This led
to a plan to halve logistics unit costs in the UK.

The value chain is an unquestioningly important tool within SCM,
affording a variety of comparisons – with customers, suppliers, competitors, distributors (see Figure 9.2). Figure 9.2 highlights that value chain
analysis must be used on both external and internal analysis – it is not
simply an internal analysis tool. However, within the SCM process it is
important not to overburden managers with too much value chain analysis
too soon, as they will produce learning overload.

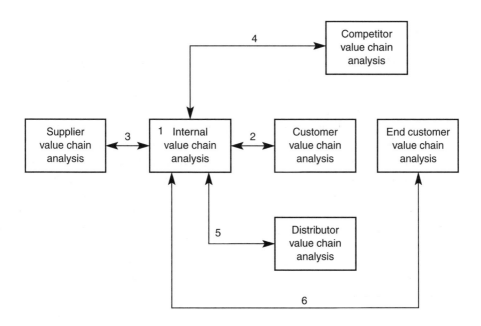

Note: each arrow shows a possible value chain analysis. Number one is in fact internal value
chain analysis. In total, six possible comparisons exist. Depending on the situation, different
value chain comparisons are more appropriate.

Fig. 9.2 Six possible value chain analyses

Capability building

Quite often businesses find it essential to build up a key capability (like information services, distribution or R&D) and find it hard to cost justify this capability. This may suggest that the company might offer its services as a mini-business to other companies in its own right. Or, there may be a case for re-examining this business function or process to see whether it is so crucial for longer term competitive advantage and, if this is questionable, whether there is a case for subcontracting out.

Finally, where it is inherently costly to support a particular business unit, then this may shift its inherent financial attractiveness. This shift can come about as a result of government regulation, environmental (green) pressures or simply shifts in customer expectations. Sometimes internal cost analysis may suggest that divestment or run-down strategic options need to be contemplated. For example, in the early 1990s parts of ICI's business were severely threatened by increased regulatory and environmental pressure. This shifted the cost base of some businesses so that it became hard to justify both new and existing investment. ICI has subsequently divested itself of or restructured many of the business units affected by this shift.

Scenario development

A way of helping identify impacts of environmental change is scenario development. This can be used not merely to look at the impact of changes in industry conditions but also to picture the impact of shifts in competitive rivalry and thus on the cost base of players. Finally, this can also be used to shape organizational scenarios which might paint the broad shape, structure and style to deliver the cost levels, quality and flexibility to meet future competitive challenge. (This is not a particularly difficult exercise and can be accomplished through a half-day to one-day workshop – see Grundy, 1994a.)

So, cost should and often does play a major role in shaping business strategies in practice. Costs are a very important ingredient of both internal, strategic analysis and also in considering external, competitive advantage. Cost analysis may also play a role in determining which industries, markets and market segments are inherently attractive to operate in, and how sustainable this attractiveness is likely to be. This has a fundamental and ongoing input into 'What business(es) are we in?'.

Financial management

Most books on cost management in any well-stocked bookshop will be found under the 'Accounting' section – probably as 'cost accounting'.

Traditional cost accounting focuses on setting budgets and standard costs, and upon subsequent monitoring and analysis of the variances. This territory is well mapped out and it is not the purpose of this chapter to reinvent the cost accounting wheel.

Activity based costing

More interesting from the point of view of strategic cost management is the attack on traditional cost accounting which occurred in the 1980s, principally by Kaplan (1987). Kaplan argued that traditional management accounting systems produce misleading management information. Historically, costs were allocated in relation to the physical use of production assets – both capital and labour. But while the service element grew as a proportion of the value chain of most businesses, the traditional bases of cost allocation became increasingly irrelevant.

Kaplan's argument is that there are often more important activities which underpinned the value added within the production process than those associated with physical operations. For instance, a particular customer might want to have a product or service tailored to some highly specific needs. The additional costs generated by tailoring delivery against these needs across a range of business processes (some tangible and some less tangible) would not be caught by conventional management accounting systems.

Instead, Kaplan proposed an alternative process which he named 'activity based costing' or 'ABC'. The key steps of ABC (Cooper and Kaplan, 1991) involve:

- first, managers need to understand how costs are generated (directly and indirectly) in the organization – hence identifying the key cost drivers;
- second, they then need to see whether processes can be simplified or changed in order to reduce costs or add more value (thus leading on into an embryonic form of business process re-engineering);
- third, having redesigned business processes they need to devise a method of tracking costs through monitoring the performance of a number of key performance indicators designed to measure the impact of key cost and value drivers.

Some applications of activity based costing (ABC) short-circuited and became merely the redesign of the accounting systems, with at best a superficial investigation of either the cost and value system, and of business process redesign. Interestingly, Shank and Govindarajan (1993) explicitly state that ABC accounting systems can actually inhibit the challenging questioning of SCM – because they often become too bureaucratic.

In my view, ABC-type approaches should not be seen as stand-alone but should be integrated with attempts to get a clearer view of what business(es) we should be in and with business process re-engineering (BPR) (Hammer and Champy, 1993; Hammer, 1995). These management programmes are usefully placed under the banner of 'strategic cost management' to position them appropriately within the strategic development process.

Although there are a lot of very good things about BPR (see Chapter 10 Cellnet case), there are three major dangers.

1. The claims for BPR are over-stated by its proponents – just because, to paraphrase some well-known gurus, it is BIG, does not mean it is EVERYTHING.
2. The difficulties of implementing BPR are woefully under-stated (I cringe when top managers suddenly react when hearing the three letters 'BPR' behave like a Christmas tree when someone has just switched the flashing electric lights on).
3. The benefits (and indeed the costs) of BPR are untargeted. When trying to research major companies who have targeted the benefits of BPR competitively, operationally and financially, I recently drew a very big blank.

Unless someone acts fast to refocus BPR and reset its expectations, we will probably remember it in the year 2000 only by its alternative definitions, such as:

'Big Personnel Reduction'; or
'Big Profitable Review' (for consultants)

I am tempted to redefine BPR as BRP – simply as 'Burn Redundant Paper (and Processes)', as 80 per cent of BPR's benefits can be achieved by simply weeding out paper and processes that don't add much value, and the mindset of increasing complexity.

Cost drivers

The idea of 'cost drivers' has also been mentioned. This notion is not self-evident, either in theory or in practice. Porter (1985) defines cost drivers as 'A number of structural factors that influence cost' (p 70).

He also lists a number of key cost drivers:

- economies of scale and learning effects;
- patterns of capacity utilization;
- linkages and interrelationships;
- integration;
- timing;

- discretionary policies;
- location;
- institutional factors.

These are relatively broad factors, and should not, as is argued by Kaplan (1988), be mistaken for more operationally specific cost drivers. Kaplan recommends (wisely) that we should concentrate on analysing the costs of primary activities between direct and indirect costs, and then focus on more specific cost driver categories, particularly in terms of indirect costs. For instance, depreciation and interest need to be traced to specific products (as suggested by Tomkins, 1991).

The moral from this is that you shouldn't get stuck on trying to use a generic framework which will apply equally well to all businesses. It is more helpful to work out the key cost drivers which are industry specific and also those which are organizationally specific. In the latter case, some of the most important cost drivers are rooted in style and are inseparable from the organizational paradigm of 'How we do things around here'.

Another useful distinction is that between the following.

- **Structural cost drivers:** those cost drivers which reflect the fundamental design of the business – operationally, technologically, and in terms of market focus and scope.
- **Executional cost drivers:** those cost drivers which hinge on the firm's ability to execute effectively.

This distinction (Riley, 1987) is useful because it helps pin-point both the internal and external 'hard' drivers of cost concerned with design, and also the more interactional 'soft' elements concerned with delivery. Not only must SCM embrace tangible issues such as product complexity and product design, but also softer issues such as organizational structure, style and management processes. For instance, when SCM was applied in a division of Mercury Communications – Mercury Messaging – the soft elements were found to be more important – especially the then management processes involved in new business development.

Cost programmes as corporate investment decisions

A second (financial) strand of thinking is that a large element of costs are actually, in effect, investment decisions (for instance, see Grundy, 1992b), yet so rarely do we see these longer term cost programmes appraised as such – even by using relatively crude measures like payback.

In reality there are many areas of cost where the bulk of the benefit is felt after the immediate, one-year budgetary period.

Examples of quasi-investment decisions include:

- acquisition costs of new customers;
- advertising and promotion;
- business process re-engineering;
- culture change;
- entry costs into new markets or segments;
- major consulting projects;
- management and organizational development;
- product development;
- research and development;
- restructuring programmes;
- systems development;
- total quality management.

An earlier chapter discussed the need to consider the 'do nothing' or 'de minimis' case for strategic development projects generally. For major cost programmes, parallel issues are raised – for instance without undertaking a particular cost programme the question should be asked – what will the adverse effects be through competitive decline? Also, what edge can be gained through cost programmes over and above competitors? For how long is that edge likely to be sustainable, and at what further cost?

If managers were prepared to appraise their internal cost programmes as if they were investment decisions, they might gain some interesting insights, for instance.

- Many cost programmes might provide a much faster payback and higher ratio of present value (of outlays) than many more tangible areas of investment. This can be appraised using a net present value/payback matrix to help managers examine their project preferences (see Figure 9.3).
- Some cost programmes have dubious benefits; many of these benefits being largely claimed to be 'intangible'. When exposed to scrutiny, however, this intangible nature might be revealed as being due to their being not very well thought through and targeted.
- On balance a project with shorter payback is preferable to one with a similar NPV but longer payback (especially if there are opportunities to do other similar projects) (see Figure 9.3). Here value can be 'turned over' faster than with slower payback projects. A proviso, however, is that managers should avoid unbalancing the portfolio of cost programmes/projects, especially where valuable projects with harder-to-quantify benefits may be at an unfair disadvantage.

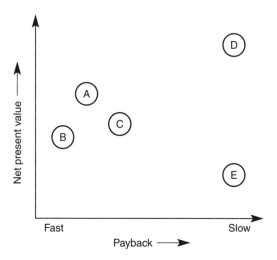

Fig. 9.3 NPV/payback matrix

A useful approach to dealing with the issue of appraisal process is to insist on major cost programmes being defined as projects and thus to require a formal business case. Cost programmes can then be more readily grouped as project sets and then subsumed into the business plan. This can be done to show both the cross-functional effect of strategic cost programmes and also the impact within each function. This should help to break down at least some of the monolithic bureaucracy which surrounds many business planning processes.

Cost structure analysis

Finally, before leaving what is financial management's contribution to strategic cost management, it is worth while just to touch on parts of cost theory which may seem to be self-evident but which are often neglected or misunderstood by managers. Here are some key points.

- Many costs are taken for granted, for instance 'fixed' costs may be fixed short term but are variable or part-variable longer term.
- There are often trade-offs between cost structure (fixed, variable and semi-variable costs) and also against operational flexibility. This is another reminder of the need to consider and challenge assumptions about operational volume by using scenarios for market size and share, and how these are likely to evolve given assumed competitive dynamics.

Not only does cost structure analysis invariably yield insights about the fundamental financial health of a business, it also yields options for shifting the balance of the cost base. These options are best explored via operational and competitive analysis.

Financial management thus provides some useful inputs into strategic cost management through ABC, through appraising longer term cost programmes as quasi-investment decisions and also through achieving a deeper understanding of cost structures.

Operations management

The main operations management themes of most relevance to strategic cost management are those of:

- quality;
- customers;
- unit cost analysis

Quality management

Turning first to quality, quality interfaces with cost management in three main ways. First, quality may add superior value to the external customer. By improving quality one might actually add more value to the customer than previously. But how will that value actually be harvested by the company? There are a number of ways in which this might occur:

- through higher prices (and thus margins);
- through reducing the likelihood and frequency of switching to another supplier;
- through reducing the costs of preventing the customer from switching (for example, through reduced advertising and promotion, and costs of customer visits).

It is rare for all of the higher prices gained through superior quality to be harvested by the company – unless of course the company has much more bargaining power than its customer. Some of the incremental value – and often most – is thus absorbed by the customer, either unavoidably or deliberately. This means that the benefits of quality management are so often felt in protecting the business rather than in generating incremental financial returns.

A second way of generating value through quality is through adding more value to the internal customer at the same or less cost. This necessitates internal bench marking of internal supply against internal market need. Internal bench marking is not analytically difficult, but it is hard in terms of process – especially in challenging preconceptions about whether existing cost programmes do or do not add value in the organization.

The third area where quality can be of financial benefit is in reducing the cost of failure and error, or the cost of (poor) quality (called 'COQ'). These costs can be considerable, particularly as the costs of undetected error compound as a product or service is processed by the organization. It is often a salutary experience to work out the cost of an error – for example in one food manufacturing company a single rubber glove dropped undetected into the production process and contaminated an entire batch. The result was the loss of a large customer who had very tight quality requirements.

According to the quality literature, investment in error prevention often adds much more value than investment in the appraisal and measurement of quality.

Customers

Another key issue is how customers are serviced and at what cost. One of the key cost drivers of any business is the choice of customers and customer need which it serves. Not only does each new customer have an acquisition cost, it also has a maintenance cost – these costs varying considerably between customers and customer types.

Despite the wealth of prescription in the marketing and strategy books about targeting customers and market segments, in practice managers are frequently deflected from pursuing these targets by thinking they need to respond to whatever customer comes through the door. This is partly due to the uncertainty factor of – 'You never know what orders will be available tomorrow' – but also because of a confusion between responsiveness and reactiveness. Responsiveness means understanding and fulfilling targeted customer demand; reactiveness means mechanically servicing the demand which happens to materialize on a day-to-day basis.

This leads us to the 'value-destroying customer' syndrome. Companies service customer needs which destroy value in many ways, for instance through:

- accepting order sizes which are uneconomic;
- agreeing to tailor customer specification beyond what competitors might do and without reward through a premium price;
- supplying customers who will be inherently uneconomic either through geographical distance, cost of distribution channels, complex after-sales servicing requirement;
- Entering into competitive bidding when, in the long run, the balance of probabilities means that you destroy, rather than create, value.

Customer analysis is a critical area of the case on Cotswold Technology, as will be seen later.

Unit cost analysis

Many important insights on cost can be attained simply by analysing what it actually costs to define a particular product or service unit. For instance, in one service organization the business managers frequently re-ran a financial model of global risk. Every time there was a significant change to some area of the world they initiated a new run of the mainframe computer model. In one particular month the computing costs seemed to go through the ceiling. Apparently no one had realized that running the model once took not only several hours of central processing time but cost tens of thousands of pounds.

The same principle of working out unit service costs can be applied to many other areas. For instance, in a major professional firm it was discovered that to send out a single memo to all 500 partners and 2,000 managers cost over £5,000. This is a classic illustration of what is a non-obvious cost driver.

Organizational behaviour

In the UK version of SCM, softer issues involving organizational behaviour play a very central role, precisely because they are harder to tackle and, at the same time, often offer bigger and more sustainable competitive benefits longer term. Chapter 5 examined how important organizational analysis was in shaping strategic development programmes. But in addition it has a pivotal role to play in managing internal costs generally.

The three main areas of impact of organizational behaviour on costs are through:

- organizational structure;
- style and culture;
- organizational change.

Organizational structure, style and culture – and organizational change – are so inseparable (because of their many interdependencies) that it is not appropriate to untangle them. Instead, one should look at organizational change as involving a single, strategic cost programme which can only really be evaluated by the following process.

- Generating a 'base case' for organizational costs – what will their costs look like without major change – given incremental changes in organizational structure, and extrapolating the existing style and culture.
- Developing an organizational strategy (see again Chapter 5) – this involves looking at how the capability of the organization can be developed to meet the external and competitive needs, and at what

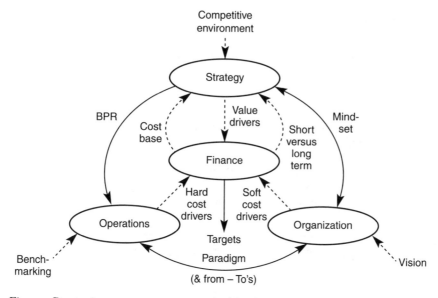

Fig. 9.4 Strategic cost management – the big picture

cost. Again, this can be supported by a higher level 'organizational scenario' as described in the section on 'strategic management'.

- Devising change programmes (for instance, operational, people-related or culture change) which might support the overall organizational strategy.
- Appraising the cost outlay of organizational change relative to illustrative benefits as a strategic investment decision.

A synthesis

Figure 9.4 now brings together the inputs to strategic cost management. This highlights how strategy, operations and organization are inseparable with finance – in terms of targeting and (ultimately) measurement. This discussion now completes the review of perspectives on costs. It is now time to take a look at the strategic cost management process.

THE STRATEGIC COST MANAGEMENT PROCESS

This framework for a strategic cost management is based on the following premises:

- without a systematic process, costs are likely to be managed on a purely or predominantly tactical basis;
- managing costs involves managers with lots of complex, cross-functional issues which need to be tackled therefore with a flexible set of tools, and also as a team process to provide more challenge to the status quo and to build ownership of the change;
- this suggests that the initial diagnosis phase is crucial, involving identifying and prioritizing issues prior to exploring and evaluating key options.

The process shown in Figure 9.5 illustrates therefore how costs can be managed strategically – showing the stages of issue definition, diagnosis, challenging options, more detailed evaluation, planning and implementation.

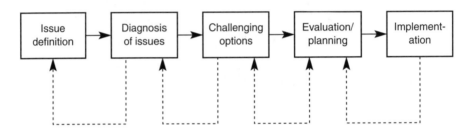

Fig. 9.5 Strategic cost management – process

Following diagnosis, the next stage is to create challenging options – this tests the status quo. This stage is separated from detailed planning and evaluation so that managers do not just reinvent the existing pattern of cost allocation in a naive way. This stage involves evaluating options using the 'AID' tool from Chapter 5 to separate out:

- **their inherent attractiveness (in cost/benefit terms):** ideally this boils down to quantitative and primarily financial indicators (these do not have to be exact);
- **the implementation difficulty:** this requires assessing how hostile or receptive the organization is likely to be to changing its allocation of resources and the timely availability of appropriate resources to achieve project goals.

The two dimensions of inherent attractiveness and implementation difficulty are once again pictured using the grid in Figure 9.6. Note that project A appears to be of medium attractiveness and relatively easy to implement, while project B looks equally attractive but much harder. Project C offers much higher net benefit, still, but because of its apparent difficulty may be placed (erroneously) by management 'on the shelf'.

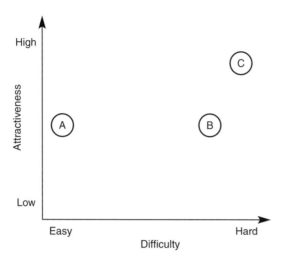

Fig. 9.6 Attractiveness and implementation difficulty grid

The process can now be fleshed out using a series of checklists for each stage. These have been successfully piloted in a number of complex organizations – for instance in the telecommunications, financial services and high technology sectors.

Each stage will be examined in turn before focusing on the Cotswold Technology case.

Strategic cost management checklists

Defining issues

Before beginning the diagnosis of issues it is necessary first of all to brainstorm the universe of areas which might be addressed before prioritizing these for analysis. You will find it useful to work through at least the early part of this checklist on your own cost issues. Avoid simply skim reading them. Allow a good half an hour for this.

Key questions to help identify the issues are as follows.

1. Which discretionary costs exist within the organization that might be managed more effectively?
2. Which overhead costs are incurred which generate limited value added?
3. Are marketing costs being well targeted and monitored in terms of their effectiveness?
4. What areas of operational cost might yield significant savings or might be refocused to add more value? Should these be selectively increased on

account of their value added? (Consider for example, distribution, purchasing and   information systems.)

5. What financing costs are being incurred in excess of what is really needed to run the business?

6. Are cost information systems genuinely effective or do these suffer from poor quality inputs, outputs and dissemination?

7. Is the prevailing culture a cost aware one? Is this one of overly frugal management or alternatively one of managing costs for both financial and competitive advantage?

8. What 'sacred cows' exist which incur cost without adding significant value to the business and also set an inappropriate example for how costs are managed elsewhere?

9. Are the costs of change evaluated, targeted and then monitored, and subject to a business case procedure?

Diagnosis of issues

1. How are costs made up and how can they be creatively resegmented, for example by activity, channels, customer types etc.?

2. To what extent are costs recurring or non-recurring, and does this suggest clues as to how both of these areas of cost can be more effectively managed?

3. What are the key cost drivers both at macro level and also at a much more micro level?

4. To what extent is poor quality or business complexity contributing to problems of controlling cost?

5. Which 20 per cent of areas of cost or cost-drivers offers 80 per cent of the potential for improvement ('Pareto' analysis)?

6. What is the gap between current cost levels and where you need to be (target cost levels)?

7. How do these target costs stack up against the improvements competitors are likely to be able to make over that period?

Creating challenging options

Once issues have been effectively diagnosed it is now timely to create genuinely challenging options.

1. Can costs be challenged either by using a zero-based approach (that is with no fixed assumptions of what is possible), or by building up from a very low base of cost?

2. Can target cost levels be established based on an assessment of how the business needs to compete effectively in, for instance, one, three and even five years' time?

3. Are these target cost levels linked to standards of output quality so that cost reduction is not pursued at the expense of a poorer quality?

4. Have these targets for cost and quality been benchmarked externally to help target them competitively?

5. Has this benchmarking process been used to generate a strategy for cost reduction which does not undermine the business strategy?

6. Has management unfrozen existing thinking about costs by encouraging a 'robbing Peter to pay Paul' climate – thus investing resources released in areas which can add more value?

7. Can costs be managed more effectively by substituting (in whole or in part) external for internal resource, thus refocusing the 'business activities that we are in'?

8. Is capacity there on a 'just-in-case' basis and is therefore considerably under-utilized?

9. Are areas of 'fixed cost' really all that fixed – especially in the long run? What trade-offs exist within the cost structure between fixed and variable costs – financially, operationally and competitively?

10. What costs are based on internal allocations and transfer prices and are these justifiable on any economic basis?

11. Are there many less tangible areas of benefit attributed to cost programmes which currently are unchallenged and loosely targeted?

12. Are there areas where new investment could generate a rapid payback through cost reduction but have simply not been considered because of the perceived financial climate?

13. Are there areas of business which you should simply get out of because external shifts in the environment have increased the cost base substantially?

14. Can the industry's or company's value chain be restructured so as to give the company (sustainable) cost advantage?

One thing to watch at this stage is that teams do not become too enthusiastic about their 'solutions' without testing them thoroughly.

Evaluation and planning

Evaluation and planning encompass not merely cost/benefit evaluation but also assessment of implementation difficulty and how this might be minimized. This phase thus combines 'hard' and 'soft' analysis as follows.

1. What are the key benefits of the cost programme, for instance:

   - strategically;
   - operationally;
   - organizationally?

2. How do these translate into financial benefits, whether these are relatively exact or inexact?
3. When will these be attained, i.e. what milestones have you set and just how realistic are these?
4. What are the key costs and risks involved both:

   - in achieving the necessary changes;
   - in sustaining the improvement?

5. What are the direct and indirect benefits, and how can these be targeted and effectively harvested?
6. What are the indirect costs and how can these be managed?
7. What might the impact be on customers', suppliers' and distributors' value chains?
8. To what extent are gains in cost advantage relative to competitors likely to be sustainable and, if so, how?
9. What are the critical barriers to implementation, for example:

   - key stakeholders and their positioning and influence;
   - organizational style;
   - sufficiency of resource;
   - overload of staff;
   - complexity of the change involved;
   - duration of the change;
   - leadership, and its active and visible support;
   - supporting measures and routines;
   - the impact generally on 'How we do things around here'?

Implementation

Implementation is a most critical phase and invites some obvious and some less obvious questions.

1. Has the project manager for the programme got the necessary time, the technical and interpersonal skills, business awareness and clout to manage this project effectively?
2. Have the key constraining forces been dealt with in the implementation plan?

3. In particular, does the implementation plan recognize the softer areas of change which also need to be managed effectively – particularly communication, feedback and motivation?
4. Are the milestones and measures of change being actively monitored, and has success (or failure) been highlighted at the right organizational level?

Cotswold Technology case study

Introduction

Cotswold Technology is a niche technology company based in the UK with marketing operations worldwide, including the US, the Far East and Japan. Over the past ten years it has been transformed from a product-led organization to one which is market-led, and with a strong commercial orientation. This has helped Cotswold achieve considerable growth in scale and in profitability – while at the same time simplifying its business portfolio.

In 1991 (the time of this case) Cotswold faced pressures to improve its financial performance following other board level changes in 1990. A new finance director had just been appointed who was given a brief by the chief executive to review costs in a number of areas including the logistics function. Since 1990 Cotswold's share price has almost quadrupled.

This case focuses on the logistics function which accounted for a considerable amount of Cotswold's costs (and its value added), particularly as Cotswold's sales were worldwide. Costs were also relatively high because of the sophisticated nature of the product which required special shipment requirements and high frequency of resupply.

The problem – and opportunity

Initially the 'problem' of driving logistic costs down was framed as simply that – cost reduction. But rapidly it was realized that costs couldn't just be managed vertically downwards like that – it was recognized that there might be unpleasant side effects, for instance loss of customer business and the rise in costs in other business processes. The last thing that management wanted was cost reduction becoming a 'dead cat' (Argyris, 1977) – where problems in one department were solved by creating them elsewhere.

In 1991 the head of Cotswold's global logistics function, who we will call Ray Scot, decided to reframe the problem as one of opportunity. He decided to shift the question from:

'How can we make major reductions in Cotswold's logistics costs?'
to
**'How can we manage logistics costs for both financial
and competitive advantage?'**

Ray Scot reflects in 1994:

*'The main thing now is that we are definitely commercially-driven. We
are in business teams now, a process which we started in 1991, meeting
three or four times a year, led by senior management.'*

This change in emphasis had a number of key implications, as follows:

- besides cost reduction, Cotswold would also be seeking opportunities
  for extra revenue generation;
- any cost-cutting measures would be carefully probed to establish
  whether they might erode Cotswold's competitive position.
- any changes in 'How we do things around here' in logistics needed to
  be managed in unison with changes in other business processes, particularly in manufacturing, marketing and information systems.

On the latter point, Ray Scot elaborates:

*'We have worked with our manufacturing colleagues and got rid of taboos;
like a product will only be available at 5 o'clock in the evening, now we can
have it at 2 o'clock. It gives us so much more [flexibility of] options.'*

The subsequent review of costs was not purely inwardly facing and was sup-
plemented by competitive benchmarking – both to establish whether Cotswold
really did have 'a problem' and also to target continuous improvement.

Looking back, in 1994, Ray Scot expands on how this has taken root:

*'Distribution effectiveness is going to be measured not only by cost but
also by service and also, of course, in how we do against our competition.
What we have done is to put in place measures, benchmarks, and as we
speak we are undertaking a major study in France and in the UK which
is trying to address all of those three issues.'*

It is now time to look at the process which proved to be a critical vehicle on
the route to success.

The process

Ray Scot orchestrated a two-day workshop in logistics preceded by one day
on manufacturing. Participants in the logistics workshops were drawn from

different parts of Cotswold's overseas operations worldwide. This proved invaluable not merely in obtaining data but also in building a commitment to effect change.

The two-day workshop was structured along the following lines.

Day 1

- Why we are trying to manage costs for both financial and competitive advantage.
- Presentation of data and distillation of issues.
- First-cut issues analysis.

Day 2

- Issues diagnosis.
- Option generation.
- Option generation – relative financial benefits and implementation difficulty.
- Action planning and conclusion

The workshop was attended by between 12–15 managers (different staff attending at different times). Ray Scot also used a facilitator who was knowledgeable both in terms of strategic and financial analysis – as it happens the author of the case.

Initially I played the role of observer/commentator (in the first half day) but was drawn into more active facilitation during the afternoon and second day. This more active involvement followed relatively extensive presentations, lasting several hours with some discussion, which primed the participants for issue diagnosis and option generation.

The initial workshop only served to get the ball rolling. Figure 9.7 shows the bigger and longer term picture, highlighting:

- the need to collect some (often basic) cost data and analyse these in new ways;
- the process of winning approval for organizational and operational change, and in how customer needs are dealt with;
- the need to focus on a small number of SCM project areas – and deliver results over a period often extending over two to three years;
- the role of external benchmarking in targeting improvement generally, ideas to reconfigure processes and as ongoing check on performance;
- the imperative to change performance measures and feedback processes to make this truly more balanced, and cross-functional.

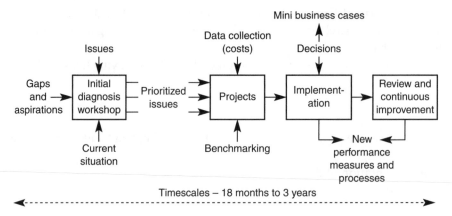

Fig. 9.7 The fuller strategic cost management process (illustrated)

This process of managing costs more strategically has since been embedded in Cotswold's culture:

> *'It is more of a process [than a system]. I think that is more important than having rigid performance measures. You can almost fiddle them [performance measures], but at the end of the day what really matters is the truth – are the customers happy?'*

Managing the outputs

The sheer amount of ideas generated by syndicate groups on that first day came as a surprise to everyone – the participants, Ray Scot and, indeed, myself. The range of opportunities generated itself became a problem for the process. As one participant said in the bar later that night:

> *'We were coming out with so many different ideas – I couldn't see how we were ever going to pull it all together.'*

In fact, this proved easier than it looked. By continually sorting out the emerging ideas into a set of issue groups, it proved possible to generate a full issue framework. One of the benefits of using a facilitator is that there is always someone who has their 'hands and brain free' to collect and structure issues and options.

The issues (and opportunities) were broken down into a number of natural areas. First, we distinguished between areas of costs which were variable, shorter term – offering relatively quick opportunities for saving. Second, there were areas of cost which might have been regarded as 'fixed' but in the longer term were variable. Thirdly, there was a big issue about service responsiveness and ensuring that customers were neither over or under-serviced. Finally, there was a need for clear objectives and performance measures to be set. Subsequent to the workshop a lot of work was done on this, particularly using competitive benchmarking.

In terms of how the tools were used, Ray Scot reflects:

'I think it is good to use some tools. It is easy to get involved in too much detail too soon. What is important is to rank things in terms of payback, importance to the business, relative importance, relative difficulty.'

One of the particularly interesting outputs was service responsiveness. First, there were areas where Cotswold was making shipments to customers more frequently than they actually needed. This was due to a number of operational practices which had not previously been challenged. Second, there were instances where customers sought 'urgent deliveries'. Cotswold responded by delivering a separate shipment without any premium price for delivery. Not only did customers subsequently not mind the premium charge for urgent deliveries, they actually welcomed the formalization of arrangements (this also helped increase Cotswold's revenues).

Ray Scot reflects that:

'We ended up with a premium (or 'tax') on certain orders. We looked at order size, timing, whether they wanted next day delivery or something special, and there was a tax put on it. In fact, the revenues generated out of it are not significant but the discipline that we put into the system is tremendous.

What we have always got to be careful of is putting ourselves in the position where it is difficult for [customers] to place an order. That is why it is important to benchmark ourselves all of the time against our competitors, to make sure they aren't offering something better.'

Third, it was realized that attempts to take a 'blunt axe' to Cotswold's logistics service levels would be financially counter-productive. As an example, because some of Cotswold's products have a longevity measured in days (not weeks or months) the effect of doubling the intervals between delivery would be very significant indeed.

In tangible terms, net cost reductions (or revenue increases) per annum of over 15 per cent of logistics costs were targeted as a result of this exercise. Interestingly, it was not altogether self-evident what the total group's bill for logistics costs was. It needs to be remembered here that Cotswold operated in many countries and that the logistics costs would be spread over a large number of cost centres. This highlights the need for segmenting costs according to business process rather than purely along the lines of the financial accounting system.

(The need to spend time pin-pointing current costs is a very common ingredient in applying strategic cost management for the first time.)

In all, over 70 options/areas of opportunity were identified which were then prioritized using the financial benefit/ implementation difficulty grid (Figure 9.6). A sub-set of these were then translated into detailed action plans and then implemented over the next two to three years. This project was managed by Ray Scot.

Reflections on the process

Looking back in 1994, Ray Scot reflects on the impact of the strategic cost process. First, he describes how the cost environment has changed and how this has been managed via continuous improvement:

> 'Things are changing in the market place, with our competitors, changes in the customer base; in our case we are moving into new technologies where we have lower gross margins than our historical products which puts more pressure on costs.
>
>   We are on a continuous improvement kick. We have some specific business issues where the distribution channel in a marketing sense is questionable in some areas, and we are evaluating whether we are in the right channel. Depending on those decisions, that will have an impact on physical distribution. So it [our focus] is now more on effectiveness rather than efficiency. Given the way we operate, we are reasonably efficient, so our opportunities for improving profit are back to effectiveness, so it all leads us back to the market place. Should you be operating through a subsidiary, should you be going direct to the market? Should you be operating a wholesale service or a retail service? These are real business issues.'

He now looks at how performance measures have been refocused in order to sustain the shift towards strategic cost management:

> 'We have to make a trade-off between costs and service and share of the market. What we try to do is we sit down with our [internal] customers once a year to agree performance measures, and those will be a combination of financial and non-financial.'

'Quarterly, we get them to give us a satisfaction rating. We also ask them are you happy – it's just a feel. If you are not happy, what is it that we are not doing? Then that might be quantified. We get a tremendous amount out of this, it can be pretty honest, quite brutal.

We ask them to pull no punches. Equally, we ask them about things that they are adding cost to or inhibiting service.'

One of the big issues which came out of the 1991 review was the extent to which distribution could or should become a strategic business unit in its own right.

'We looked at it [distribution as a business strategy in its own right], but at the end of the day we discarded it. We have decided that distribution is a core competence, we are not going to dilute it by offering services to other companies elsewhere. The amount of money that we might be able to make relative to the business is not worth while. We had divested a business which had left a great big hole in terms of unrecovered overheads, particularly in our overseas subsidiaries. For a while we focused on whether we could pull in other companies to fill this gap. What we found is that we would have to put a tremendous amount of effort into it. At the end of the day that was too big a distraction.'

Distribution costs were also perceived to be a key strategic issue in post acquisition management itself key to strategic development:

'Acquisitions bring their own problems; there are synergy benefits. For example, by combining our buying power for one acquisition we could save almost half a million dollars, however there was a cost to the acquired company (which was much less). So we had this debate, who was right and who was wrong, so that is just one small example.'

The above highlights once again the considerable barrier of managing the organizational politics generated non-intentionally from traditional, perhaps inflexible, control processes. As one measure of success, it can be seen that strategic cost management has exceeded its original expectations in terms of benefits, even if it has taken longer to deliver these and harder than was originally anticipated.

'When we started out at 1991, we were running at something in the order of [distribution costs], a percentage of sales just over 10 per cent. We are now at 8 per cent.'

The impact of the savings in distribution costs represents about 15 per cent of Cotswold's annual profits in 1994, highlighting the significance of strategic cost management just in one key business function alone.

Some key lessons from the case

A number of key lessons for how strategic cost management can play a role in managing strategies for growth emerge from this case.

- How the original problem is framed is of vital importance – to manage costs for both financial and competitive advantage is non-trivial.
- The current situation needs to be defined very clearly – for instance, what exactly are your current costs?
- Sufficient time must be created for both workshop preparation, and for issue generation, diagnosis and evaluation.
- The process frequently yields a very large number of opportunities which then have to be skilfully evaluated and prioritized.
- Some large opportunities may be longer term or may be perceived to be relatively difficult. However, these do not tend to go away but need to be brought back on to the agenda (for instance, the implications for 'What businesses are we in?').
- It is crucial to get the right people involved – from a variety of functions – so that they own the need for change and for continuing improvement.
- It may be extremely advisable to have an internal or external facilitator (avoid do-it-yourself brain surgery) – it is absolutely imperative to have a project manager.
- The strategic cost team needs to proactively influence upwards to shape the expectations (and sometimes the perceptions) of key stakeholders and to bring them on board rather than to adopt a 'leave alone' strategy.
- There is invariably a good deal of organizational politics associated with making SCM work. This needs to be tackled directly, otherwise much of the potential gains will not be harvested.
- To sustain the benefits, key performance measures need to be reshaped and also made more externally orientated, for instance by competitive benchmarking.
- There is invariably more work than the managers anticipate in the detailed planning and implementation process – there is a danger that some of the areas for greatest financial benefit do not get addressed because of perceived implementation difficulty.

On the final point above – implementation – Ray Scot reflects:

> I think that the honest truth is that we under-estimated [the amount of work required in implementation]. This was double at least what we expected. Then you have to rationalize the situation and you say 'what's important', and you agree with your [internal] customers what is important and, in our case, the customer is the commercial people. They set the direction and then we figure out the optimum solution. It doesn't mean to say that all good ideas come from the marketplace, they don't.

Figure 9.8 highlights the typical difference between perceived and actual implementation difficulty. Note that diagnosis difficulty is much reduced by application of analysis tools (like the attractiveness/implementation difficulty grid). But the difficulty really comes in sustaining the momentum of reshaping the cost base.

After an initial focus on increasing efficiency it may be a natural evolution to shift more into reviewing effectiveness – are you doing the right things (as opposed to doing things right)?

CONCLUSION

By now the argument for managing costs strategically through SCM is both overpowering and, I hope, complete. You will have seen how costs can

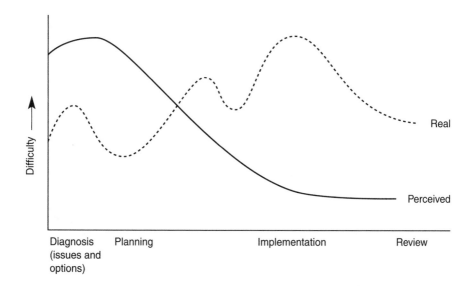

Fig. 9.8 Strategic cost management – perceived versus real implementation difficulty

be managed as a coherent process – for both financial and competitive advantage. Strategic cost management is a vital tool in seeking breakthrough strategies for growth which genuinely add value. The SCM process draws in a variety of analysis tools and recipes for diagnosing cost issues, for creating challenging options and for testing implementation plans.

Costs have often been relegated within finance as a 'systems' or budgetary issue. To a large extent they have been viewed as being merely operational and tactical. But they can actually play a major role either in enabling or frustrating strategies for growth.

However, the increasingly competitive pressure of the past few years has put the spotlight very much on costs. This increase in competitive pressures has been accompanied by stagnant economic conditions, deregulation in many sectors and also many formerly growth industries reaching maturity. Sometimes this spotlight has been focused purely internally and in the short term was without regard for the interdependencies within the business system. More rarely has cost management been sensitized to avoid the negative impact on competitive position. A way forward here is to highlight and amplify the message that this generates weaker financial performance – not only longer term but also indirectly through impact in other functional areas.

Strategic cost management is therefore not merely a philosophy which integrates perspectives from strategic management, financial management, operations and organizational behaviour. It is also a practical approach which enables managers to rise up above the narrow and political budget games that hold back strategic development from achieving its full potential.

ACTION CHECKLIST

- What levels do you need to drive your costs down relative to your competitors in order to compete strategically two, four, six years out?

- How can you align your cost structures, programmes and budgets better with your generic strategies (differentiation versus cost leadership)?

- Which business activities absorb disproportionate costs relative to the value they add in support of your existing strategy and strategies for growth?

- Which of your major areas of cost can (and should) be appraised using a mini-business case methodology?

- To what extent are customers over or under-serviced on account of your budgetary policies and practices?

- Can you capture more value where you add (or might add) disproportionate value via the customers' value chain (i.e. via your pricing structures)?

- Where have you grown your business at the expense of underlying high unit costs and what does this mean for reconfiguring your business?

- How does organization structure and style and change impact over cost levels, and how can these softer cost-drivers be managed more effectively?

- What specific areas of cost can now be managed more strategically – for both financial and competitive advantage via strategic cost projects?

- How attractive are the net benefits less costs of these projects relative to their degree of implementation difficulty?

'Finance can play a most central role in formulating and implementing strategy.'

10

REACHING FOR
VALUE – VALUING
BUSINESS CHANGE

INTRODUCTION

This chapter now aims to generate a new debate in strategic management. It seeks to breathe fresh life into discussion of how internal, organizational strategies are managed – through the perhaps unlikely help of finance.

Traditionally, business finance has been seen by strategic management as a discipline which comes to the fore primarily once strategic thinking is done. Finance is thus seen as costing out the strategy and setting financial constraints. This is an essential but more tactical role. But finance can be interwoven fully with strategic thinking and evaluation.

I aim to demonstrate that finance can play a most central role in formulating and implementing strategy. The idea is to focus particularly in finance's role in helping shape strategies for organizational change. That role is most effectively executed via the notion of valuing business change (or 'VBC').

A BRIEF OVERVIEW OF PREVIOUS THINKING

A good deal of work has already been done to link competitive and financial strategies for external strategic moves (Barwise, Marsh *et al*, 1987; Grundy, 1992ab; Grundy, 1993b; Grundy and Ward, 1994. The focus of this research has been strategic investment decisions. This stream of research suggests that:

- many areas of investment are not evaluated financially because they are not treated as 'capital' (on the balance sheet), or because many of the benefits are perceived to be 'less tangible';

- projects associated with organizational change often escape the valuation net entirely, not only because they are not seen as 'strategic investment decisions' (as above), but also because they have medium term, as opposed to longer term, benefits;
- in these cases, while many of the benefits (and costs) appear at first sight to be less tangible, invariably there are alternative ways of targeting them both financially and non-financially.

However, this previous research does not provide either a framework for diagnosing and targeting the value of business change projects, nor has it explored how companies in practice are tackling this specific problem area.

But before taking a look at an empirical case to help generate a theoretical framework, it will be useful to briefly re-examine why managers would profit from valuing business change projects and programmes.

WHY VALUE BUSINESS CHANGE?

There appear to be five key reasons for valuing business change:

- targeting the outputs;
- reshaping the change strategy;
- prioritizing change programmes;
- monitoring the results;
- learning – from both outputs and process.

Targeting the outputs

First, there is a very strong argument for targeting business change, both (a) so that managers define what kind of effects they are seeking to achieve within the business system and (b) to assess how valuable (or costly) those effects are likely to be. The business system is the network of external and internal value drivers which are realigned through the change process. This notion comes partly from systems theory (Senge, 1990) and partly from the concept of alignment of value drivers (Grundy, 1992b).

Schaffer and Thomson (1992) performed a great service to the cause by suggesting that change programmes should be quite specifically targeted in order to bring results, otherwise their effects are liable to be diffuse. This chapter moves somewhat further than this by suggesting the explicit valuation of change projects and programmes as a means of sharpening up this targeting.

This does not mean, however, that a precise or near-precise valuation of change projects is being suggested. These valuations are on a continuum between being exacting through to indicative.

Reshaping the change strategy

Second, by valuing business change it is perhaps more likely that the initial concept of a change programme will be reshaped, rather than just taken as a given. This reshaping process is likely to be an ongoing process (see, for instance, the case of Prudential Life Administration, Grundy 1993a, where the change programme went through a number of overlapping phases, each time involving and refocusing of change initiatives). There is thus likely to be a continual need to revisit the value of business change. This is particularly true as strategies for internal changes are likely to be fluid – a mix of both deliberate and emergent change (Mintzberg, 1994).

Prioritizing change programmes

Third, at any point in time any organization may be exposed to an excess of possible (and desirable) change programmes relative to its capacity to digest change. This means that VBC can be of service in prioritizing business change. By mapping the interdependencies between change projects, this also enables managers to gain a better fix on whether the various change initiatives represent one of three different things. First, are they (a) a series of projects which add value principally on a stand-alone basis? Or are they (b) projects having many close interdependencies (so all have to be implemented – but not all at the same time and in the same mix)? Or, alternatively, (c) are they really an integrated package and have to be implemented in unison to both achieve momentum for change and to deliver the intended value? Figure 10.1 illustrates this by reference to a number of the most common areas of deliberate change currently being implemented by large companies.

Monitoring the results

Fourth, VBC can assist in helping monitor the effects of business change. Some of these effects (positive and negative) might be intended, and some unintended. Also, VBC may help open up the debate about why value was not generated as previously believed would happen. This may well be because of a raft of interdependencies which might have not been managed or which may not have been within management's control.

For an analysis of the organizational interdependencies impacting on a telecommunications business undergoing 'deliberate' strategic change, see the two cases on Dowty – before and after – in Grundy (1993a) and Grundy (1994a). This case highlighted that much of the value of the change was emergent – especially through learning about the business's competitive

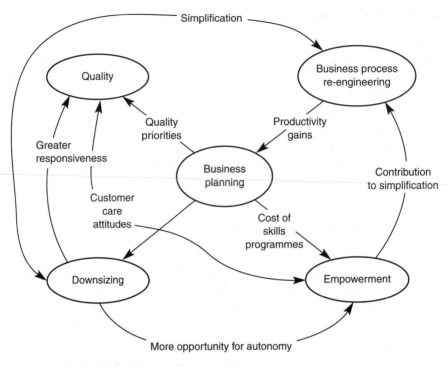

Fig. 10.1 Some key interdependencies between change programmes

position. (The intended result of the strategic review was a strategy for growth. The actual result was a strategic restructuring and turnaround.)

Finally, VBC offers at least some handle for enabling managers to learn from what they did to manage change. Because change is seen as an active 'let's get on and do it' process by many managers, it appears not to be a natural habit to stand back from any change programme and ask, 'What value did it add, what value did it destroy, and why; and what lessons can we learn for how we conduct future change programmes?'

HOW MIGHT BUSINESS CHANGE BE VALUED?

This next section outlines how business change might be valued, based on the current state of knowledge. This draws together techniques from strategy, finance and organizational change. These techniques could be used either in the diagnosis, planning or implementation and control phases of change management (Grundy, 1993a).

But first, it may seem to be a most daunting task to value business change because of the difficulty of defining (a) the key objectives of many change programmes and (b) the key organizational shifts necessary to achieve these objectives.

A five-stage approach may help simplify these hurdles.

1. **The objectives:** the change objective may be set by applying a balanced score card (Kaplan, 1992) approach to defining the key objectives of the change.
2. **The underlying shifts on 'how we do things around here' or the paradigm (Grundy, 1993a):** 'from...to' analysis may be to diagnose the key organizational shifts necessary to underpin the change.
3. **Valuing the change:** value-based techniques may be applied to the cost/benefit analysis of the proposed change.
4. **Assessing the implementation difficulty:** the likely implementation difficulty might be evaluated (and thus, by implication, the time scales) through analysing the organizational forces impacting on implementation.
5. **Building a business case:** a business case methodology may be applied to appraise the value of the business change and to prioritize it against other change projects using an attractiveness/implementation difficulty grid.

The balanced score-card

First, a balanced score-card approach to the change helps the change to be more effectively targeted in terms of identifying the:

- specific and tangible, financial benefits;
- softer improvements in market and competitive position;
- operational benefits (e.g. greater speed and flexibility) – tangible in nature but hard to quantify financially;
- innovative capability in building new ideas which offer contingent value (Grundy, 1992b) – that is value which will only crystallize by alignment of a number of internal and external value drivers.

These objectives might become more specific and financially quantifiable by the stage of preparing the business case.

Refining the underlying organizational shifts

Second, 'from and to' (or 'FT') analysis can help identify the degree of underlying change necessary to support the specific change objective of a particular project. 'FT' analysis helps to identify the softer interdependencies which need to be aligned in order to reap the potential value of the change. 'FT' analysis will also help identify the key uncertainties and risks, for instance that change projects elsewhere in the organization distract management's attention so that the particular change project is halted or deflected.

Valuing the change

Third, in valuing the change, we need to consider (a) targeting the benefits and (b) estimating the costs. Taking first (a), Figure 10.2 illustrates the need to separate out incremental value added versus costs saved. Also less easily measurable benefits of speed and responsiveness need to be assessed.

Value added may need to be tested out to ensure that value added in theory (for instance, via improved quality of service to customers) is harvested via incremental volumes or premium prices. This value is shared (Ghemawat, 1991) between customers and the company. The outcome of this sharing is interdependent with relative supplier versus buyer power, competitor activity, and the company's marketing and pricing strategy.

Next, cost saved invites an analysis of the key cost-drivers impacted upon by the change (Shank and Govindarajan, 1993). This might involve identifying the most fundamental cost-drivers. For instance, one might ask what impact does apparent duplication of functional activities between corporate centre and business units have on operational costs.

Service times and responsiveness can also play an important role in contributing to value (Stalk, 1990). Speed or responsiveness may create possible value (for instance, increased speed might enable a company to service either more customers or more needs in the same time). Actually harvesting this value may, however, be interdependent with more effective

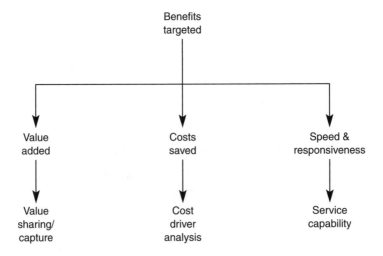

Fig. 10.2 Benefits targeted

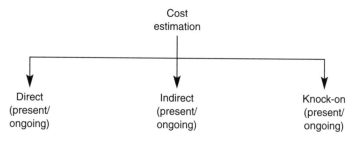

Fig. 10.3 Cost estimation

marketing strategy or tactics. A new marketing strategy and tactics may also be needed to create more potential demand. Greater speed and responsiveness may therefore generate incremental value when assigned to other areas of change.

Turning next to (b) or cost estimation (see Figure 10.3), costs might be either directly attributable to the change project or may be indirect (but within the same operation). There might also be knock-on costs, in other business units. Each one of these cost areas might be either a function of the change process or might be an ongoing cost. For example, there might be ongoing and indirect costs of a total quality management programme as a result of ongoing compliance costs.

The point of assessing the overall attractiveness of the change is therefore to capture the broader and longer term benefits and costs of the change programme. Looking only at the direct and immediate costs of the programme, and the direct benefits may provide a most misleading picture (positively or negatively) of the potential value of the change. Again, cost estimation of indirect and knock-on costs requires in-depth analysis of the underlying cost drivers.

Assessing the implementation difficulty

The next stage in the analysis is to assess the difficulty of the change using an approach derived from 'implementation forces' analysis.

IMF analysis displays the key hard and soft forces which might enable or constrain effective implementation. (Note that the constraining forces are not called 'resistances', because this suggests active hostility as a natural organization property – constraining forces can be things like inadequate resources, a lack of project management etc. See Figure 10.4 for an example of IMF analysis. The length of the arrows depicts the perceived strength of the force. IMF analysis can be used both as a management tool and as a means of collecting data.)

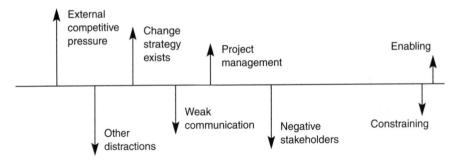

Fig. 10.4 Implementation forces analysis

Building a business case

The final stage of the process is to capture the attractiveness of the change, the assessment of implementation difficulty and the key assumptions in a business case. As part of a wider analysis of change programmes, it is also possible to map a number of these programmes on an attractiveness/implementation difficulty matrix (see Figure 10.5). Figure 10.5 suggests that restructuring may be of medium attractiveness and in the 'not so difficult' zone; whereas, business process re-engineering is considerably more difficult but of higher attractiveness. A culture change programme is very difficult and is also of lower net benefit (remember Figure 10.5's examples are illustrative).

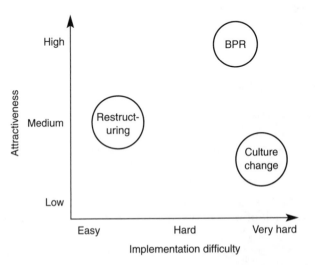

Fig. 10.5 Attractiveness/implementation difficulty matrix (AID)

As part of the business case, a useful sanity check is the use of an uncertainty/importance grid to prioritize assumptions (Mitroff and Linstone, 1993; Grundy, 1994). While more commonly applied to external competitive strategy and decisions, this grid is perhaps even more vital for surfacing and challenging underlying assumptions. Figure 10.6 is a useful example of the grid as applied (with hindsight) to downsizing simplification and culture change at Prudential Life Administration over the period 1989–92. Notice that some of the assumptions in the high importance and very uncertainty quadrant (the 'danger zone') are not so obvious, for instance the continuity of top management.

A sceptical reader may ask at this juncture 'How feasible is it to apply such a structured process to a fluid thing like organizational change? Aren't we better off just making our act of faith and then managing change on an emergent basis?" This book strongly dissents from this view. It is precisely because change is typically such a fluid process with ill-defined objectives that more discipline is called for to target it. Value gives an important handle over change which hitherto appears to have been under-exploited.

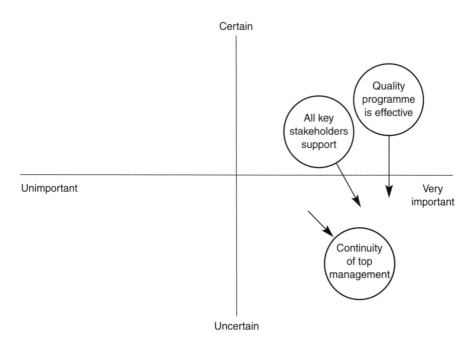

Fig. 10.6 Uncertainty/importance grid – change at Prudential Life Administration

Cellnet case study

Introduction

The next step is therefore to explore how one company has used elements of a VBC process. In the following case study there are some interesting gaps in this process which are highlighted.

The methodology was to interview a key manager involved in planning and co-ordinating a major change programme.

Interestingly, it was hard to find companies who claimed to have used a formal business case methodology to target and shape major change. Where companies were identified they were loath to admit access to a researcher – large change programmes are currently seen as (a) important ingredients of competitive advantage and (b) politically sensitive.

Strategic change at Cellnet

Cellnet was founded in 1985 to exploit the mobile telecommunications market in the UK. The company is a joint venture between British Telecommunications and Securicor, the security company. Securicor has done very well out of the venture with a good portion of its group profits generated by Cellnet.

Cellnet is the second largest player in the market and in 1994/5 significantly closed the gap with the market leader, Vodafone. The market has now gone through its emergent stage and is still going through high growth (Porter, 1980). But the threat of early maturity is a very real one, with its attendant implications for cost base and ways of competing.

Geoff Lane, currently operations director, was the head of Cellnet's paradigm project, which aimed at redesigning Cellnet into a much lower-cost, and more responsive and quick organization. Geoff Lane begins:

> '*I suppose it was a classic thing, we began with some throwaway techniques that you don't particularly think will lead anywhere special. We began by looking at some business processes to see if we could do a lot better. Basically, certain business processes were very sick. You have to remember that Cellnet is only a ten-year-old company, and it has grown extremely rapidly. This growth has involved a mass of processes, many of which have been simply plastered on.*'

The focus on operational analysis then received a major strategic impetus:

'The urgency increased when we realized we needed to do something quite drastic when we put together our strategic plan in (1992/3). We had always produced longer term business plans before, particularly for shareholders. But in the past our plans had been principally financial documents.

Our previous long-term plan had been number-driven. What number do you want to see coming out at the end? It was mainly aspirations and needed more [strategic] substance. In the new strategic plan we took a very in-depth look at market trends and changes, what the competitors were doing, what future product road maps we needed both to remain competitive and get ahead...'

Cellnet was able to project a 'what if' of decline with strategic 'do nothing':

'Out of the strategic plan we got a much more realistic view of the financials. With falling prices and more competitors coming in we needed to take a substantial slice off our cost base to achieve the kind of returns that our shareholders were looking for. Because of the magnitude of the reduction it was realized that you simply couldn't do that without some combination of downsizing or business process re-engineering (BPR).'

There was also a major strategic gap in the revenue side which was also linked to new organizational responsiveness and speed:

'A second thing was that we also planned to introduce four times as many products in the next two years as we had launched over the past eight years. We obviously had a major mismatch between what we had set out to do and what we had done in the past.'

This was further reinforced by underlying attitudes in the organization:

'So we had identified a lack of capability in being able to respond fast enough to market change. We then had a new MD on board saying that we had to be a lot closer to our customers and sensitive to market change. We also had an explosive growth in the market and in competition.'

The result of this diagnosis of the 'do nothing' situation (strategic and financial decline) was the 'paradigm project':

'This is what brought about the paradigm project to reshape how we do business. It was obvious at the time that we were looking at pretty

radical change. We began by asking the individual members of the management team what shifts in 'how we do business' (our paradigm) we needed to make – between the current position and the future. This job was facilitated by a firm of management consultants – to help us generate more ideas. We wanted to dig down to how the management team really felt about things rather than merely what they would say on the surface.

We were then able to arrive at both an 'old frame' and a 'new frame' for doing business. This flagged up some key gaps between old and new frames and enabled us to decide whether it was a big or little change we were looking at – it was a Big One.'

The change process was initially an emergent one:

'Until that time the team had been working on business process 'hotspots', helping fix things which were broke. We wanted to see first of all whether BPR could get us there. Second, we wanted to train our process review team. This also served to sort out those in the team who were going to be good at it from those who were less good.'

Geoff Lane describes how the change strategy became more and more deliberate, detailed and targeted:

'It was very helpful to have an overall model of what we were trying to achieve. This began with purpose, vision and objectives and then moved through the process of what work we needed to perform and how we would organize it.

If I can turn to the mechanics of the process, we first formed a macro design team to define the future work of the business. [This team was a subset of the management team.] Not only did this have 17 steps but it kept on splitting out when we went down and down to a more detailed level. One of the beauties of the process was that the external consultants did not say 'This is rubbish' – we were learning the whole time that we went along.

In the space of four weeks this analysis developed into nine core steps, two of which were concerned with scanning the external environment, two with developing the 'proposition' (to the market), two with internal processes and capability development. Two were concerned with integrating and packaging the solution and a final one with market release.

Under these nine core work steps we then identified the specific things which needed to happen to achieve the new frame. We then handed it over to the business, involving 50 key managers, and asked them what they were going to do with it.

We broke all the big steps down into smaller steps, defining at each stage what support work needs to happen. When our managers had completed that, we gave it back to the senior management team and then turned to the difficult issue of what to do about the organizational structure.'

Quite rapidly the project encountered some organizational constraints, particularly in defining the core processes of the organization:

'Out of our initial analysis came some quite challenging things. For example, engineering were saying that you had to do certain things in particular ways. But given the change in performance that the business needed to achieve, we had to find some fundamentally different ways of doing things.

One thing that we kicked off right away was the difference between what we called 'core work' and 'support work'. 'Core work' was the fundamental work which enabled the company to exist, whilst 'support work' is the work which enabled the 'core work' to be completed.

This distinction between core work and support work caused a lot of interesting debate. For instance, when our network people found that what they were doing was support work rather than core work, they didn't like this, at least at first. We explained that core work was work which supported customers directly and that everything else was built around that. There has to be a lot of education...'

This shows the important interdependencies between processes and structure:

'Before and up until the paradigm project and the strategic plan we had 11 departments which made for a very complex structure. We asked each one of the top team to have a crack at the new organization structure. What we said is that we needed a 'strategic development entity' – a kind of think tank. This was about the early steps in the overall processes of the business which explored what was going on in the outside world. Then we have the customer entity, the technical entity and the business services entity. All the organizational links are drawn from the customer entity.'

When asked what the value of these changes is, Geoff Lane explains:

'The value of these changes comes in several ways. First of all, before paradigm the company looked at the financials very much as being the

concern of the MD and the finance director. They handled all the major interfaces with the shareholders. The other managers weren't as closely involved in the numbers so there wasn't real ownership. Now we are all looking at all the numbers across the business (not only financial) but there is still some way to go.'

Besides having a more commercial mindset generally across the company, another element of value is derived from speed:

'Second, we are shortening time scales to develop products and the network infrastructure. Previously we used to hand each new product over several [functional] walls. The result was, of course, that all the inefficiencies occur at each interface and accumulate over the whole process. No one really has a full line of sight throughout the process, and we saw the true customer need diluted. Now the customer operations group take the decisions (pointing to the new organizational structure, indicating their pivotal role), even when technology group are building it.'

The business case for the change was then integral with the strategic and financial plan for the company:

'We did take a hard look at [in the strategic plan] what was likely to happen if we didn't go ahead with the paradigm project. We looked at what would happen in terms of the profits. We looked at what was likely to happen if we didn't get the cost savings. We considered the likely costs of incentives and discounts, our average acquisition costs per new customer and, of course, anticipated price decreases.'

But Geoff Lane admits that there is still work remaining in valuing business change:

'We have identified tools like activity-based management as being important to assess costs. But we do need to avoid a whole heap of bureaucracy with time sheets for everyone and for everything that moves. We will need to measure time, cost and quality in our new business processes. Where we have, for example, a whole portfolio of propositions we don't want to lose sight of the overall profitability of the proposition. We still want to keep that identity.'

So not only is it necessary to perform a macro level view of the value of change, it is also necessary to target it at a micro level:

'But here I am talking about the more detailed control of operations improvements – before we began, we drove the project off the strategic plan, which was backed up with broad financial projections and targets. In the plan we looked very closely at market share, our responsiveness to market need and the overall level of reduction required in our cost base.'

There is also potential value in targeting the value added by specific individuals once business processes have been simplified:

'On the topic of feedback, many of our people couldn't see, however, how doing their job better contributed to the overall scheme of things. If we can give people that quality of understanding that it really does make a difference I think we really will have made progress.'

One of the costs avoided now that the organization has become more responsive is that of less hierarchy and closer responsibility:

'But all of that hierarchy slowed the organization down. When something had to be done up, it went up a stove pipe [in the organization] and then landed eventually somewhere else. And if it didn't work, then who was responsible? Now they all know when something does work and we can reward everyone in the team. And if it doesn't work and if there is blame, then we know where it went wrong.'

But these successes have been far from painless:

'But achieving this kind of shift is really hard ... [pausing for thought], you know it is funny how things get back to you. I have even heard the word 'Waco' used about the project [after the US cult seige that went wrong] and myself referred to as David Koresh [the cult leader].'

Geoff Lane also describes the importance of change in style throughout the organization:

'Sometimes people start to slip back [to their old ways] but they soon start to see themselves slipping back. Once they achieve the breakthrough they often then say, 'I can't see why we ever had all the old problems'. We really had to change at the top, to get our top management to manage as a virtual team. Unless we actually achieve this we will never cross the gap.'

The Cellnet case study highlights a number of key lessons. First, a change programme often begins in an emergent, fragmented way. Managers are often learning at that stage and may not have defined the change's strategic objective, what value it hopes to get out of the change and the full implementation strategy.

Change projects like BPR are so interdependent with other areas of change that their value is often not practicable to assess separate from the value of the new (versus the old) business strategy. BPR is typically a part of the 'strategic project set' which also involves:

- new organization structure and roles;
- change in management style;
- skills training;
- changes in product and service portfolio;
- new management controls and measures of value added versus cost.

Returning briefly to Figure 10.1, it now becomes clear how many of these elements were drawn into the Cellnet case, particularly BPR, business planning, empowerment and downsizing.

Because of external competitive change, companies are often forced to invest in major internal change merely to protect existing revenues and cash flows. The rate of decline of the 'declining base case' is a fundamental value driver to the change project. What might actually enable Cellnet to generate incremental value over its present cash streams will be:

- its ability to achieve changes faster, cheaper and more effectively than its rivals;
- its dependence on its ability to maintain the integrated process it set out with.

Unfortunately, many change programmes go through periods of reconfiguration, especially when there are blocks from the old culture. Or, there may be a hold-up in progress because of 'bits missing' – in this case, the absence of micro-measures of value.

Another key issue is when to 'freeze' the design of the new organization. Although there might always be an element of 'continuous improvement', it is no doubt costly and disruptive to mount major business and organizational redesign. Also, it is perhaps hard to see how one can establish a process of micro-measures of value added versus cost in such a fluid organizational context.

Finally, to track the change process calls for some milestones or indicators of progress. For example, milestones might be established like:

- new structures in place and considered by the majority to be working better than previously;
- a doubling in products to market;
- cost targets hit;
- customer service targets met and exceeded.

Although valuing business change calls for some overall financial valuation of change projects, this does not mean that everything has to be valued with precision.

CONCLUSION

Valuing business change brings a new discipline to change programmes which are frequently embarked on because of 'acts of faith'. Financial analysis should not supplant informed judgement, but should steer it. Unlike Hammer and Stanton (1995) (who still see BPR as very much vision driven and inherently hard to pre-target financially), I believe BPR should be much more value-targeted in advance. If the issue of interdependencies and potentially the declining base case are addressed, then many of the concerns which managers might have about applying 'hard' analysis techniques to a 'soft' problem dissolve.

ACTION CHECKLIST

- Which of your major areas of business change clearly targeted strategically, organizationally and financially, and which of them did not?

- To what extent are these held together by an overall view of the shifts in 'How we do things around here'?

- Are there too many areas for breakthrough or are the different areas too fragmented?

- Or, are there just a small number of mammoth projects which are patently (or, at least, probably) unachievable?

- What does the business case for the change reveal about the most important and uncertain assumptions?

- To what extent is the value generated incremental or of a protective nature?

- What measures and indicators are in place to track delivery of value?

- At what stage is it appropriate to stabilize the new way of doing things (moving from 'breakthrough' mode into 'continuous improvement' mode) in order to prevent value loss through management exhaustion?

Part IV

TURNING THOUGHT
INTO ACTION

'Avoid stratophrenia!'

11

CHANNELLING
THE BREAKTHROUGH

This final chapter looks at the role of breakthrough business planning, project management, and indicators of strategic health and financial performance. Looking at how to measure or track both strategic health and financial performance helps avoid stratophrenia! Then it is time to reflect on all the lessons of this book, specifically linking this with the implications for action. The conclusion is an examination of Your Next Steps.

BREAKTHROUGH BUSINESS PLANNING

Despite all the books and advice on strategic planning, with relatively few exceptions most companies' business plans are short term, financial and predominantly inwardly focused. They often suffer from a primarily tactical focus, being a consolidation of actions rather than presenting a coherent picture. Very few are actually lively and exciting. Even when they are, they are frequently typically under-tested and vulnerable to becoming at best part-realized.

It is now necessary to set out various tools for managers' breakthrough in the context of the business planning process.

Figure 11.1 fills this gap. Breakthrough business planning (BBP) enables companies to select from the menu of tools those best suited to the planning process and business challenges.

Figure 11.1 highlights the interdependency of issue analysis, vision and objectives in setting the process for delivering the plan. It also highlights the importance of communication planning early on, which then moves through the entire process, needing continual attention. In some instances effective communication requires between 20 and 30 per cent of total effort.

Communication subsequently covers a wide range of areas including the overall business goals and insights into external opportunities or threats. It also helps communicate agendas openly as a prelude to any decisions and

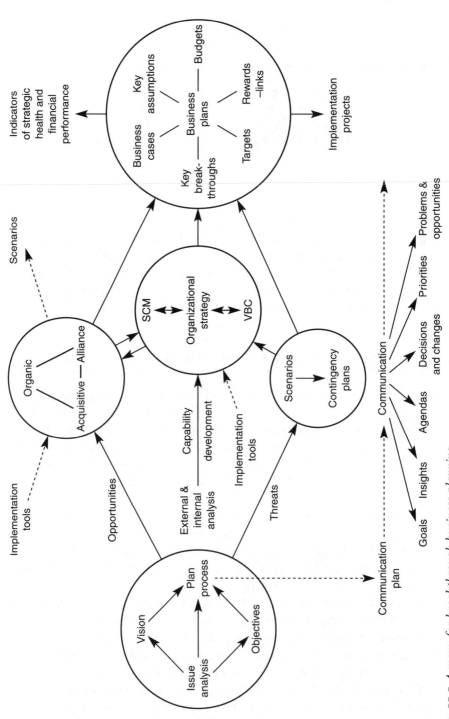

Fig. 11.1 A menu for breakthrough business planning

changes. New opportunities can also be highlighted using FT or ('from...to') analysis. Problems and opportunities can be circulated more freely, not only before key decisions have been made but also in shaping detailed implementation plans.

Besides the analysis of specific opportunities and threats (with selective mini scenarios being undertaken) the core of breakthrough business planning is driven by the development of organizational strategy. This core captures the internal breakthrough opportunities, and is assisted by tools from both strategic cost management (SCM) and valuing business change (VBC) frameworks.

Finally, breakthrough business plans spell out the key breakthroughs, integrate the results and rationale of the various specific business cases, and set targets (which link to rewards). The business plans are dovetailed to specific implementation projects, and to indicators of strategic health and financial performance.

Note that budgets themselves form only one of the outputs. Of equal importance are the key assumptions which underpin the business plan, especially those which are most important and more uncertain.

Figure 11.1 does not imply a massive planning bureaucracy. Nor does it imply a strictly linear process – breakthrough business planning is highly iterative. For instance, if a new issue crystallizes (as did cost levels during a major review of Dowty Communications (Grundy, 1993a)), then it is imperative to refocus and, if necessary, widen the scope of business planning decisions and implementation programmes.

Nor does Figure 11.1 imply that for every decision that occurs, there is a business case or that there is a panoply of implementation projects. Applying *hoshin* once again, each business area focuses on no more than between one to three breakthrough projects. The other issues are then the focus of continuous improvement or development programmes.

Ideally, the initial launch of the process (see the circle far left in Figure 11.1) should take no more than a couple of days. The bulk of the work occurs in the centre. The amount of work depends essentially upon the degree to which the company understands its target markets, change in these markets and the extent to which management believes it to be necessary to challenge assumptions. It also depends upon the potential for, and the urgency of, internal breakthrough.

Scenario development need not and must not become an industry (refer once again to Appendix II).

Finally, the importance of thinking through what will be communicated, how, and to whom and through whom (towards the right) cannot be over-stressed. This is where leadership comes truly to the fore in the equation of success (or failure). Strategic droop often begins at the communication interface and the weakest link in the chain is typically business leadership.

After this overview of breakthrough business planning, it is time to continue the process of managing implementation projects.

A PROJECT MANAGING STRATEGIC DEVELOPMENT

Introducing everyday project management

Breakthroughs in strategies for growth do not happen merely by analysis, however well-oiled the decision process is. Ideas and solutions must be transformed into action. This transformation is facilitated through project management.

When one mentions the two words 'project management' often the alert eyes of senior managers begin to dull and cloud over. It is as if these two words joined together at once summon up a vision of over-sophisticated and impossibly bureaucratic, over-regimented processes. This raises the question as to why 'project management' is seen as another form of an unwanted, MBA-type disease (or 'management by asphyxiation').

Although at some stage in their careers managers are invariably exposed to project management, this is invariably a fleeting experience. Because project management is usually presented as complex, technical and intricate, most managers are turned off for life. Even the technical terms themselves (like 'Gantt Charts', 'Critical Paths' and 'Float Time') are off-putting – to say the least.

But over the last five to ten years there has been a major resurgence of interest in project management. Project management master's degree courses with eager managers have proliferated and are bursting at the seams.

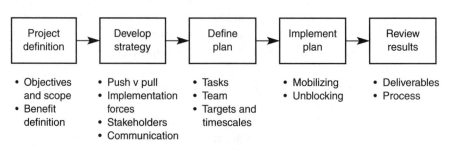

Fig. 11.2 Everyday project management – the process

Fig. 11.3 Setting project objectives

Project management of major corporate initiatives does not have to be rocket science. Instead, you are invited to practise 'everyday project management' (see Figure 11.2), which is altogether a much clearer, simplified and workable process. So, below is an overview of project managing strategic development and then you will have a chance to flesh out your own strategic development plans.

A strategic development project is defined as being 'any programme aimed at achieving a breakthrough in both corporate scope and financial performance ("the result") to a pre-planned time and cost'.

The classic triangle in Figure 11.3 which depicts the result, the time and the cost, suggests that there are inherent tensions in project management. One can, for instance, develop a new aeroengine to a particular target performance (the result) and in targeted time, but then blow the cost budget. Or you can skimp on the cost and deliver results on time, but with either shortfalls in quality or quantity or both. Alternatively, you might achieve the result at the targeted cost but it may take a lot longer to deliver this.

Project management – the key phases

Figure 11.2 shows the five key phases of everyday project management which can be used to help manage strategic development more effectively during implementation:

- definition;
- project strategy;
- define plan;
- implementation;
- review.

Each of these stages is highly iterative. For example, during feasibility there is typically a good deal of project redefinition. Also, at the stage of making a formal proposal the key elements of definition (including objectives and constraints, strategy and ownership) are revisited.

Taking each phase in turn, project definition involves:

- setting the key strategic, operational, organizational and organizational objectives of the project;
- exploring and testing the constraints;
- developing an implementation strategy.

Project objectives and constraints

The objectives of any strategic development project are typically a mix of hard to soft. Some objectives are more readily measurable (such as to build relative market share – this being a strategic objective, or to achieve a particular financial result – a financial objective). Other objectives are less tangible (such as to develop a new capability or to learn about a particular area of market development – both being strategic objectives). It is a fruitful discipline to define all of these objectives explicitly.

Quite senior managers often balk at defining project objectives with clarity, perhaps because they are shy, because they feel that being really clear and specific is babyish, or perhaps because they want to preserve political elbow room. In any event, deliberately fuzzing up project objectives is a dangerous game. It is hard enough anyway to communicate clear and explicit objectives for strategic development projects. You don't need to give yourself an even greater handicap than you already have.

Short exercise

For *one* possible strategic development project which you have already identified ask these questions.

- What are the key strategic objectives (for instance, repositioning a product, penetrating a new market, defending an existing market position)?
- What are the key operational objectives (for instance improving efficiency, increasing flexibility, increasing capacity, achieving operational leverages)?
- What are the key organizational objectives (for instance, simplifying a process or developing a capability)?
- What are the key financial objectives (for instance, reducing the cost base, improving margins, generating an NPV, achieving an IRR, delivering a target, payback etc.)?
- How consistent are these objectives as a whole and do they reinforce each other?

Turning next to project constraints, again these might be so severe as to make it impossible – right from the very start of the project – to achieve success. (In my earlier career I used to relish a 'mission impossible' project but in more recent times I have sought to avoid the 'Houdini project'.) Any constraints which may derail the project need to be identified extremely early on.

This is another example of the 'it's not going to happen' factor (a term coined by Hewlett Packard). It is far better to say it isn't going to happen than to adopt what has been previously called a 'Nietzsche-Pollyanna' approach (Carter, 1971). Nietzsche was the philosopher who prescribed 'The Will to Power' as a guiding light for one's highest aspirations. There are many parallels with strategic development – managers frequently begin major projects to achieve strategic development breakthrough in a 'Will to Power' mode. Then when things start to go wrong, they resort to the Pollyanna doctrine (as in the *Peter Pan* story) of 'Don't worry, it will all turn out all right in the end'.

Project strategy and ownership

There are different options for project strategy. Returning to Chapter 5, one should pose the question: 'Is the project going to be pursued as a "push" project, I driven almost entirely top-down, or is it going to involve intensive participation before the project strategy is defined?' The choice of a primarily push or pull strategy is likely to be decisive in determining eventual success or failure. Obviously the reality is that one adopts a mixture of both 'push' and 'pull' approaches, but the mix should be a deliberate one and not arrived at by default.

Another key variable is the ownership of the project. There should always be a project sponsor (unless that is the project manager), so that there is a clear definition of whom the project is delivering benefits for. Where there are a number of interested stakeholders (especially where the project's objectives impact on different parts of the organization), then it would be wise to do a stakeholder analysis of the key players (see Chapter 5).

Short exercise

For a specific strategic development project you are currently (or have been) involved with, either directly or indirectly ask these questions.

- Which stakeholders have a major interest in all the deliverables of the project at different stages of its life cycle?
- Which stakeholders are involved in the process of making the project work?

- Using the stakeholder analysis, which of these players are most/least influential, and is their attitude to the project favourable, neutral or unfavourable?
- How can these patterns of influence and attitude be reshaped?

Defining the plan – feasibility

The feasibility appraisal leads to more detailed and specific targeting of the costs and benefits of the project. This also leads into risk assessment. Again you might wish to use the uncertainty/importance grid (see Chapter 4) to identify and evaluate the key vulnerabilities.

During the feasibility stage you will need to match the resources and team to the needs of the project. A classic trap is to pick a team (or specific individuals) which is quite capable technically, but which is politically unskilled or lacks a sufficiently strong power base.

During the feasibility stage, it is also a useful sanity check to do an 'IMF' (see Chapter 5) to assess the key enablers and constraints impacting on the project. A useful checklist for identifying key enablers and constraints for a specific project follows.

1. How clear are the project's objectives, and how well and consistently do the key stakeholders understand the objectives?
2. Is there full and timely communication throughout the project?
3. Are project management skills adequate?
4. Is there continuity of the team?
5. Are resources genuinely sufficient (especially at critical phases of the project)?
6. Are the milestones actually realistic?
7. Has a 'pilot' phase been included?
8. Just how genuinely open to learning are the project managers, the team and key stakeholders?
9. How susceptible is the project to organizational politics?

Defining the plan – project proposal

The project proposal should contain two key ingredients:

- the business case
- the project plan.

The business case has been covered at some length in Chapter 4. The key point at this juncture is to stress that the main links between the business case and the project plan are:

- the resource requirements (not merely in terms of quantity but also quality and timeliness);
- the milestones for delivery of project benefits;
- the assumptions surrounding implementation difficulty.

The project plan should avoid getting bogged down in inappropriate, over-complicated and misleadingly precise networking of activities. Few strategic development projects (and, for that matter, few management projects) are amenable to full-blown critical path and activity network analysis. Because of the relatively high levels of uncertainty surrounding the timings of most project activities, scientific modelling of activities is invariably frustrated.

Everyday project management does however provide a most important role in listing activities, in targeting approximate timings and durations, and in sorting out the order in which things must happen. Rather than call this Gantt charts it is a lot more accessible to call these 'activity road maps' (or, if you prefer acronyms, ARMs).

Implementation and review

During implementation the tools introduced in Chapter 5 (particularly IMF analysis, stakeholder analysis) need to be continuously revisited, otherwise a project which has been running extremely well can begin to drift and be deflected off-course.

During review these tools are equally valuable in understanding how and why a particular strategic development project got into trouble. They can also suggest what could still be done to generate mass value from it.

So many strategic development projects become unguided as soon as they begin to track off-course. It is as if as soon as they deviate, managers feel that 'the error' cannot be discussed and is uncorrectable. Some projects actually go so wrong that they become such a bundle of 'self-sealing errors' (Argyris, 1991) and the whole programme becomes a corporate cover-up. The irony is – everyone in 'the know' can read through the smokescreen being generated at the top or the middle, but still no one has the heart or the courage to move fast to kill the project and cut the losses. The paradox of project management is therefore:

The more things go wrong, then the more they tend to go wrong – resulting in a disaster curve.

Tracking strategic and financial performance

In a famous video on *Competitive Strategy* (Emerson Electric's Integration of Skill in the US), Michael Porter of Harvard reflects on the lack of tools and frameworks for relating strategic and financial health. This is another example of 'stratophrenia', where management teams have two distinct perspectives of the same business(es), sometimes at different times, sometimes at the same time. With stratophrenia these views can be inconsistent.

During the Harvard video Michael Porter interviewed the chief executive of Skil Corporation. This corporation staged a major turnaround in the 1980s. Michael Porter reflects that:

- a company can be in the process of achieving a strategic turnaround but its financial performance may lag, sometimes for up to several years;
- a company might be financially profitable and performing well, but be 'strategically bankrupt'.

Strategic health is defined as:

The underlying competitive position of a business set against the emerging competitive forces and its stream of opportunities.

The notion of strategic health thus compares present capability against future challenge. This is different from the traditional notion of 'strategic fit' that compares present capability with current environment.

Financial performance is defined as:

The underlying profit stream in relatlon to current capital base and current and future cash flow.

Financial performance is thus not a single indicator but balances conventional short-term, accounting-based measures against future, economic cash flows (see once again Chapter 4).

Most businesses (even up to the largest groups) find problems in balancing different financial measures of performance. They also find it very hard (if they do this formally at all) to link the financial measures of performance to indicators of strategic health (and vice versa).

The causes of lags between strategic health and financial performance are not hard to find. These are likely to be due to the benefits of investment in strategic change taking a while to materialize. Also these benefits are offset by continued strategic drift and decay. Conventional measurement tools (both from strategy and finance) appear to fall well short in helping track both strategic health and financial performance – and simultaneously.

Although Kaplan's 'balanced score-card' (Kaplan and Norton, 1992) offers some clues, this more operationally-based approach may fail to capture 'strategic health' as it is defined.

This section gives a practical overview of how strategic health and financial performance can be integrated. This is achieved by breaking down strategic health into:

(a) present competitive position; and
(b) future strategic potential.

Taking (a), present competitive position is then analysed between the business's position in terms of its competitive software and its competitive hardware.

The future strategic potential of the business (b) is then analysed between its future competitive pressure and also the quality of its opportunity stream.

Next, financial performance is broken down between:

- return on capital (measured via return on net assets) ;
- cash flow.

Return on capital can also be broken down still further, in terms of return on sales versus turnover divided by net assets. Remembering the textbooks on accounting ratios, these show that (as the sales figure nicely cancels out):

$$\text{Return on capital employed*} = \frac{\text{Operating profit}}{\text{Sales}} \times \frac{\text{Sales}}{\text{Net assets}} \times 100\%$$

*If measured as return on net assets.

It is also possible to split out cash flow into another grid to disaggregate operating cash flow (before depreciation) from investment requirements. This helps to highlight the constituents of cash flow. Financial performance should then be broken down by strategic business units down to the key fighting units in the organization (frequently this is done at too high a level and needs to be taken down a level more)

The more novel of the grids (which are now focused on) are those concerning strategic health. Figure 11.4 (on 'strategic health') maps present competitive position against future strategic potential for M&S, Tesco and Rover.

M&S has a medium to high strategic potential across its businesses, especially in exploiting its own brand. It has a very strong opportunity stream, particularly internationally, but it also faces increasing competitive pressure as it extends from its existing core markets (see Figure 11.5).

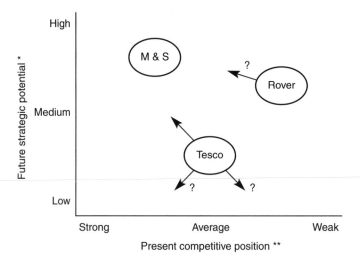

*   Opportunity stream plus future competitive pressure
** Competitive hardware plus software

Fig. 11.4 Strategic health

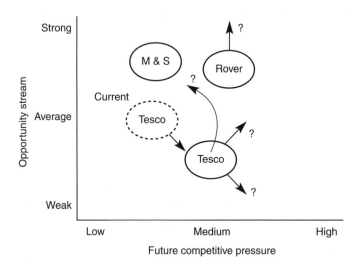

Fig. 11.5 Future strategic potential

M&S also has a very strong competitive position (Figure 11.6), particularly in terms of its competitive hardware. This competitive hardware includes its:

- products;
- service quality;
- channels (its retail network);
- customer base;
- operations;
- cost base.

These dimensions require further benchmarking of current position and thus collecting external as well as internal data (selectively). This process should, however, avoid becoming an industry in its own right.

Tesco's competitive software is not quite as strong as that of M&S (as our longer case study earlier in the book highlighted). M&S's own position in Figure 11.6 is shown as a cucumber-type shape. Its competitive position in Figure 11.4 is thus shown slightly to the right of 'very strong'.

Tesco's future strategic potential (Figure 11.4) is not quite as high as that of M&S. (M&S is now very well placed to exploit opportunities for international development, while Tesco has only just begun to do this.) Figure 11.5 controversially shows Tesco as facing fairly tough competitive pressure and a more limited opportunity stream than M&S in the UK. (Obviously Tesco managers may like to challenge and debate these judgements. But these are not absolute positionings – they require further refinement in terms of indicators and measures of strategic health. It is much more important to have this debate than to do precise positionings.)

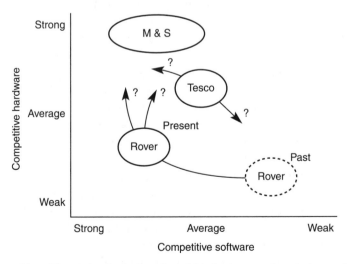

Note: this needs to be broken down (a) to business and product group level (vertically) and separated (b) by area of competitive support.

Fig. 11.6 Present competitive position

Tesco's present competitive position also appears weaker than M&S (which is not surprising, considering M&S's competitive might) (see Figure 11.4). While Tesco's competitive hardware is perhaps slightly better than average within the industry, its competitive software appears little different from other players (Figure 11.6). Tesco's competitive software (again this may require selective benchmarking) comprises of its:

- brand, and image and reputation;
- skills and style;
- responsiveness and team-working;
- systems and processes;
- leadership and management;
- innovation.

(This positioning may need some further qualitative/semi-quantitative rating.) Tesco might be pleased to come out of this well against M&S.

Rover, by contrast, is moving through a strategic turnaround Its competitive position has moved from being relatively weak to just below average (overall) – Figure 11.4 – because of its relative small size even *vis-à-vis* its target niches and its past dependency on Honda technology. Its future strategic potential is high, especially given its good opportunity stream, although future competitive pressure is very similar to that facing Tesco (Figure 11.5) – this pressure is pretty tough.

From Chapter 8, Rover's competitive hardware is a little below average but improving rapidly (in some aspects – especially product quality – it is probably ahead of certain of the competition). Its competitive software is also getting strong, especially through team-working and flexibility (Figure 11.6).

The Rover example shows how useful it is to split out the hardware and software sides to competitive advantage. Rover's turnaround is based to a great extent on its strong competitive software (and to some extent its newer products). But its competitive hardware also incorporates its cost base and relative scale, which have traditionally disadvantaged it as a business.

A key missing ingredient now is financial health. Figure 11.7 shows the estimated financial health of the three businesses.

M&S has a very strong return on capital and cash flow. Its programme of major international expansion may shift it over to the right slightly (but for good reasons) as cash flow becomes less strong – it is not necessary to have very strong cash flow. Tesco has average return on capital and cash flow. Rover has weaker return on capital (uneven and not high over the three years to 1994), and its cash flow is not strong (although in 1995 Rover's financial performance is improving considerably, this is at a time of economic recovery).

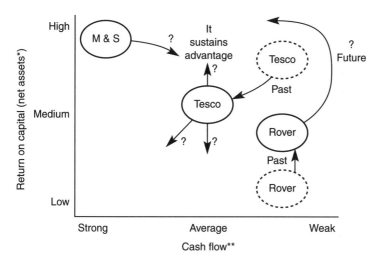

* Can be split between return on sales, and sales divided by net assets (asset turnover)
** Can be split between operating cash flow and capital investment/acquisitions.

Fig. 11.7 Financial performance

Figure 11.7 can have quantitative as opposed to qualitative measurement scales. One way of doing this is to relate net operating cash flow to turnover as a percentage (for comparability across business units).

Figure 11.8 now integrates the picture of both strategic health and financial performance. M&S is positioned as having strong strategic health and strong financial performance. Tesco is not so well positioned, having an average strategic health and financial performance – and may slip on both dimensions, especially if attacked by competition more fiercely. It might be fruitful for the Tesco board to review where they need to take the business on both axes of 11.8 and how, and when (business area-by-area).

Rover is staging a major improvement which (with BMW backing) is likely to move it north-westwards towards better strategic health and improved financial performance. A number of provisos should not be made on this shift, particularly:

• Rover's cash flow does not move very strongly negative, mainly due to massive investment requirement;
• Rover's competitive software is not dissipated during the post-acquisition management phase (see the more detailed BMW and Rover case in Chapter 8);

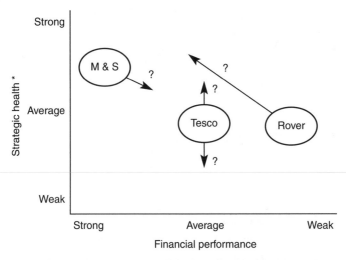

Fig. 11.8 Strategic health and financial performance

- competitive pressure in Rover's niche markets (for example in four-wheel drive) does not intensify significantly

Figures 11.4 to 11.8 thus show how the debate about linking strategic and financial performance can be initiated. These figures also highlight the benefits which this yields, particularly in comparing different business units, and in taking a multi-perspective view of position, performance and prospects. They also help raise strategic issues to prompt thinking for paths for future development.

In addition to Figures 11.4 to 11.8, other grids can be constructed for comparing strategic health and financial performance. For instance, we might compare:

- present competitive position (Figure 11.4) against return on capital (Figure 11.7), or against cash flow (Figure 11.7) or against overall financial performance (Figure 11.8);
- the opportunity stream (Figure 11.5) against return on capital (Figure 11.7);
- the opportunity stream (Figure 11.5) against present competitive position (Figure 11.4);
- investment cash flow (subset of Figure 11.7) against return on capital employed (Figure 11.7);
- operating cash flow (Figure 11.7) can be split between current and future.

These grids bring alive (in a pictorial way) the positioning and performance of different business areas from a number of perspectives. They also challenge the existing pattern of resource allocation. Finally, they may help explain why resources do need to be deployed in a certain way, or why certain trade – offs in time are necessary

Although the various case studies are used as examples, the parallels with your own business(es) should be evident. More specifically, the strategic health/financial performance grid can be used for:

- reappraising past performance (as part of a strategic review);
- monitoring current business performance and future profits – across the portfolio of business areas;
- evaluating the impact of new areas of strategic development, particularly in new markets, channels, services and products.

Exercise on your own company

For one or more than one business area(s) ask these questions.

- How is this positioned in terms of its opportunity stream and future competitive pressure (Figure 11.5)?
- How is it positioned in its competitive hardware and software (Figure 11.6)?
- How is it therefore positioned in terms of its future strategic potential and present competitive position (Figure 11.4)?
- What is its financial health (in terms of cash flow, return on capital) (Figure 11.7)?
- How is it therefore positioned overall in terms of its strategic health and financial performance (Figure 11.8)?

KEY LESSONS FROM THE BOOK

In this book the need for a process for managing breakthrough strategies for growth was exposed. This process needs to be managed strategically rather than incrementally and 'all in bits'.

But to manage strategies for growth it was first necessary to become clear about what 'strategy' meant. Strategy was defined in terms of a constant striving to achieve (and keep) competitive advantage, rather than primarily in terms of pure business growth. Also, the need to target strategic development on generating longer term financial value, rather than primarily on short-term accounting returns was emphasized.

A single, mechanistic process for managing strategic development was not prescribed. Chapter 1, however, highlighted the trade-offs between adopting different kinds of strategy (particularly deliberate versus emergent). There are some considerable downsides in holding on to an extremely fluid and emergent approach, and for too long. Also, the problems of an inappropriate deliberate strategy were highlighted at London International.

Key implication 1

Use the deliberate, emergent, emerging, submergent and detergent framework for strategies for growth to monitor which mode your company may have defaulted to.

Strategic recipes were found to play a major, and often tacit and unconscious, role in shaping strategies for growth. It was fruitful to expose these recipes so that a more objective review of what had and had not worked well in the past could be examined. (See the first part of the Marks & Spencer case in Chapter 2.)

Key implication 2

Expose and re-examine your implicit recipes for strategic development explicitly and openly within your management teams.

Then the strategic analysis toolkit was used to shine light on the future direction of, and opportunities for, strategic development. In Chapter 3 a number of tools for analysing the external and internal environment were explored – and with a powerful visual effect. Some specific tools included the competitive forces, the 'grow-earnings' grid, the onion model of competitive advantage and the strategy health check (or 'STAIR' analysis).

These tools offered a novel picture of strategic development both in the once gloomy but now innovative undertaking industry, and also in analysing the current position and future potential of Marks & Spencer. (For strategic development workshops, see Appendix III.)

Key implication 3

Use the strategic analysis tools intuitively and informally whenever thinking about a strategic development opportunity. But also be prepared to use them formally and explicitly to share and test the management team's strategic vision – check it out.

Chapter 4 looked at strategies for growth from yet another angle – from the perspective of value analysis, avoiding the trap of assuming that growth strategies could be easily and precisely collapsed into 'the financial numbers'. Yet by linking the the financial (or 'value') analysis directly to the earlier strategic analysis, it was possible to provide some powerful reality checks on what might otherwise become a 'strategic mirage' (and not, after all, strategic vision).

To achieve this some of the most knotty problems of value analysis were focused on – for instance dealing with the declining base case and protective value, with interdependencies (for instance in the Alton Towers case), with intangibles, and with value of a future and highly contingent nature.

Key implication 4

Do not be tempted to slide from 'it is hard to put a value on this strategic development opportunity' to 'we don't need to think about in what circumstances we might generate value, how, and what might prevent value from crystallizing.'

Chapter 4 introduced the notion of mapping assumptions in terms of degrees of uncertainty and importance. This tool (and its 'danger zone' of very important and very uncertain assumptions) can be used to help evaluate strategic development at the decision stage and throughout implementation. So often the assumption that 'we can do it' is not only very important but also very uncertain.

Key implication 5

Whenever you sense discomfort about a particular strategic development project, do spend five minutes with a single piece of A4 to map the key assumptions in terms of uncertainty and importance. See this as a strategic (but cheap) insurance policy.

The uncertainty and importance grid also provided links with the third key perspective on strategies for growth – organizational analysis. A number of closely interrelated tools were explored – including implementation forces (IMF) analysis, stakeholder analysis, and the attractiveness-implementation difficulty (AID) tool. These tools then provided a foundation for examining implementation issues throughout the remainder of the book. These tools are equally applicable to other areas of implementation in your jobs – don't forget this!

Key implication 6

For all strategic development projects do at least take the precaution of exploring the key implementation difficulties, either informally or, better still, formally.

Without the infrastructure of key capabilities it was highlighted that strategic development was very likely to fail. The final part of Chapter 5 highlighted the need to evaluate capabilities in an holistic way, rather than to split this up into HR, and other, functionally based strategies.

The next topic was organic growth (Chapter 6). Using the Tesco case the strategic analysis tools were again practised – linking the results with the analysis of Tesco's financial performance. The impact of strategic and growth recipes was once again highlighted, particularly in providing the momentum for both organic development, and for acquisitive forays both in France and in Scotland. The case study also illustrated the influence of the prevailing industry mindset – the sixth force, which was added to Michael Porter's set of five (in Chapter 3).

Key implication 7

Always bear in mind when attempting breakthrough strategies for growth the perhaps insidious influence of the industry mindset. What shared assumptions do you need to challenge, if not actually reject?

Chapter 7 moved step-by-step through the process of managing acquisitive growth. This related closely to the analysis tools from 'the strategic toolkit' (Chapter 3) and to the need to be objective about how value would be generated (Chapter 4) through the acquisition, particularly through the 'three V's'. The organizational issues which surround the post-acquisition management phase (from Chapter 5) were also addressed. The checklist of acquisition deal do's and don'ts is essential reading, for newcomers and for the experienced (see also Appendix IV on value).

The two mini case studies, Hanson and Sketchley, underlined the imperatives of maintaining absolute clarity of purpose, managing commitment levels of the assessment of risks and uncertainties. Again, there is no one single approach to acquisitions – this book does not advocate the Hanson route. ICI and Zeneca also brought together the lessons from demergers – avoid the strategic clutter which then leads to value dilution and subsequent need for demerger, wherever possible.

Key implication 8

Acquisition is rarely, if ever, the only route for effective strategies for growth. Not only are there usually organic options but there may be others too, including licensing and joint ventures. Be especially clear about your acquisition 'do's and don'ts'.

The BMW and Rover case (in Chapter 8) leads into joint discussions of organic and acquisitive strategies for growth – this time in an international context. As further reinforcement to learning the strategic positions and prospects were analysed (separately) for BMW and Rover, the strategic impact of the acquisition, and the potential value generated. The onion model of competitive advantage helped identify just how much BMW brought to the deal. The analysis of key uncertainties also highlighted some downsides which commentators may have identified but not as fully exposed. In particular, the issues of how difficult post-acquisition management of Rover might become were highlighted as appearing both very important and, at the time of the deal, also very uncertain.

Key implications 9 and 10

- Never give in to strategic temptation without fully thinking through the potential impact, right into the relatively distant future.
- Do not confuse markets becoming global with an imperative to 'have a global strategy' and therefore to have a significant presence in all key markets. This can lead to major strategic and financial dilution

The next step on the journey was to examine two key infrastructure issues for strategies for growth – strategic cost management and valuing business change.

Cost management is so often an area of profound mismanagement which impedes breakthrough strategic development. By managing cost management strategically this threat is turned into an opportunity. Costs can, and should, be managed for both financial and competitive advantage – as in the Cotswold Technology case.

Valuing business change (Chapter 10) is another and closely related area of internal development which may be essential to pre-empt external change. The Cellnet case illustrated how business process reengineering can be more effectively targeted and evaluated by combining strategic, financial and organizational analysis.

Key implication 11

Apply the same rigour and holistic thinking to internally facing strategic development as you did to externally facing development.

Finally Chapter 11 shows how project management (in its everyday form) could be simplified and applied in the strategic development arena.

Project management is not about putting management on the moon; it is about working backwards from the future. More importantly than any rocket science, it is about sensing the soft (as well as the hard) implementation forces which continually threaten to destabilize the project in mid-flight.

It also explored how strategic health and financial performance can be used as turn indicators of business success.

Key implication 12

Those who practise strategic development without applying project management techniques run the same risks as those who once practised 'free love' in the 1960s and 1970s. The environment has changed. Do apply 'everyday scenario planning' (ESP) (Appendix II).

Key implication 13 (lucky for some)

For those who rely upon luck as the core ingredient of strategic development (for instance, Barings merchant bank in the UK): it's really simple – don't.

BRINGING IT ALL TOGETHER

Figure 11.9 now integrates all the main ingredients in this book, which began by looking at the fit between the three key areas of analysis – strategic, financial and organizational. There were many linkages between these different tools (see Figure 11.10).

Figure 11.10 shows how strategic analysis helps to focus financial analysis on the right issues, particularly through injecting strategic thinking by setting strategic objectives. Financial analysis in turn helps to value the strategy. Strategic analysis also targets the key capabilities for development while organizational analysis checks whether it can be implemented.

Finally, organizational analysis challenges the financial assumptions with 'When and how can we implement?' In turn, the financial analysis can help test out the cost/benefit of developing particular capabilities, so that these capabilities are not just developed on a just-in-case basis.

Finally, the key interfaces between internal breakthrough are pictured in Figure 11.11. Internal breathrough is very frequently triggered by intensified competitive and financial pressure (as well as organizational politics). Organizational strategy, which integrates the shift in people processes, structures and capabilities, does foster a coherent response to these external processes.

Organizational strategy then helps to identify the softer cost-drivers and also to define the specific organizational shifts that are needed (the from – to's).

Valuing business change helps to target change and strategic cost management helps to protect strategy-critical capabilities. Finally, strategic cost

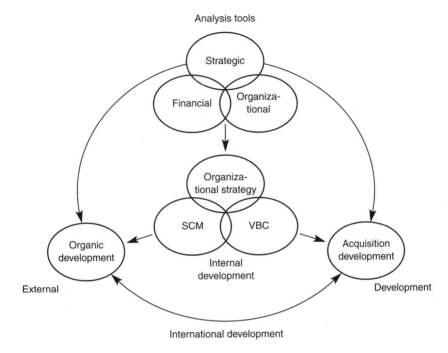

Fig. 11.9 Breakthrough strategies for growth – the big picture

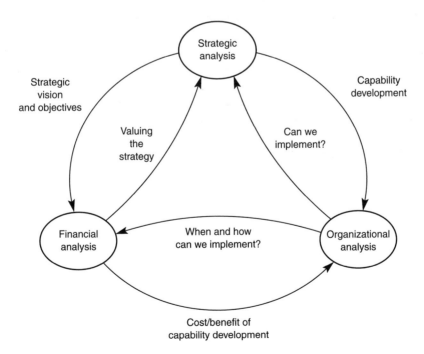

Fig. 11.10 Integrating the analysis process

management projects provide the meat (alongside other change programmes) for valuing business change.

Both organic development and acquisitive development (see again Figure 11.9) are greatly assisted by an integrated approach to internal breakthrough. For instance, we can easily imagine the relevance of both strategic cost management and valuing business change, say, to the post-acquisition management of Rover (by BMW) and William Low (by Tesco). Also, in the Marks & Spencer case the intuitive application of strategic cost management throughout M&S's operations was drawn out. At Cellnet, valuing business change (particularly BPR) played a major role in supporting Cellnet's ambitious external plans – through providing Cellnet with a keenly competitive, future cost base.

Breakthrough Strategies for Growth thus provides a process for exploiting opportunities for capturing both financial and competitive advantage. It also provides an integrated set of tools and recipes for challenging existing direction, and generating and probing opportunities in new directions (so do now check you have used the detailed checklists in Appendix I).

Unlike other guides, which primarily take either a strategic, market-led, financial or organizational perspective, it offers a full road map. This full road map gives you the complete picture rather than one which just shows the roads, the towns, or just shows the mountains or rivers. Hopefully, your own mental map is now considerably fleshed out which you began to explore in Chapter 1 with the cartoon map of 'What is Strategy?

So what does *Breakthrough Strategies for Growth* now mean to you? It could mean two things. First it could mean that you feel more confident that your organization's existing external (and internal) strategy for growth (whether deliberate, emergent or perhaps even 'detergent') is sound. Or it could mean that you have begun to head off projects or programmes that take you into major danger zones. If the latter is the case, then you may be some way to avoiding your strategy management from becoming: **(S)TRAGEDY MANAGEMENT.**

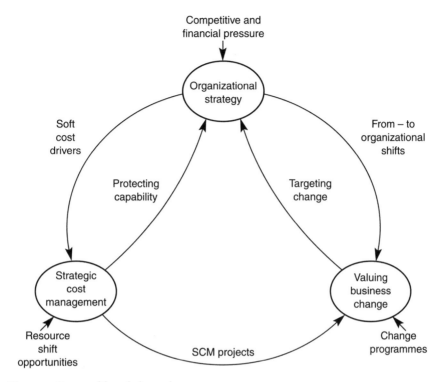

Fig11.11 Internal breakthrough

APPENDIX I

Diagnosing your own strategies for growth issues

SELF-DIAGNOSIS OF YOUR ISSUES

Having worked through the book it is now time for you to apply these to your own business. Give yourself at least an hour's run at these questions.

Revisiting the past

These first four questions explore the basis of past (successful and unsuccessful) strategic development in your business.

- In the past, which 20 per cent of activities has generated 80 per cent of profit (for example, by geographic area, type of market or need, products, customer segments, specific customers etc.)? (You may have to think hard about 'what business you are in', not merely in terms of organizational structure but rather product/market/customer needs.)
- What has been the basis for this past success (for instance, has it been having a distinct competitive edge, good timing, favourable market and competitive trends, getting the implementation of the strategy right etc.)? Consider using the STAIR analysis tool, Porter's competitive forces and the onion model of competitive advantage.
- What have the causes been of any notable failures or disappointments (for example, lack of clear competitive edge, lack of critical mass in resources, poor implementation, competitor reaction etc.)?
- What types of activity might not have worked in the past but are now perhaps both feasible and attractive (perhaps because of market change or increased capability)? Consider analysing the growth drivers behind market demand and also PEST analysis.

Reviewing present position

The following three questions evaluate the opportunities which are more evident currently.

- What are the current opportunities for strategic development (in terms, for example, of extending existing markets, exploiting the existing customer base, product or service innovation, new distribution channels, challenging the cost base and thereby the basis of price competition)? (This suggests a brainstorming exercise – possibly a SWOT analysis will help.)
- What are the key routes to exploiting these avenues to development, e.g. by organic growth, acquisitions, by joint ventures or licensing?
- How important (in terms of financial and competitive impact) are these opportunities likely to be and how difficult are they likely to be to exploit?

Rethinking the future

The next series of four questions helps to explore opportunities which are 'around the corner' but which can provide a major contribution to corporate development long term.

- What emerging opportunities exist which might together generate 20 per cent or more of business activity within five years' time? (Consider developing a future scenario using PEST, Porter's competitive forces and the onion model of competitive advantage.)
- What key growth drivers have an impact on shaping (or constraining) the growth of these opportunities?
- To what extent are these options likely to offer sustainable financial and competitive advantage, given known and suspected competitor activity. (This invites an analysis of not merely obvious but also less obvious competitors.)
- What level of competitive rivalry will this opportunity exhibit? (Use Porter's five competitive forces.)

Refocusing the strategy

The following five questions now challenge existing corporate development strategies in order to rebalance the portfolio.

- What business activities now naturally suggest themselves as being areas to harvest, run down or get out of? (Apply the GE grid here – Chapter 3.)
- What other areas of the business(es) can be fruitfully reinvigorated and how?

- What overall shifts in the nature of the business(es) and in the underlying competencies are implied by the new strategies ('from x to y')?
- What level of profits, investment and cash flow could the refocused set of strategies offer?
- What are the key risks and uncertainties which need to be considered or managed? (Use the uncertainty and importance grid from Chapter 4.)

Retargeting efforts

- What are the critical success factors (things to get right or avoid getting wrong), which are implied by the refocused strategy? (These can be distilled from the analysis of Porter's five competitive forces.)
- What simple messages to the organization are now appropriate and how can these be conveyed in an exciting (but not over-hyped) way?
- What new targets and indicators of success need to be established? (This suggests a balance of measures – competitive, financial, operational, organizational.)
- How can these targets and indicators be continuously revisited?

Analysing your results

If you have done the above homework properly then you will no doubt have gained some insights into the key opportunities and constraints. You should now have come up with some specific ideas for strategic development which will now be probed more systematically with the strategic analysis tools in Chapter 3.

APPENDIX II

Growth scenarios

INTRODUCTION

This appendix gives a practitioner's overview of the use of scenarios as a strategic development tool. Scenarios have been well popularized for many years (particularly by Shell managers and planners (see Grundy, 1994), but for many the notion of scenario development appears difficult, time-consuming and one of uncertain benefit. It is perhaps ironic that the most effective tool for dealing with uncertainty is rarely used because managers are so uncertain as to how to use it, and about what value it will be. In fact, scenario development can be rapid and add disproportionate value relative to effort, especially in 'everyday scenario planning' (or 'ESP').

The key questions which are now therefore addressed are as follows.

- What are scenarios?
- How can scenarios help?
- How can scenarios be developed – and quickly?

WHAT ARE SCENARIOS?

Scenarios are

- internally consistent views of the future,
- which focus on discontinuity and change (not on continuity),
- which also involve exploring how the underlying systems in the business environment may generate change,
- views of how the competitive players (existing and new) might behave.

Scenarios are not static and comprehensive views of the future. Scenarios are in many ways more like a video film – they are of necessity selective but contain a dynamic storyline. Scenarios thus contain a series of views (pictures) of the future. This is fruitfully presented as a series of pictures, not as a single one. Also, there is a storyline which enables these pictures to hang together.

The story can be run (again like a video film) forward or, alternatively, backward. By replaying the story you can work backwards from a particular scenario to see what events might bring about a particular outcome. (These events are called 'transitional events').

Just as 'strategy' is frequently defined as a pattern in a stream of (past and current) decisions, so a 'scenario' is a pattern of future events, and of the interaction between customers, competitors and other key players in the industry.

Next, although many managers understand change they are frequently bemused by the idea of 'discontinuity'. Discontinuity simply means a major break between past and future. Discontinuity can occur imperceptibly (for example just as a train may be switched from one line to another). Or, it can happen abruptly – with a big jolt (or, even in its most extreme form, through derailment).

But the main point is that discontinuity is not about (predictable) trends – it is about surprise and occasionally corporate shock (as in the ICI case study when the chairman Sir Denys Henderson realized that his world view had suddenly shifted).

Scenarios naturally involve a lot of thinking about how the external environment actually works. For example, how might a change in regulation bring about market growth, changes in prices and margins, the levels of competitive rivalry and the pattern of competitor dominance? This is not about just applying standard PEST or competitive forces analysis and looking at the output in a static and isolated manner; it is very much about looking at industry dynamics, the impact of lags (for instance in recognition of what is going on and subsequent behaviour) and in changes in the industry mindset.

Finally, scenarios are not about creating abstract pictures. (This is not modern art.) As in cartoons, scenarios shows players in the market doing specific things and behaving in specific ways.

Scenarios are not therefore an excuse to make broad or vague generalizations – as they are pictures they have a clarity about them which will enable recognition. Managers need to know which world they are entering into – the resolution thus has to be sharp, not fuzzy. In Ansoff's terms, they are ways of picking up, amplifying and interpreting weak signals in the environment.

Scenarios, like all pictures, will thus have a foreground and a background, some features of central interest, and others which are more peripheral.

By now it should have become evident what scenarios are not. Scenarios are not:

- mere forecasts;
- projections from past trends;

- fixed or rigid world views;
- complete in all details;
- static.

When doing scenario analysis for the first time with a management team, it is imperative to make these distinctions – particularly to avoid the rabbit warren of projections and forecasts.

HOW CAN SCENARIOS HELP?

Scenarios can help in a number of ways. Scenario planning at Shell is principally known for its very 'big picture' analysis – particularly for global or industry-broad scenarios, or for country-specific scenarios. In addition, managers can also perform issue-specific scenarios (for example, the impact of regulating/environmental pressure). Or one can do scenarios specific to a particular strategic development decision. For instance, in this book scenarios might well have been developed for:

- London International Group – the impact of recession on photo-processing;
- Marks & Spencer – scenarios for the financial services industry or for entry into new service-based markets;
- Rolls-Royce Aeroengines – the impact of international telecommunication;
- Tesco – the impact (and timing) of home shopping;
- Hanson – the take-over battle with ICI as a scenario (before the event);
- BMW/Rover – the evolution of the four-wheel drive market;
- Cellnet – an implementation scenario for BPR.

HOW CAN SCENARIOS BE DEVELOPED – AND QUICKLY?

About two years ago, I was asked by the head of strategy development for a very major technology company to discuss how one might set about accelerating scenario development. The company had used scenarios to a limited extent in the past, but had found them to be slow and arduous to create.

The challenge set was this: how could one create a small number of scenarios for a key market in under a day?

A small (but hand-picked) team was assembled which included the representatives, technical experts and planning staff – and an external consultant. (The consultant's task was to design and facilitate the process, not to give expert input on scenario content.) Once the issue had been defined, a number of key questions aimed at probing views of the future were defined. These were supported by the process in Figure II.1. It is also useful to have two small teams working in parallel on the scenario – with core common assumptions but with deliberate divergence at the later stages of the process.

Figure II.1 begins by setting the broad background to the scenario. Just because it is looking at a scenario of the future doesn't mean that all assumptions are left open.

Next, the key driving systems impacting on the environment are identified. For instance, for the do-it-yourself UK retail market (in the late 1990s) the following could be identified:

- changes in social and demographic lifestyles (e.g. the breakdown of the 'nuclear' family);
- the impact of the housing market;
- change in leisure patterns;
- the pattern of rivalry in the market place (for example, now that the grocery chain Sainsbury has bought the out-of-town, DIY retailer, Texas, in the UK).

This kind of analysis is best done in a pictorial way. Figure II.2 outlines some pictures of this industry. This figure highlights not merely the complexity of the external systems impacting on the industry, but also the

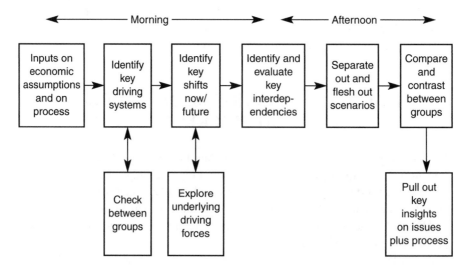

Fig. II.1 Scenario planning – process building/testing

Fig. II.2 Underlying drivers of the UK Do-It-Yourself market

influence of key clusters, particularly those around the housing market and the economy, family leisure patterns, and also competitive rivalry.

Here is a quick run-through of the scenario storyline, imagining (the time of writing being 1995) during 1998:

- a Labour government, with slightly higher taxes but with these eroding the incomes of income-rich people, but not specifically DIY fanatics;
- reducing unemployment, making it hard to get tradespeople to do things at a reasonable price in the home;
- a continuing deterioration in the UK social fabric, resulting in a 'fortress home' mentality and renewed growth in DIY;

- so that the (now) dominant player, as it happens Sainsbury's, begins to make very good profits out of DIY, especially as no new sites can be opened (due to planning restrictions) so profitability per outlet goes up.

Once this analysis has been performed, it is then possible to identify those variables which are likely to be particularly unstable (that you can annotate as a green 'U') and high impact (and annotated as a red 'I'). Variables which are either or both U and I may then suggest some possible key shifts between 'new and future'.

Another phase is to identify the biggest and most sensitive areas of inter-dependency. This helps identify these clusters of variables (and thus the shifts in 'from...to') which, once begun, could have an unstoppable momentum.

In order to separate out and flesh out specific scenarios, it is useful to turn once again to the 'uncertainty/importance' matrix (see Chapter 4 and also Figure II.3). This enables the identification of the one or more assumptions which are both extremely uncertain and very important. This assumption (the 'danger zone') normally suggests a specific scenario route.

A practical issue is the need to make sure that each scenario work group works together as a coherent team to define and then evaluate each assumption and its positioning on Figure II.3. Frequently managers are tempted to delegate the positioning of each assumption to different individuals who would then work independently. This may lead to confusion

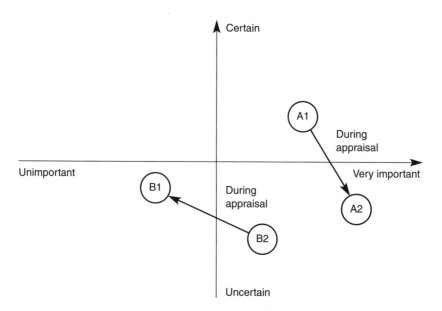

Fig. II.3 Mapping assumptions

over both what the assumption really means and why it has been positioned in a certain way. It is often faster and more effective to work together as a small team rather than to do fragmented individual work.

Once that route is chosen, fleshing out the various scenarios involves reviewing the key interdependencies, the potential major shifts and then creating a storyline about how the scenario could actually come about. This storyline would entail considering things like the following.

- What will the industry (or niche, or organization) really look like?
- How will the key players behave?
- What transitional events might bring this scenario about?

A most useful technique is to role-play competitors and how they might behave in the storyline of the scenario (and, for that matter, other key players like major customers, suppliers or the regulator). This helps inject more life and dynamism into the scenario picture.

Once a small number of scenarios have been developed, they should be then exposed to cross-testing by the two teams. This will help:

- Reveal why particular assumptions were thought most important and most uncertain (and, conversely, those which are less important and most certain)?
- draw out the implications for strategy, and for the critical success factors;
- begin to bring out the financial implications of the scenario.

Financial analysis does have a role to play in scenario development. This should not be so much as part of artificial sensitivity analysis (or 'playing the numbers game'), but to begin to value and cost out the impact of a particular scenario, not only on your particular business but indeed on the whole industry. Some key lessons from scenario development in the past are that you need to:

- bring line managers and planners together to create scenarios;
- examine key shifts in your views of the world;
- ensure that it feeds directly into planning/decision-making processes;
- avoid too many views of the future (preferably keep to two);
- manage concerns that 'we will never get the right (precise) answer' – scenarios are not about doing forecasts;
- use a few analysis tools – also avoid lots of detailed data input – free the mind to be creative;
- refine and revisit scenarios, especially where new signals are detected in the business environment.

In conclusion, it is now opportune to ask yourself these questions.

- What issues would be useful to work on as part of a scenario analysis for my business?

- What are the external systems driving this particular strategic development issue?
- How are these liable to interact?
- Which are most unstable and have highest impact?
- What key shifts in the environment may occur?
- What are the key assumptions about the future out of all this analysis?
- Which one to three are most important and most uncertain ('danger zone')?
- What overall scenario(s) is both plausible and challenging?
- How will the individual players in this scenario behave?
- What transitional events might bring this scenario about?
- What are the implications for our strategy, and particular options, and for the degree of flexibility (room for manoeuvre)?
- What are (in the broadest terms) the practical financial implications?

Scenario Postscript: Importance and Influence

Besides importance and uncertainty mapping, it is also useful to examine specific strategic events. Managers can then evaluate the relative importnace of these events (which may be external or internal), and their own degree of influence over them. Figure II.4 maps this relative importance and influence for a specific business venture. Clearly this tool poses issues for:

- Gaining more influence over key strategic events (externally – and internally, via key stakeholders).
- Challenging whether the strategy is viable (too many events in the South-East quadrant or "impotence zone" spells acute danger).

The importance and influence tool is a natural addition to Everyday Project Management (Chapter 11).

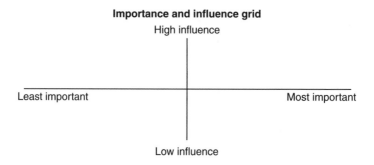

Importance and influence grid

High influence

Least important   Most important

Low influence

APPENDIX III

Strategic development workshops

This appendix gives some very practical advice on design, running and getting maximum value out of strategic development workshops.

Although workshops can generate disproportionate value (and vision), this can be diluted considerably where:

- there is inadequate pre-planning (of issues, process and outputs);
- there is no facilitation or where this is ineffective;
- there are no plans in place to deal with the output and to move it on into the next phase;
- there are no tools to help managers make progress (use the tools and checklists contained in this book).

Twelve key questions on 'how to run a workshop' are as follows.

1. What is the objective of the workshop?
2. How does it relate to other initiatives?
3. What are seen as the key outputs (learning, problem definition, action plans, behavioural shift etc.), and how will these be documented and communicated, and to whom?
4. Who needs to be involved?
5. How will it be positioned in the organization and by whom?
6. Who will facilitate, and are they seen as competent and impartial?
7. Where should it be held and what facilities are required?
8. What are the next steps following the workshop likely to be?
9. What key barriers and blockages may arise, and how will these be dealt with and by whom?
10. What specific activities will be undertaken and what will this input require?
11. How will these be broken down into discussion groups and who will be in each one?
12. How long is required to make substantial progress on each issue and what happens if tasks are incomplete?

Experience shows that it is essential to consider all these questions at length, rather than rushing into a workshop on a particular issue with merely a broad agenda. The questions emphasize both content and process, and involve thinking through how these interrelate. They also involve analysing both current and future context – this provides high quality feed-in of data, and also helps to think through feedback into the management process in detail and in advance.

It is vital to structure the content of each workshop to contain key questions. An example of this for a bank is as follows

Morning

- What is our current position in derivatives trading?
- What options exist for us to develop new products for new or existing markets?
- What competitive advantage would we be able to achieve and sustain, and how?

Afternoon

- What would the implementation implications be, and what would the direct and indirect costs be?
- Broadly speaking, what are the likely financial implications (and risks) of any new developments?
- What are our next steps?

Where you are dealing with a sensitive issue(s) in a workshop, it is advisable to set up some ground rules for interaction. One method (as in Chapter 5) is to write key words on flipcharts beginning with 'P': things to avoid will include being political, picky, procrastinating, pedantic; while things to practise are being positive. Having set up these process rules there is, typically, very little need to refer to them. When this is done, tension can be diffused through a good dose of humour.

Where you are dealing with particularly important or sensitive issues (or both) it may be advisable to use an external facilitator. There are situations where an external facilitator can help not merely in terms of objectivity, but also to orchestrate the process so that it is genuinely a level playing field politically (otherwise you may be attempting the equivalent of do-it-yourself brain surgery).

The benefits of using an external facilitator (over an internal one, or not one at all) are as follows.

- **Speed:** the team should make progress much faster.
- **Outputs:** these should be more thorough, well tested and complete.

- **Insights:** a skilled external facilitator should be able to oil the flow of ideas, identify blind spots and provide ideas of their own.
- **Openness:** an external facilitator should be able to elicit doubts which may have been exposed and be able to generate a balanced but incisive discussion.
- **Implementation:** an external facilitator should be capable of anticipating what the key implementation requirements feel like relative to capability.

The costs and risks of using an external facilitator are as follows.

- **Search costs:** to find someone with the necessary skills and whose style fits the management team.
- **Actual costs:** which can vary dramatically from the small independent to the large consulting firm.
- **Risks:** of the facilitator not being as good as the marketing presentation suggested.
- **Overdependency:** the facilitator is relied upon to the extent that the team become dependent upon them, in order to make progress.
- **The Holy Grail:** by hiring a facilitator, management see them as being the primary agent of progress (not merely the conductor of the orchestra but also first, second and third violin).

APPENDIX IV

Acquisitions and value

This final appendix explores the kinds of value at which acquisitions can be targeted. These ideas are an extension of earlier work on strategic investment decisions at Cranfield School of Management (Grundy, 1992b).

Figure IV.1 attempts to map different acquisition styles. This highlights the four key dimensions of:

- protective and enhancing value;
- synergistic value;
- future opportunity value;
- sweat value.

Figure IV.2 shows the estimated profile of Lloyds Bank's acquisition of the large building society, the Cheltenham and Gloucester. The primary value of the acquisition appears to be to protect and enhance Lloyds Bank's

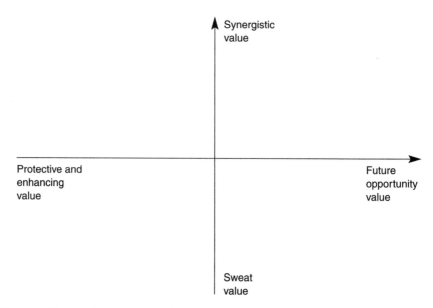

Fig. IV.1 Types of acquisition value

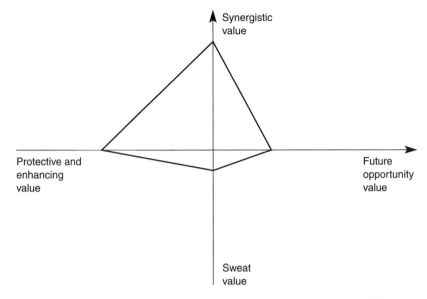

Fig. IV.2 Lloyds bank's acquisition of Cheltenham and Gloucester Building Society

competitive position and to reap synergistic value. There would appear to be less of a thrust towards creating future opportunity and even less opportunity for creating (stand-alone) sweat value. Cheltenham and Gloucester is already a very efficient organization.

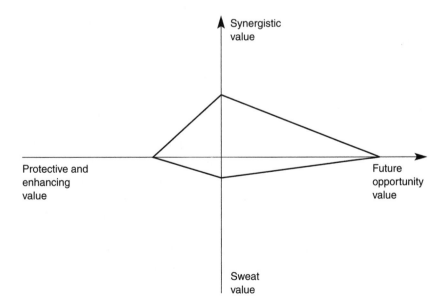

Fig. IV.3 BMW's acquisition of Rover group

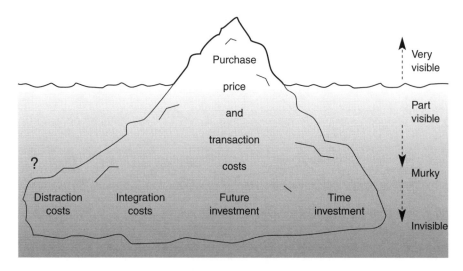

Fig. IV.4 The iceberg of acquisition investment

Figure IV.3 shows a different profile for BMW's acquisition of Rover Group. This acquisition helps bring BMW into the smaller car and four-wheel drive market, so it does have some protective and enhancing value. It also has certain limited synergies (in terms of distribution and sourcing), but these are limited because of the perceived need to maintain separate brands (and dealer networks). Rover is also an efficient organization, so there is little real opportunity for sweat value. The major thrust for BMW is therefore to exploit Rover's future opportunity value – that is as a platform for launching new models into different market areas.

Companies like Hanson would probably show almost exclusively sweat value. But even Hanson may have emergent synergistic value, for example by integrating all of its UK brick operations recently or by generating some future opportunity value by learning about a particular sector.

The final thing is to explore how the total acquisition investment is often underestimated. Figure IV.4 shows how this is typically perceived. The 'Early Learner' will see this investment typically as being the up-front acquisition price (plus more obvious transaction costs). The 'Adolescent Acquirer' will recognize also the need for investment post-acquisition change and development, but may not fully recognize the scale of investment required in this and also underestimate the time investment. Only the 'Experienced Player' can fully scope total investment cost, together with the distraction costs, thus seeing the whole iceberg.

BIBLIOGRAPHY

Ansoff H. I., Managing Strategic Surprise by Response to Weak Signals, *Californian Management Review*, XVIII, pp 21–33, Winter 1975

Argyris C., Double Loop Learning in Organisations, *Harvard Business Review*, pp 115–25, September–October 1977

Argyris C., Teaching Smart People How to Learn, *Harvard Business Review*, pp 99–109, May–June 1991

Barwise P., Marsh P., Thomas K., Wensley R., *Managing Strategic Investment Decisions in Large Diversified Companies*, London Business School, 1987

Barwise P., Marsh P., Wensley R., Must Finance and Strategy Clash?, *Harvard Business Review*, pp 85–90, September–October 1989

Bowman C., Charting Competitive Strategy in *The Challenge of Strategic Management*, pp 84–96, Faulkner D. and Johnson J., Kogan Page, London, 1992

Brummer A. and Cowe R., *Hanson – A Biography*, Fourth Estate, London 1994

Carr C., Tomkins C., Bayliss B., *Strategic Investment Decisions*, Avebury, 1994

Carter E. E., Project Evaluations and Firm Decisions, *Journal of Management Studies*, Vol 28, pp 253–79, 1971

Cooper R. and Kaplan R. S., Profit Priorities from Activity-Based Costing, *Harvard Business Review*, Boston, May–June 1991

Copeland T., Koller T., Murrin J., *Valuation – Meaning and Managing the Value of Companies*, J. Wiley, 1990

Ellis J. and Williams D., *Corporate Strategy and Financial Analysis*, Pitman, 1993

Faulkner D. and Bowman C., *The Essence of Competitive Strategy*, Prentice Hall, 1995

Ghemawat P., Building Strategy on the Experience Curve, *Harvard Business Review*, pp 53–8, March–April 1985

Ghemawat P., *Commitment – The Dynamic of Strategy*, The Free Press, Macmillan, New York, 1991

Goold M. and Campbell A., *Strategies and Styles*, Basil Blackwell, Oxford, 1987

Goold M., Campbell A., Alexander M., *Corporate Level Strategy*, J Wiley and Sons, 1994

Goold M., Campbell A., Alexander M., Corporate Strategy – The Question of Parenting Advantage, *Harvard Business Review*, Boston, pp 120–42, March–April 1995

Grundy A. N., Strategic Cost Management – The Land that Strategy Forgot, *Strategic Planning Society Journal*, 1992a

Grundy A. N., *Corporate Strategy and Financial Decisions*, Kogan Page, 1992b

Grundy A. N., *Implementing Strategic Change*, Kogan Page, 1993a

Grundy A. N., Putting Value on a Strategy, *Long Range Planning*, Vol 26, No 3, pp. 87–94, 1993b

Grundy A. N., *Strategic Learning in Action*, McGraw-Hill, 1994a

Grundy A. N. and Ward K., Beyond the Numbers Game, *Financial Times*, 28 December 1994b

Grundy A. N., Ten Easy Ways of Destroying Shareholder Value, *Long Range Planning*, Vol 28 no 3 pp 76–83, 1995

Hamel G. and Prahalad C. K., *Competing for the Future*, Harvard Business School Press, 1994

Hammer M. and Champy J., *Reengineering the Corporation*, Nicholas Brealey Publishing, London, 1993

Hammer M. and Stanton A., *The Reengineering Revolution*, Hammer & Co., 1995

Haspeslagh PC and Jemison, DB *Managing Acquisitions*, The Free Press, Macmillan, 1991

Jemison D. B. and Sitkin S. B., Acquisitions: The Process can be a Problem, pp 107–16, *Harvard Business Review*, Boston, March–April 1986

Johnson G. and Scholes K., *Exploring Corporate Strategy*, Prentice Hall, 1989

Johnson G., Managing Strategic Change: Strategy, Culture and Action, pp 202–19 in Faulkner D. and Johnson G., *The Challenge of Strategic Management*, Kogan Page, 1992

Kaplan R. S. and Johnson H. T., *Relevance Lost – The Rise and Fall of Management Accounting*, Harvard Business School Press, 1987

Kaplan R. S., *One Cost System Isn't Enough*, Harvard Business Review, February 1988

Kaplan R. S. and Norton D. P., The Balanced Scorecard – Measures that Drive Performance, *Harvard Business Review*, Boston, pp 71–9, January–February 1992

Kuhn T. S., *The Structure of Scientific Revolutions*, Chicago University Press, Chicago, 1962

Lewin K., *A Dynamic Theory of Personality*, McGraw Book Company, New York, 1935

Lorange P. and Roos J., *Strategic Alliances*, Blackwell, 1992

McTaggart J. M., Kontes P. W., Mankins M. C., *The Value Imperative*, The Free Press, Macmillan, 1994

Mills R. W., *Strategic Value Analysis*, Mills, Henley, 1994

Mintzberg H. and Waters J. A., Of Strategies, Deliberate and Emergent, *Strategic Management Journal* 6(3), pp 257–72, 1985

Mintzberg H., *The Rise and Fall of Strategic Planning*, Prentice Hall, 1994

Mintzberg H. and Westley F., Cycles of Organisational Change, *Strategic Management Journal*, Vol 13, pp 39–59, 1992

Mitroff I. I. and Linstone H. A., *The Unbounded Mind*, Oxford University Press, 1993

Ohmae K., *The Mind of the Strategist*, New York, McGraw-Hill, 1982

Owen G. and Harrison T., Why ICI Chose to Demerge, *Harvard Business Review*, pp 133–41, March–April 1995

Piercey N. P., Diagnosing and Solving Implementation Problems in Strategic Planning, *Journal of General Management*, Henley, Vol 15, No 1, pp 19–38, Autumn 1989

Porter E. M., *Competitive Advantage*, The Free Press, Macmillan, 1985

Rappaport A., *Creating Shareholder Value*, The Free Press, New York, 1986

Reimann B., *Managing for Value: A Guide to Value-based Strategic Management*, Basil Blackwell, Oxford, 1990

Riley D., Competitive Cost Based Investment Strategies For Industrial Companies in *Manufacturing Issues*, Booz, Allen and Hamilton, New York, 1987

Schaffer R. H. and Thomson H. A., Successful Change Programmes Begin with Results, *Harvard Business Review*, Harvard, pp 80–9, January–February 1992

Senge P., *The Fifth Discipline: The Art and Practice of the Learning Organisation*, Century Business, 1990

Shank J. K. and Govindarajan V., *Strategic Cost Management – The New Tool for Competitive Advantage*, The Free Press, Macmillan, New York, 1993

Spender J. C., *Strategy Making in Business*, unpublished PhD thesis, University of Massachusetts, 1980

Stacey R., *Strategic Management and Organisational Dynamics*, Pitman, 1993

Stalk E., *Competing Against Time*, The Free Press, 1990

Tomkins C., *Corporate Resource Allocation – Financial, Strategic and Organisational Perspectives*, Basil Blackwell, 1991

Wright W., Sketchley was Taken to the Cleaners, *Long Range Planning*, Vol 25, No 3, pp 108–16, 1992

INDEX